OVID AND THE RENAISSANCE BODY

Body has been one of the main preoccupations of current Renaissance historiography and current critical theory. Both the literary representation of the body and the construction of the material body in Renaissance anatomical and medical discourses have been used to explore the dynamics of early modern sexuality, gender, and society. Yet the influence of Ovid's texts on the construction of the Renaissance discourses of gender, sexuality, and subjectivity has not been fully explored.

This collection of original essays uses contemporary theory to examine Renaissance writers' reworking of Ovid's texts in order to analyse the strategies used in the construction of early modern discourses of gender, sexuality, and writing. The volume is divided into three parts. Part I explores literary and dramatic allusions to Ovid in relation to early modern ideologies of subjectivity and anxieties about identification and desire. Part II illustrates the appropriation of Ovidian myths by poets and dramatists interested in the articulation of agency. Part III demonstrates how various points of intertextuality between Ovid and English Renaissance writers ranging from Marlowe to Milton contributed to early modern epistemologies and discourse of embodiment, spectatorship, and print culture.

GORAN V. STANIVUKOVIC is Assistant Professor of English at Saint Mary's University.

Ovid and the Renaissance Body

EDITED BY GORAN V. STANIVUKOVIC

UNIVERSITY OF TORONTO PRESS
Toronto Buffalo London

Toronto Buffalo London

Reprinted in paperback 2019

ISBN 978-0-8020-3515-8 (cloth)
ISBN 978-1-4875-2419-7 (paper)

National Library of Canada Cataloguing in Publication Data

Main entry under title:

Ovid and the Renaissance body

ISBN 978-0-8020-3515-8 (bound.) ISBN 978-1-4875-2419-7 (paperback).

1. Ovid, 43 B.C.–17 or 18 A.D. – Influence. 2. European literature – Renaissance, 1450–1600 – History and criticism. 3. English literature – Early modern, 1500–1700 – History and criticism. 4. Body, Human, in literature. 5. Sex in literature. I. Stanivukovic, Goran V.

PN721.O94 2001 809′.9335 C2001-930064-6

The author gratefully acknowledges financial support received from Saint Mary's University.

University of Toronto Press acknowledges the financial assistance to its publishing program of the Canada Council for the Arts and the Ontario Arts Council, an agency of the Goverment of Ontario

Canada Council for the Arts Conseil des Arts du Canada

ONTARIO ARTS COUNCIL
CONSEIL DES ARTS DE L'ONTARIO
an Ontario government agency
un organisme du gouvernement de l'Ontario

Funded by the Government of Canada Financé par le gouvernement du Canada

Contents

Acknowledgments

I would like to thank all the contributors in this volume, whose enthusiastic response to the idea of this book made the project possible. I am especially grateful to Valerie Traub for her generous help with, and support of, this project from its inception. Staff at the Folger Shakespeare Library and at the Huntington Library went out of their way to help me use their libraries' superb collections of Ovidiana. These two libraries also supported some of my work on this project, for which I am grateful. I thank Laura Syms and Mary Campbell, of the University College of Cape Breton Library, who patiently, efficiently, and with good humour, dealt with all of my requests to 'rush' the inter-library loans. For their advice, support, and interest in this project, I would like to thank Steven Bruhm, Lynn Enterline, Elizabeth Harvey, Natasha Hurley, Mary and Richard Keshen, Talia Rodgers, and Peter Schwenger. I am also grateful to Margaret MacLeod, Jennifer MacGillivary, and, especially, Pamela Wetzel, who stepped in at some crucial moments to solve various computer glitches. I am grateful to Geraldine Thomas for her help with Latin. I am indebted to Jane Couchman, David MacNeil, Marjorie Stone, and Linda Vecchi for making it possible for me to organize a special, double session, 'The Politics of Ovid's *Metamorphoses* in the Renaissance,' at the 1997 Congress of the Canadian Learned Societies at Memorial University of Newfoundland in Saint John's. I gratefully acknowledge the financial support I received from Saint Mary's University. I thank The Special Collections of the Robinson Library of the University of Newcastle upon Tyne for the permission to reproduce the figure in Michael Pincombe's essay, and the Folger Shakespeare Library for the permission to reproduce the engraving on the book cover.

OVID AND THE RENAISSANCE BODY

Introduction

GORAN V. STANIVUKOVIC

Ovid ... had a way of writing so fit to stir up a pleasing admiration and concernment, which are the objects of a tragedy, and to show the various movements of a soul combating betwixt two different passions, that, had he lived in our age, or in his own could have writ with our advantages, no man but must have yielded to him.

John Dryden, 'An Essay of Dramatic Poesy'

There are many reasons for Ovid's renewed appeal ... [His stories] offer a mythical key to most of the more extreme forms of human behaviour and suffering, especially ones we think of as peculiarly modern: holocaust, plague, sexual harassment, rape, incest, seduction, pollution, sex-change, suicide, hetero- and homosexual love, torture, war, child-battering, depression and intoxication form the bulk of the themes.

Michael Hofmann and James Lasdun, *After Ovid*

Towards the end of Shakespeare's *Titus Andronicus,* Lavinia – raped, her tongue cut out, and with stumps for hands – 'busily ... turns the leaves' of Ovid's *Metamorphoses* looking for the story of Philomela (4.1.45).[1] At this moment, the stage becomes the site of a powerful and disturbing image of two preoccupations of Renaissance literature and arts: Ovid and the body. This scene of reading Lavinia's ravished and mutilated body through Ovid, and of staging a failed attempt to articulate the pain and fate of femininity at the end of this profoundly Ovidian and misogynistic play, anticipates some of the major trajectories of this project: the collusion of the physical with the sexual body; the Ovidian erotic body as a site for the inscription of ideology; the Ovidian body as an instrument for producing multifaceted sexualities; the interweaving of sexuality, power, and nation building; and the intersection of the body, textuality, and voice. *Ovid and the Renaissance Body* joins the burgeoning scholarship on the Renaissance body as eroticized object, and it enters into dialogue with criticism about the construction of the early modern subject.

The essays collected here regard Ovid as more than an agent of change in Renaissance fantasies about the body and sexualities. They explore the Ovidian influence through contemporary theory, especially poststructuralist theories of sexuality, historicism, and writing. It thus represents a significant methodological shift from the scholarship which explores Ovid only as a stylistic and thematic model. This collection is *not* concerned with what Stephen Greenblatt calls the 'elephants' graveyard of literary history,'[2] that is, source study. Rather, these essays demonstrate how Renaissance writers manipulate Ovid's stories in order to develop new arguments about bodies and sexualities; they show, too, how we can study Ovid as constitutive of a history of the body, and how theory informs this historicist method. This collection, then, primarily focuses on what has been called not the aesthetic, but the 'psychological' value of an influence, whereby 'evaluating an influence we are engaged in judging its genetic function.'[3]

Thus the essays in this collection suggest that the discourse of the Ovidian body was independent of, but complemented by, other discourses of the body in the Renaissance, building on what we can already call an archaeology of the Renaissance body in current scholarship. Reading the Renaissance body through Ovid, they unsettle and expand different cultural representations of the body that dominated or were emerging in the Renaissance. In that sense, the Ovidian body became a resource for new ideologies of the body at the time when other cultural and political conditions were enabling the shaping of Renaissance subjectivity. Thus the essays in this collection show that in Renaissance culture the Ovidian body 'functions as a kind of "spoiler," always baffling or exceeding the ways in which [the body] is represented.'[4]

The sources of Ovid's revival in the Renaissance lie in the renewed attention to paganism and metamorphoses. Mutability, as Leonard Barkan suggests, was one of the causes of renewed interest in Ovid during the Renaissance.[5] This dovetails with the revival of the elegy, and of erotic and satirical literature, a revival which was part of the growing urban culture. Because Ovid was central to humanist education and the Renaissance practice of imitation, and because there was then no authoritative edition of Ovid's works, Ovid's myths were especially open to various interpretations and versions. In a recent book on Marlowe's uses of Ovid, for example, Patrick Cheney explores 'the idea of a literary career; the practice of professional rivalry, and the writing of nationhood.'[6] Yet the essays in this collection show that 'writing of nationhood' was complicated and often subverted by Renaissance writers' use of the Ovidian body's erotic manifestations. Another instance of the idiosyncrasy of Renaissance readings of Ovid is Arthur Golding's 1567 translation of the *Metamorphoses*. Golding substitutes English equivalents for the landscape, characters, and ideas of the Latin original, in effect reinventing Ovid 'as the author of very English stories.'[7] One might then argue that this English Ovid enabled Renaissance writers to treat his myths as representative of their own nationhood. Consequently, later English writers treated the Ovidian love stories in Golding as a domestic repository of topics, passions, and characters. As a result of such unbridled interpretation, Ovidian narratives of the body became particularly suitable vehicles for constructing new discourses of sexuality, discourses which countered the rigidity that characterized much of the religious writing on the body. While the roots of the Renaissance ideas about the body were in the long and complex history of the Christian idea of 'sexual renunciation,' Ovidian discourse challenged that Christian idea, prefiguring a discourse that resisted the body's subordination to orthodox norms of sexuality, and opening the way for a new Ovidian history of the early modern body.[8] The precursor to the Renaissance fascination with, and revisionism of, Ovid can be found in the widespread medieval tradition of the moralized Ovid, tradition which turned Ovid into Christian moralized tales.

What further attracted Renaissance writers to Ovid was the morality of his works, especially the *Metamorphoses,* and his treatment of the pastoral. Arguing that the *Metamorphoses* is not a 'moralistic' but a 'moral' poem, Charles Paul Segal refers 'to the poem's recurrent concern with human suffering and helplessness.'[9] It is precisely through that suffering that the Ovidian subject emerges as transformed. The misfortune of many of Ovid's characters, on the one hand, renders them vulnerable, erotic outcasts from the world of the gods. On the other hand, their misfortunes force them never to stop questing for their selves, however dire the circumstances of the world they inhabit. Ovidian characters challenged the limits of normativity, thus offering models to Renaissance writers wanting to represent new subjects being shaped by the complexities of Renaissance culture. As well, Ovid's pastoral settings are full of 'trappings,' hardly evocative, as Segal points out, of 'a genuine peacefulness or tranquility.' Rather, they 'create an atmosphere given over to strange powers and pervaded by sensuous lassitude where both physical and moral energies seem sapped and helpless.'[10] With all the ambivalence, anxiety, pain, and pleasure that it entails, Ovidian discourse of the body and self was the closest to the complex, often contradictory ways in which Renaissance subjects were constituted. The multidimensional world of the changing cultural, social, and political conditions in the sixteenth and seventeenth centuries were mirrored in the pleasures and anxieties of the Ovidian world. Indeed, for the same reasons, two contemporary poets, Michael Hofmann and James Lasdun, have attempted the renewal of Ovid today, implying that Ovid can still inspire literary imagination, and that his work has much to communicate to contemporary culture.[11] Today's revival of Ovid comes at a time when in North America and Britain we have started to challenge and redefine arguments about the stability of gender and the binarism of sexuality; when we have begun to scrutinize the nature, ambiguity, and articulation of desire, and violations of the body; and when there has been more visible political battle for social legitimacy of gay and lesbian sexualitities.[12] *Ovid and the Renaissance Body* contributes to this moment of cultural challenge and revival.

Of all the discourses that shaped the early modern subjects – medical, anatomical, matrimonial, theological, legal, political, scientific – the Ovidian discourse was the most widely available,[13] and the closest to the Renaissance idea that the gender of the body does not determine the erotic nature of that body's desire. No other discourse of subjectivity so explicitly focused on the terms that constitute self: body, libido, and agency. Indeed, in its use of the Ovidian love myths to represent the complexities and ambiguities of desire, Renaissance Ovidianism was a kind of proleptic psychoanalysis.

The Renaissance Ovidian discourse of the body burgeoned alongside the two most dominant discourses of the body: theological and medical. For the church, sexuality and the physical body were linked to morality. For medical theorists and anatomists, the physical body was a reflection of gender hierarchy, in which the male body was considered the norm, superior to the female. And as Patricia Crawford argues, the medical and theological discourses of the body were connected, the medical discourse influencing the theological.[14] The Renaissance revival of Ovid (one might say that that revival was a continuation and expansion of the medieval obsessiveness with Ovid) occurred between mid-1500 and mid-1600, at the time of what Jonathan Sawday calls 'the *discovery* of the Vesalian body,' that is, at the time of 'the belief that the human body expressed in miniature the divine workmanship of God, and that its form corresponded to the greater form of the macrocosm.'[15] The Ovidian body provided a discourse that countered the Vesalian, or the anatomical body. The Vesalian anatomical body showed people the godly norm within themselves, as Sawday suggests, and it confirmed Renaissance assumptions about the normativity of the male body. The concept of the Vesalian body, thus, works with the concept of the Ovidian body to make what the Ovidian figures make even more explosive, even metaphysical, than they are already when considered separate from, or counter to, the Vesalian body. If the body with its Ovidian potential is still a godlike body, as it often is, the Ovidian body's intersection with the Vesalian might borrow that metaphysical aspect from it. Ovid's figures showed the perils and pleasures that bodies produce in passionate contact with other bodies – against the will of the gods. This was especially evident in Renaissance interpretations of the *Metamorphoses*, the Ovidian epic about creation repeatedly condemned for its pagan hedonism. Their chaos notwithstanding, the Ovidian bodies, with their paganism and their overt eroticism, and not the ornate Vesalian (Christian) anatomy, became predominant in imagining bodies in literature and art. Yet this collection demonstrates that even Ovidian discourses of the body were never completely cohesive. In drawing distinctions between the classical and the Renaissance body, Gail Kern Paster argues that, '[i]f the classical body – opaque, closed off, finished, a body all surface and no interior – instantiates the bodily ideal of Renaissance absolutism, it does so more as a denial of common bodiliness *tout court* than as a new form of bodiliness individualized.'[16] The essays in *Ovid and the Renaissance Body* argue in fact that the classical bodies of Ovid's stories made possible the very individualized bodiliness denied to the classical body to emerge as a new and powerful discourse of the body in competition with other discourses of corporeality.

Current criticism of the body tends to examine the intersection of social power and the construction of the body by focusing on the materiality of the body, especially its humoral and physiological traits within the Renaissance discourses of anatomy or medicine. This criticism also treats the body as a synecdoche for the Renaissance ideas of, and fantasies about, sexuality and gender. Although the writers in this collection also explore the body as a social construct, they do so by emphasizing the ways in which the Ovidian discourse constructs the body. They examine the body within the context of the social and political forces at work in Renaissance England, and they take as their objective an exploration, following Foucault, of the early modern technologies of power that regulated, and were inscribed in, the Renaissance body.[17] Working thus within the Foucauldian tradition of the invention of sexuality, Thomas Laqueur, for example, examines the history of the biological body as the history of culturally and socially constructed ideas about the generative physiology of the material body.[18] Yet even current scholarship, whether it treats the body as anatomical, humoral, or signifying matter, rarely links it to Ovidianism which, especially in the *Metamorphoses*, treats the body both as malleable matter and as a metonymy of erotic identification.

The landmark in contemporary Ovid criticism is Jonathan Bate's book, *Shakespeare and Ovid.*[19] Because Bate's reading of Shakespeare's Ovid focuses on the humanist practice of imitation, his treatment of the narratives of love and the psychology of desire in Shakespeare is primarily grounded in philological examination, leaving aside much of the social and cultural impact of the discourse of body and sexuality. Although Bate's work is important to many essays in this collection (and, indeed, for the work on Renaissance Ovid in general), the essays in *Ovid and the Renaissance Body* offer a different pluralism of critical methodologies and approaches for exploring the Ovidian body as an agent of a simultaneous *cultural* and *textual* discourse of the body, sexuality, and protocols of desire.

Leonard Barkan's study of metamorphoses and paganism represents a thematic approach to Ovid, illuminating the ways in which Ovid's myths of pagan love and sexuality in the *Metamorphoses* became subjects of the medieval and Renaissance poetics and allegories of desire. While Barkan analyses the hermeneutics of Ovidian desire, Richard A. Lanham traces how Ovid's rhetoric of the *Metamorphoses* provided a model for Renaissance eloquence, concluding that, to Renaissance writers, Ovid is '[o]nly the style.'[20] Renaissance writers took to Ovidian rhetoric because of its naturalness and flexibility, but they also embraced him as a storehouse of ideas about bodies and desires: he was used not just as a catalogue of rhetorical devices or classical topoi of love. Lanham's rhetorical criticism is important but limited in that it does not consider that, besides emulating Ovid's myths and styles, the Renaissance was engaged in a larger creative transformation, an adaptation of Ovidian ideologies of body and desire. As the essays in this volume demonstrate, the Renaissance imitation of Ovid's rhetoric was but one step towards a more complex process: reliance on Ovid as a resource for constructing new embodiments and subjects.[21] In its examination of that process, *Ovid and the Renaissance Body* also differs significantly from the only two other volumes on Ovid in the Renaissance, *Ovid Renewed*, whose essays expand philological criticism, and *Shakespeare's Ovid*, whose essays are a contribution to source criticism, for they explore the ways in which Shakespeare adapts the *Metamorphoses* in the plays and poems.[22]

That past critical tradition, representing as it does a modern version of *Stoffgeschichte*, of the quest for sources and their imitation, typifies the scholarship on Renaissance Ovid. The tradition belongs, one might say, to a pretheoretical phase of scholarship on Ovid. Although this kind of scholarship supplied much of the necessary philological groundwork, it has not addressed the processes and goals in the Renaissance writers' uses of Ovid from the standpoint of current critical theories, nor has it discussed the cultural forces which initiated a shift in Renaissance conceptualization and fantasies about the body. The new approach to Ovid, to which this collection contributes, has been made possible by the proliferation of critical theories, especially feminism and queer theory, that have changed our ways of historicizing and theorizing bodies and sexualities.

Ovid and the Renaissance Body appears just as criticism and theory have made us increasingly aware of the complexities of exploring sexuality and gender, especially in texts from historically distant periods. It comes too just when we feel the need for an expansion of terms so that we can better capture the discontinuities in the early modern construction of the body. In fact, scholarship's turn to Ovidianism comes just as the new historicist and cultural materialist claims about social construction are being questioned by more specific forms of historicisms (the study of early modern print culture and habits of reading, for example); when queer theory seems to have peaked and is looking for fresh nuances for its arguments about bodies, sexual practices, and identities that seem nonnormative (at least from the distance of our culture) within a heteroerotic culture; and just as feminism seeks to diversify its critical methodologies.

Poststructuralist theories of sexuality, in Judith Butler's articulation, destabilize the body as 'the firm foundation' for gender and normative sexuality.[23] Butler's theory of the performativity of the body and of gender roles sometimes questions any signification of the body prior to discourse (body as an 'inert matter'); it has expanded the possibilities for the study of identification and desire, and has thus enabled the rise of performativity in queer theory. But it did that, initially at least, from an ahistorical position. Most of the contributors to this volume, while not necessarily and explicitly following Butler, work within the larger concept of the performativity of the body, all looking for ways to historicize and question the body's materiality and to theorize historical Ovidian corporeality. *Pace* Lanham, one could say, then, that the theoretical approach to Ovid demonstrates that, for the Renaissance, instead of 'only the style' Ovid was 'only the body.' Thus the challenge of theory invites the return to Ovid this anthology represents, and it is in this context that Valerie Traub argues in her afterword for 'a new Ovidianism' at this moment in Renaissance scholarship.

One might say that an aetiology of the body, where the gendered body is separate from desire, which we find in Ovid, is a historical precursor both to queer theory's centredness on erotic identification rather than on gender, and to separation of gender and sexual desire in the Renaissance. Both feminist and queer theories carry some ideological weight, marking as they do a difference between analyses of gender (in feminism) and, on the other hand, analyses of erotic identification and of nonnormative sexual practices (in queer theory). The essays in this anthology explore malleable sexualities and desires in ways which resist ideological divisions of gender and sexuality, by analysing voice, desire, and writing. In so doing, this collection expands the critical possibilities for both feminism and queer theory, as well as for historicism.

The theoretical implications of the Ovidian body have only very recently been studied. Elizabeth Harvey acutely reads Donne's challenge to Ovid's myth of Sappho by pairing Sappho with Philaenis, and constructs her as a lesbian. Such a reading departs from philological and thematic criticism and centres more on a theoretically informed analysis.[24] Examining the male writers' cross-gendered ventriloquism, Harvey shows how applying theories of voice and embodiment to Ovid can expand our analysis of Renaissance sexuality, textual identification, and desire. This new interest in Ovid is evident also in Valerie Traub's examination of the ways in which early modern culture reshaped the Callisto myth from the *Metamorphoses* in ways which show 'a range of attitudes toward sexual violence, deception, jealousy, all-female communities, and same-gender eroticism.'[25] And Debora Kuller Shuger has explored 'the eroticized Ovidian representation of abandoned females' on the model of the body of Mary Magdalene and the trope of the abandoned woman in Ovid's *Heroides*.[26] The 'Christian Ovidianism' of the Mary Magdalene narratives, Shuger argues, suggests how the rhetoric of biblical erotic spirituality, fused with the paganism of Ovidian corporeality, produced, in new ways, the female subject as erotic.[27] New theoretical implications also emerge in Mario DiGangi's analysis of 'Ovidian comedy' and the 'homoerotics of marriage' in early modern literature and drama. DiGangi uses the 'Ovidian comedy' to describe late sixteenth-century comedies (*Twelfth Night* and *As You Like It*), focusing on gender and sexual ambiguity.[28] Pushing the boundaries of the study of Ovid and the body further, Lynn Enterline has recently argued 'that the violated and fractured body is the place where, for Ovid aesthetics and violence converge, where the usually separated realms of the rhetorical and the sexual most insistently meet.'[29] While these and other critics have helped to define this new field, *Ovid and the Renaissance Body* expands it.

The essays in this volume have been grouped in three categories: identification and desire; speech, voice, and embodiment; and textualization. What unites these essays, however, is, first, their aim to historicize the multiplicity of Renaissance uses of Ovid by arguing for a diversity of discourses on body and sex in the Renaissance. The variety of approaches in this collection – feminist, speech-act, queer, cultural materialist, gender, and print culture – demonstrates the wide applicability of Ovidianism in the study of the Renaissance body: Ovidianism speaks to the theories of identification and desire, to discussions of normative and nonnormative sexuality, and to analysis of the relationship among body, writing, and printing. Each essay challenges the terms of a specific theory and reveals the tensions within a specific methodology. The collection deals with most of Ovid's major works, *Metamorphoses, Ars Amatoria, Amores, Fasti,* and the *Heroides,* and it discusses a number of English, French, and Italian Renaissance writers, as well as different genres in the sixteenth and seventeenth centuries.

'Identification and Desire,' the opening section, analyses sexuality and erotic writing. Six essays in this section engage with queer theory, focusing on the construction of the 'lesbian' subject and male-male erotics in lyrical poetry and drama, reconfiguration of heterosexuality in Renaissance epyllia, and Ovidian eroticism. Two essays look at the construction of masculinity in relation to Renaissance anxieties over erotic writing. Carla Freccero reviews the queering of the poetic voice as a route towards same-sex desire, and she argues against the Freudian distinction between identification and desire. Instead, in her exploration of polymorphous desire in Ovid and Renaissance Petrarchism, she calls for the use of textual identification and desire. This enables her to show how Louise Labé's use of the *Metamorphoses* and the *Heroides* often 'crosses,' and reconstitutes, through Petrarch, the gendered identification of the already travestied female voices in the *Heroides.* Jim Ellis argues that a similar 're-crossing' of the subject from Petrarch, via Ovid, to a Renaissance text is at stake in the construction of heterosexuality in the Renaissance Ovidian minor epics (or epyllia), in Thomas Lodge's *Scillaes Metamorphosis* and John Marston's *The Metamorphosis of Pigmalion's Image.* For Ellis, the denial of the Petrarchan alienation of the subject from language in Ovidian poetry and the distance between the subject and desire in Ovidian erotics create in epyllia a space within which Renaissance writers renegotiate heterosexuality. Ellis uses Luce Irigaray's and Monique Wittig's rethinking of heterosexuality as part of his theoretical framework. The Ovidian male subject's stories of amorous woe become, in Renaissance epyllia, rhetorical strategies for substituting women for men, introducing into epyllia homoerotic desire that circulates within the homosocial culture of the epyllia's courtier-readers.

While Ellis calls for a renegotiation of heterosexuality, Mark Dooley argues for the renegotiation of female same-sex erotics in John Lyly's play *Gallathea.* This renegotiation is defensible, Dooley contends, because of Lyly's radical recasting of the myth of Iphis and Ianthe. Dooley's essay represents a new push in the study of the early modern 'one-sex' model, one which in turn destabilizes earlier new historicist claims of it.[30] He challenges the neoclassical medical arguments of the 'one-sex' model of the body with the possibility of the sex change, from male to female, suggesting that its representation of female same-sex desire is limited. Arguing that Lyly finds corporeal metamorphosis a limitation to female same-sex erotics – as evident in his transformation of the Iphis and Ianthe to Phillida and Gallathea relationships – Dooley demonstrates that Lyly's play promotes a female same-sex model as autonomous and non-threatening. In so doing, Dooley suggests that 'lesbianism' was not altogether silenced and not always invisible in the Renaissance.

Morgan Holmes explores the erotics of 'pastoral Ovidianism' in the female-female erotics in Andrew Marvell, whose use of Ovid has not yet been the subject of much critical analysis. Holmes examines the 'multiplicitous erotic desires and practices' in Marvell's lament, *The Nymph Complaining for the Death of her Faun.* Holmes sees the fawn and the nymph as the loci of Marvell's employment of Ovid to challenge the normativity of cross-gendered embodiment and virtue. He shows how Marvell's gendering of the two mythical creatures as females enjoying the pleasure of each other's bodies subverts 'sexual orthodoxy.'

Holmes's essay examines female same-sex desire, but it also challenges how we define the pastoral and how we look at pastoral erotics.

Mario DiGangi discusses the link between courtly pride, and male homoeroticism, and physical deformity in Ben Jonson. Tracing the history of the Renaissance use of the Narcissus myth until Jonson's transformation of it, DiGangi shows how Jonson associates Narcissus with the proud courtiers in *Cynthia's Revels* and *Poetaster.* DiGangi discusses narcissism not as a pathology, but as a social signifier of contemporary social anxieties about the reputation of the court and its power. He argues that, as a socially disruptive figure, Jonson's Narcissus is associated with courtiers whose bodily practices transgress standards of acceptable courtly behaviour, passions, and language. DiGangi's analysis of narcissism represents a departure from the customary treatment of Narcissus, the figure invariably associated with homoeroticism, a departure from the psychoanalytical to historicist queer theory. The last essay in this section, Ian Moulton's analysis of the Ovidian eroticism of John Harington's translation of Ariosto's *Orlando Furioso,* examines how the Renaissance writer's cancellations of Ovid's texts affect the construction of masculinity, and what ideological forces were at stake in such imitations. Moulton argues that the playfulness with gender and eros in Harington's translation of *Orlando Furioso* should be read in the context of the humorous treatment of eroticism in the Ovidian erotic epyllia, especially in Shakespeare's *Venus and Adonis* and Marlowe's *Hero and Leander.*

The anthology's second section, 'Speech, Voice, and Embodiment,' features three essays. Gina Bloom analyses the myth of Echo, primarily in George Sandys's 1632 translation of the *Metamorphoses.* Contrary to some current feminist criticism, which treats Echo as an example of a silenced female subject, Bloom's analysis of articulation and agency is based in the trope of Echo's 'echoic sound.' Echo's disembodied voice becomes a challenge to misogynistic silencing of her voice, and it represents a way of articulating agency despite patriarchal impediments to women's access to power. Bloom's essay thus offers new ways of looking at the issues of national poet (in ways different from Patrick Cheney) as well as male poet's appropriation of the female body. Such interpretation opens the way for historicist feminism to find new models of female assertion of voice against the ideology of silencing. Michael Pincombe's and Bruce Boehrer's essays explore the relationship between the body and masculinist anxiety about female sexuality. Michael Pincombe explores the hermaphrodite in Edmund Spenser's *The Faerie Queene* and

Thomas Peend's poem *Pleasant Fable of Hermaphroditus and Salmacis* (1565). Pincombe analyses Peend's satirical transformation of Ovid's hermaphroditus as a eunuch, which provides the context for his analysis of Scudamor in *The Faerie Queene.* Both Pincombe and Boehrer challenge, though in differing ways, some of contemporary criticism's claims about effeminacy as a site of male anxiety about female sexuality. While Pincombe argues that effeminacy spurs male attraction towards women, Boehrer sees effeminacy as a specific position of the husband in Jacobean city comedy. Arguing that the discourse of cuckoldry in Jacobean drama originates in the 'the dilemma of the cuckold' in Ovidian verse – the dilemma is that the married man absorbs some of his wife's character flaws – Boehrer examines the cuckold in Thomas Middleton's play, *A Cheap Maid in Cheapside,* and Ben Jonson's *Volpone.* Relating the cuckold in drama to the one in *Amores,* and discussing the effeminized cuckold-husband of Jacobean drama, Boehrer argues that the cuckold is an exemplary masculine figure who attempts to regain what he had repressed through marriage, and that he is also an image of failed husbandry. The implication of Boehrer's analysis is that the Ovidian cuckold in Renaissance drama and culture operates not just in the realm of individual desire, but also in the sphere of domestic and public space, in both the micro and macro commonwealth.

The collection closes with four essays in the section 'Textualization,' all of which explore how the Ovidian body enabled discourses of writing, translation, poetic identity, and print culture. Looking at Donne's and Marlowe's use of the *Amores,* Raphael Lyne analyses the Ovidian body as a writing medium and writing surface. Lyne discusses Ovid as a basis for 'the corporeal associations of the wax,' for the ways, that is, in which malleable bodies and flexible desires are inscribed on the writing surface of warm wax. The heat of the lovers' desires in Donne's *Elegies* and in Marlowe's translation of *Amores* is metaphorically embodied anew in wax. Through such an embodiment, the poets inscribe Ovid's linking of the lovers' physical and spiritual conditions. Lyne's thesis expands the current arguments about writing technologies and print culture in the Renaissance by demonstrating how Ovid is central to the overlapping cultural practices of shaping texts and representing desires. Elizabeth Sauer's essay contributes to a hitherto less explored area of Milton's Ovidianism and the gendered construction of the poetic persona. Sauer argues that Milton's 'struggle' with the metamorphosis as a destructive force in *Paradise Lost* helped him 'reinvent' his masculine poetic identity rejecting in the process the feminine side of his persona.

The reinvention of poetic identity is the subject of Judith Deitch's essay, too, although she examines through a revisionist approach to literary imitation within the context of male poet's appropriation of female body. Deitch demonstrates how Spenser's 'facile and fragmented' imitation of Echo in *Epithalamion*, imitation which can figure the poet as epigone, is transferred as an 'ineffectual image onto the available woman.' If in many of the essays Ovidianism is treated as a discourse for a body that is absent, silenced, and suppressed, in Lori Newcomb's essay Ovid provides a resolution for fixing the text and embodying gender on the stage of Renaissance theatre. In the case of Pygmalion, which Newcomb examines, the process is that of reversal of the process of silencing the body and of making it absent. Looking at Hermione's transformation from an absent woman to a materialized statue, and then to a real woman, in *The Winter's Tale*, Newcomb explores how Shakespeare's use of Pygmalion from the *Metamorphoses* shifts between the construction of a textual body of the play, theatrical embodiment of gender, and a celebration of the human body.

This collection was undertaken in an attempt to reconfigure Renaissance Ovidianism and to explore a number of arguments about subjectivity and sexuality. Earlier literary criticism applied the term 'Ovidian' to formalist and thematic influences ('Ovidian rhetoric' or 'Ovidian love'). This anthology regards Ovid as an influence in the cultural production of new subjects, that is, Ovidian identities or Ovidian sexualities. Yet *Ovid and the Renaissance Body* aims not merely to bring together different methodologies for analysing Ovid and the body in Renaissance studies; it seeks also a new course in our present debate about the history and theory of the body and sexuality.

NOTES

1 G. Blackmore Evans, ed., *The Riverside Shakespeare* (Boston: Houghton Mifflin, 1974).
2 Stephen Greenblatt, 'Shakespeare and the Exorcists,' in *Shakespeare and the Question of Theory*, ed. Patricia Parker and Geoffrey Hartman (London: Methuen, 1985), p. 163.
3 Claudio Guillén, 'The Aesthetics of Influence in Comparative Literature,' *Comparative Literature* 1 (1959): 187.
4 Catherine Gallagher and Stephen Greenblatt, *Practicing New Historicism* (Chicago and London: University of Chicago Press, 2000), p. 15.

5 Leonard Barkan, *The Gods Made Flesh: Metamorphoses and the Pursuit of Paganism* (New Haven: Yale University Press, 1986), p. 172.

6 Patrick Cheney, *Marlowe's Counterfeit Profession: Ovid, Spenser, Counternationhood* (Toronto: University of Toronto Press, 1997), p. 3.

7 Raphael Lyne, 'Golding's Englished *Metamorphoses*,' *Translation in Literature* 5 (1996): 183.

8 For a detailed history of continence in Christian tradition, see Peter Brown, *The Body and Society: Men, Women, and Sexual Renunciation in Early Christianity* (New York: Columbia University Press, 1988).

9 Charles Paul Segal, *Landscape in Ovid's Metamorphoses: A Study in the Transformations of a Literary Symbol* (Wiesbaden: Franz Steiner Verlag, 1969), pp. 2–3. Because of the ethical stance adopted in translation, Arthur Golding's 1567 and George Sandys's 1632 translations of *Metamorphoses* can be called 'moralistic.'

10 Segal, *Landscape in Ovid's Metamorphoses*, p. 82.

11 The second epigraph at the beginning of this Introduction demonstrates this. Michael Hofmann and James Lasdun, eds., 'Introduction,' *After Ovid: New Metamorphoses* (New York: The Noonday Press, Farrar, Straus and Giroux, 1994), p. xi.

12 In addition to Hofmann and Lasdun, Ted Hughes (*Tales of Ovid* [New York: Farrar, Straus & Giroux, 1997]) demonstrates the power of Ovid's verse to inspire contemporary poetic imagination. Other examples of contemporary literature's interest in Ovid include David Malouf's *An Imaginary Life* (New York: Georg Braziller, 1978, 2nd ed. 1992), and Cees Nooteboom's *The Following Story*, trans. from Dutch by Ina Rilke (San Diego, New York, and London: Harcourt Brace, 1993). I am grateful to Tony Telford Moore for sending me a copy of Malouf's novel inspired by Ovid's exile to the shores of the Black Sea, and to Bradin Cormack for drawing my attention to Nooteboom's novel of metamorphosis.

13 Numerous editions, versions, and translations, that circulated in print and manuscript and that were used in humanist classrooms, and a rich tradition of visual representations of Ovid in paintings, sculptures, engravings, and tapestries, suggest both the immensity of Ovid's impact on the Renaissance and the association of the rise of urban culture with the revival of Ovid. In European literature and culture, as Charles Martindale suggests, 'Ovid is everywhere' (p. 1). See Charles Martindale, ed., 'Introduction,' *Ovid Renewed: Ovidian Influences on Literature and Art from the Middle Ages to the Twentieth Century* (Cambridge: Cambridge University Press, 1988), p. 1. See also Edward Kennard Rand, *Ovid and His Influence* (New York: Cooper Square Publishers, 1928); Ernst Robert Curtius, *European Literature and the*

Latin Middle Ages, trans. Willard R. Trask (Princeton: Princeton University Press, 1973), pp. 28ff.; and Ann M. Blair, 'Lectures on Ovid's *Metamorphoses*: The Class Notes of a 16th-century Paris Schoolboy,' *Princeton University Library Chronicle* 59 (1989): 117–44.

14 Patricia Crawford, 'Sexual Knowledge in England, 1500–1750,' in *Sexual Knowledge, Sexual Science: The History of Attitudes to Sexuality,* ed. Roy Porter and Mikuláš Teich (Cambridge: Cambridge University Press, 1994), p. 84.

15 Jonathan Sawday, *The Body Emblazoned: Dissection and the Human Body in Renaissance Culture* (London and New York: Routledge, 1996), p. 23.

16 Gail Kern Paster, *The Body Embarrassed: Drama and the Disciplines of Shame in Early Modern England* (Ithaca: Cornell University Press, 1993), p. 15. For the social and symbolic analyses of the body parts in the Renaissance, see also David Hillman and Carla Mazzio, eds., *The Body in Parts: Fantasies of Corporeality in Early Modern Europe* (New York and London: Routledge, 1997).

17 Michel Foucault, *The History of Sexuality: An Introduction,* vol. 1, trans. Robert Hurley (New York: Vintage Books, 1990), p. 47.

18 Thomas Laqueur, *Making Sex: Body and Gender from the Greeks to Freud* (Cambridge, MA: Harvard University Press, 1992).

19 Jonathan Bate, *Shakespeare and Ovid* (Oxford: Oxford University Press, 1994).

20 Richard A. Lanham, *The Motives of Eloquence: Literary Rhetoric in the Renaissance* (New Haven and London: Yale University Press, 1976), p. 64.

21 For an analysis on the impact of the Renaissance imitation of themes and styles found in Ovid on the formation of poetic genres, see Clark Hulse, *Metamorphic Verse: The Elizabethan Minor Epic* (Princeton: Princeton University Press, 1981).

22 A.B. Taylor, ed., *Shakespeare's Ovid: The* Metamorphoses *in the Plays and Poems* (Cambridge: Cambridge University Press, 2000).

23 Judith Butler, *Gender Trouble: Feminism and the Subversion of Identity* (New York and London: Routledge, 1990), p. 129.

24 Elizabeth D. Harvey, 'Ventriloquizing Sappho, or The Lesbian Muse,' in *Ventriloquized Voices: Feminist Theory and English Renaissance Texts* (London and New York: Routledge, 1992), pp. 116–39.

25 Valerie Traub, 'The Perversion of "Lesbian" Desire,' *History Workshop Journal* 41 (1996): 27.

26 Debora Kuller Shuger, *The Renaissance Bible: Scholarship, Sacrifice, and Subjectivity* (Berkeley, Los Angeles, London: University of California Press, 1998), p. 170.

27 Shuger, *The Renaissance Bible,* p. 177.

28 Mario DiGangi, 'The Homoerotics of Marriage in Ovidian Comedy,' *The*

Homoerotics of Early Modern Drama (Cambridge: Cambridge University Press, 1997), pp. 29–63.

29 Lynn Enterline, *The Rhetoric of the Body from Ovid to Shakespeare* (Cambridge: Cambridge University Press, 2000), p. 1.

30 Recently, the Renaissance 'one-sex' model has been subjected to revisionist scrutiny. See Janet Adelman, 'Making Defect Perfection: Shakespeare and the One-Sex Model,' in *Enacting Gender on the English Renaissance Stage*, ed. Viviana Comensoli and Anne Russell (Urbana and Chicago: University of Illinois Press, 1999), pp. 23–52; and Winfried Schleiner, 'Early Modern Controversies about the One-Sex Model,' *Renaissance Quarterly* 53.1 (2000): 180–91.

PART I

Identification and Desire

Ovidian Subjectivities in Early Modern Lyric: Identification and Desire in Petrarch and Louise Labé

CARLA FRECCERO

Recent studies in the history and theory of sexuality have returned to a famous Freudian formulation of sexual development to examine key aspects in the formation of subjectivity: identification and desire. Freud wrote of the Oedipal complex that it was the phase of an individual's development whereby these were accomplished in the subject: through the Oedipal phase and the castration complex the infant learns to identify with one sex and desire the other. Elsewhere, however, Freud's discussions of identification reveal that it is not so easy to separate the two: identification turns out to be the form possession takes of an object that is lost. In 'An Example of Psycho-analytic Work,' Freud asserts, 'If one has lost a love-object, the most obvious reaction is to identify oneself with it, to replace it from within, as it were, by identification.'[1] Further, in 'On Narcissism,' he argues that the ego-instincts, which take the 'self' as their object and therefore testify to what Freud calls the 'primary narcissism' of every person, prop up or support the sexual instincts or drives, which eventually will invest in other objects.[2] Thus there is said to be both an ego-libido and an object-libido, the former taking the place of primary narcissism as an ego-ideal, the latter directing itself towards an object outside the self (pp. 75–6). In a later work, *The Ego and the Id* (1923), where Freud further develops his theories of subjectivity based on his observations in 'Mourning and Melancholia,' he restates the relation between desire and identification more forcefully as the replacement of an object-cathexis by an identification:

> When it happens that a person has to give up a sexual object, there quite often ensues an alteration of his ego which can only be described as a

setting up of the object inside the ego, as it occurs in melancholia ... It may be that this identification is the sole condition under which the id can give up its objects. At any rate the process, especially in the early phases of development, is a very frequent one, and it makes it possible to suppose that the character of the ego is a precipitate of abandoned object-cathexes and that it contains the history of those object-choices.[3]

Thus, although in its form as identification it is foreclosed, it is possible to argue, as theorists such as Judith Butler have done, that a residue or trace of desire haunts identification, and that that desire is – as Freud himself suggested – same-sex desire: 'Large quantities of libido which is essentially homosexual are in this way drawn into the formation of the narcissistic ego-ideal' ('On Narcissism,' p. 76). Thus Butler argues that normative gender (same-sex identification) is constitutively melancholic, maintaining the traces of a foreclosed (lost and refused as lost) same-sex object of love.[4]

If identification and desire are two ways of describing self/other relations, then it may be possible to think of the scene of the lyric love poem in these revised terms, since lyric is a privileged domain of subjectivity that takes as its specific focus the constitution of a desiring subject by means of an object. And indeed, in early modernity, it is Petrarch, 'in many respects the most influential poet in the history of Western literature,'[5] to whom might be attributed precisely the explicit thematization and formalization of the ways identification and desire are finally inseparable in the constitution of subjectivity.

Petrarch's *Canzoniere*, or 'Song Book,' is said to have fixed, for subsequent generations, a set of poetic and descriptive norms for the love lyric. Nancy Vickers argues that petrarchism's influence is so authoritative that 'the contemporary lyric "I" follows every move we make: it is predominantly gendered as male; its message, for the most part, reminds us of the pain of adolescent love; and its discourse often strikingly appropriates classic tropes of petrarchism.'[6] The tradition Petrarch inherits, notes François Rigolot, posits a certain heteronormative arrangement of gender and sexuality:

il ne sera pas déraisonnable de poser qu'en règle générale le discours amoureux s'organise autour de modèles thèmatiques et formels établis depuis longtemps, en théorie et en pratique, par la tradition essentiellement masculine de la *fin' amour*: les publics masculin et féminin ... s'attendent à ce que le poème mette en scène un Amant, que cet Amant parle à la première personne de sa situation amoureuse, et que ce soit une Dame qui incarne l'objet de son désir.[7]

[It would not be unreasonable to hypothesize that, as a general rule, the discourse of love organizes itself around thematic and formal models that have been established for a long time – in theory and practice – by the essentially masculine tradition of *fin' amour*: both masculine and feminine audiences ... expect the poem to feature a Lover, expect that Lover to speak in the first person about his amorous condition, and they expect it to be a Lady who embodies the object of his desire.]

Within the tradition, therefore, insofar as the 'you' (or 'she') is necessary to the 'I' in the lyric, the ordering principles of differentiation between the two are sexual difference and heterosexual desire. Or we might say that sexual difference and heterosexual desire are produced as an effect of the necessary division of the 'I' and 'you' in the lyric utterance.

The masculine subject in the Petrarchan lyric thus constitutes itself in relation to a feminine object. It is the reiteration of the subject in the repetition of a series of lyric stances, the seemingly endless reoccupation of the lyric 'I' in relation to the object, that fixes and stabilizes this subject.[8] As John Freccero remarks ('The Fig Tree and the Laurel,' p. 34), the content of this lyric poetry – 'the idolatrous and unrequited passion for a beautiful and sometimes cruel lady' – is neither innovative nor original; rather, what distinguishes Petrarchan lyric is its (exclusive) preoccupation with the constitution of the poet himself:

The persona created by the serial juxtaposition of dimensionless lyric moments is as illusory as the animation of a film strip, the product of the reader's imagination as much as of the poet's craft; yet, the resultant portrait of an eternally weeping lover remains Petrarch's most distinctive poetic achievement ... It remained for centuries the model of poetic self-creation ...

That reiteration, or 'serial juxtaposition,' however, ultimately suggests not a dyadic relation between a subject and an object that is other but a split subject, a subject whose object is the creation of that subject.[9] In the Petrarchan situation this is made manifest by the inscription of fame (*lauro*, gendered masculine) in the name of the beloved (*Laura*, gendered feminine). As Jonathan Culler has noted of the apostrophic address of the lyric, 'apostrophes ... work less to establish an "I-Thou" relation ... than to dramatize or constitute an image of the self.'[10] 'This figure,' he notes of the 'you,' 'which seems to establish relations between the self and the other can in fact be read as an act of radical interiorization and solipsism' (p. 146).

Thus what is articulated in the Pertrachan lyric 'exchange' between an 'I' and a 'you' or 'she' is as much a relation of identification as of desire.[11] As such, it converges with what recent theorists of sexuality have argued 'queers' subjectivity in relation to the hegemonic heterosexual matrix (whereby gender, desire, and sex are imaginarily unified according to the identification/desire split) by troubling those categories, such that Laura comes to resemble, not so much an 'other' object of desire, but a kind of Petrarch in drag.[12]

One of the privileged figures for the conflated boundaries of such a relation is, of course, Narcissus, from whose Ovidian tale Freud derives the disorder that consists in loving what one ought instead to identify with as an ego-ideal. 'The presence of a myth in a work of art,' Leonard Barkan asserts, 'testifies to a problem, a mystery, a complexity, even a self-contradiction,'[13] and indeed, centuries of western interpretations of myths best known through their Ovidian formulation attest to this assertion. While in an earlier European tradition, Barkan claims, Ovidian myth lent itself to rationalizations of social and economic problems, and in the form of the *Ovide moralisé* was also read typologically as allegories of the divine, for lyric poets such as Petrarch, the Ovidian legacy is primarily an erotic and profane one.[14]

Ovid, in fact, pointedly articulates the dilemma of identification and desire represented by the narcissistic subject, for Narcissus laments: 'uror amore mei: flammas moveoque feroque. / quid faciam? roger anne rogem? quid deinde rogabo? / quod cupio mecum est ...' (III, ll. 464–6; 'I burn with love of my own self; I both kindle the flames and suffer them. What shall I do? Shall I be wooed or woo? Why woo at all? What I desire, I have ...').[15] The convergence of the two, the inability in other words to produce a separation between desiring subject and desired object results, Ovid suggests, in death. Petrarch accords Laura, as reflection, those same death-dealing properties Narcissus discovered in the realization that the image he desired was himself ('iste ego sum'; l. 463); Laura's eyes are 'micidiali specchi' ('homicidal mirrors,' Canzone 46): 'the lady celebrated by Petrarch is a brilliant surface, a pure signifier whose momentary exteriority to the poet serves as an Archimedean point from which he can create himself' (Freccero, 'The

Fig Tree and the Laurel,' p. 39). Thus in Freccero's description, Petrarch creates a poetics from Lacan's 'mirror stage' which itself rewrites, after a fashion, Narcissus's specular confrontation.[16]

Thus, in spite of the pretext of a normative organization of identification and desire according to the binary of sexual difference, Petrarch's is a 'perverse' model of desire. Barkan convincingly makes a case for the association, in Renaissance humanism, of the cultural confrontation between the present and the classical past with figures of the erotically perverse:

> One of the keystones of pagan myth is the privilege of the gods to break the essential human prohibitions. As I have argued elsewhere, unorthodox instances of endogamy and exogamy, including homosexuality but also such very different practices as incest and cannibalism, are related to this pattern of definitions for the human and the divine. Once mythic behavior is defined in terms of erotic unions among parties either too little or too much related, whether by tribe, gender, or blood, then the history of the myths may itself be played out via cultural dynamic that operates between consciousness of self and of other. The homosexual aspect of the myth of Ganymede, in other words, may express the *identity* or *sameness* that is a condition of the meeting of two apparently distinct selves, while the fact that this union is figured as between god and man (or man and boy) may express the *difference* that is likewise a condition of such meeting ... Taken together, these possibilities establish a cultural field in which the narrative of the myth may become a cultural allegory for precisely that historical confrontation between self and other which I characterized ... as a kind of humanist anthropology.[17]

In his reading, then, Ovidian narrative becomes not only the figural source for an erotics of the perverse, explicitly associated with poetry, but also a trope for the uncanny historical and cultural confrontation between two alien cultures separated by time and invested with a relation of identification ('sameness') and desire ('difference').[18]

If in Renaissance lyric poetry, classical myth can be thought of as allusively figuring an intersubjective relation that is both erotic and perverse, then it would seem that Ovid's *Metamorphoses* in particular serves as a figural paradigm for the transformations of poetic subjectivity and the instability of the boundaries between identification and desire. Commenting on a passage concerning the metamorphoses of the gods in Lactantius's *Divine Institutes,* Barkan notes, 'The otherness of pagan narratives becomes an occasion both for defining poetry and meditating on its dangers. By this logic the myths came in some respects to be metonymic for poetry itself' (*Transuming Passion*, p. 49). In fact, the poem of the *Canzoniere* most distinctively associated (by Petrarch himself) with the inscription of Petrarchan subjectivity, Canzone 23, 'Nel dolce tempo de la prima etade' ('In the sweet time of my first age'), is frequently referred to as the canzone of the metamorphoses for its deployment of Ovidian myth.[19]

Canzone 23 – the longest poem in the collection – is a kind of poetic manifesto, 'a spiritual autobiography of the poet-lover figured forth in a series of Ovidian transformations,'[20] with metamorphosis signalling an ultimately cyclical series of self-transformations involving mobility and voice. A distinctive feature of the poem is that, until the envoy, the poet is most often the mortal punished by a divinity, or the feminized object of violent and punitive transformation: first, like Daphne, he is transformed into a laurel; then, like Cygnus, into a swan; like Battus, into a stone; like Byblis into a fountain; like Echo into a disembodied voice, and then, upon returning to flesh to feel more pain, he is, like Actaeon, transformed into a stag which, were it not for the envoy (where he undergoes another set of transformations), he ought still to be ('et ancor de' miei can fuggo lo stormo,' l. 160; 'and still I flee the belling of my hounds,' p. 66).

The poem problematizes Petrarch's narcissistic and idolatrous poetics, and does so through an Ovidian problematization of subjectivity that destabilizes the boundaries between identification and desire articulating, as it does, Freud's assertion of the homoerotics of narcissistic subjectivity. Love (*Amor*), finding the poet impregnable to his assault, takes a powerful lady (*Donna*) as his patroness, and:

> ei duo mi transformaro in quel ch' i' sono,
> facendomi d'uom vivo un lauro verde
> che per fredda stagion foglia non perde (Canzone 23, ll. 38–40)

> those two transformed me into what I am, making me of a living man a green laurel that loses no leaf for all the cold season (p. 60)

Love and the Lady initiate the transformation of the poet into the laurel/Laura of eternal poetry, a metamorphosis (Daphne's) that effects a subject/object reversal and a movement away from the human and the voice and into inscription and immobility; each subsequent transformation similarly stresses the inhuman and the prohibition on speech (cf. Vickers, 'Diana Described,' p. 278). The culmination of the poem, to which I will return, invokes Actaeon's crime of beholding the goddess Diana naked and reiterates the manifesto of repeated transgression and nonrepentance that characterizes the poet's stance throughout: 'non ben si ripente/de l'un mal chi de l'altro s'apparecchia' (ll. 130–1; 'he does not repent well of one sin who prepares himself for another' p. 66). The envoy describes an apotheosis that invokes what Barkan calls *the* 'emblem for transcendent troping': Ganymede carried aloft by Jupiter (Barkan, *Transuming Passion,* p. 72). This figure, Barkan notes, comes to represent the sublimating activity of figuration itself in the context of an allusive relation between cultures. It is thus the quintessential example of 'transumption,' a response 'to an allusive culture that generates figural relations between individual acts of apparent free volition and a history whose omnipresence doubles their meaning' (pp. 42–3). But whereas in Dante's *Purgatorio,* the most immediate source for the image, the poet is Ganymede who is 'rapisse,' or 'rapt' (*Purgatorio* 9. ll. 13–30), in Canzone 23 the poet is the eagle of Jupiter himself and it is the Lady ('lei che ne' miei detto onoro' l. 166; 'her whom in my words I honor') who occupies the place of Ganymede. This temporary reversal of roles, whereby the poet occupies the god's place and heterosexualizes the dynamics of the (Dantesque or) Ovidian scene, then returns to the seemingly static, idolatrous, and narcissistic 'figure' of the initiatory transformation in the poem:

> né per nova figura il primo alloro
> seppi lassar, ché pur la sua dolce ombra
> ogni men bel piacer del cor mi sgombra. (ll. 167–9)

> nor for any new shape could I leave the first laurel, for still its sweet shade turns away from my heart any less beautiful pleasure. (p. 68)

The reassertion of the poet's identification with the laurel as the masculine embodiment of the beloved's name and the emblem of poetic glory suggests the inextricability, in this poetics, of desire and identification. Further, it collapses the mediatory term of the Lady in such a way as to rehomoeroticize the Ovidian episode of Jupiter and Ganymede, which, according to Barkan, troubles the separation of identification and desire in the 'monumentally awkward syntax that struggles to express both the difference and the interchangeability of the two lovers' of the lines: 'inventum est aliquid, quod Iuppiter esse, / quam quod erat, mallet' (10, ll. 156–7; *Transuming Passion,* p. 22). Thus (masculine) Love, through the agency of the Lady, inflicts violent punishment upon the unrepentant poet/lover who seeks out such violence and, in turn, becomes the god who wreaks it on a version of the self as other (or the other as self) in order to return to the 'figura' of poetry as eternal and unchanging. Freud writes of the narcissistic subject that he may love 'what he is himself,' 'what he once was,' 'what he would like to be,' or 'someone who was once part of himself,' 'object'-choices, which he also suggests (simultaneously and so somewhat in contradiction, but also later, in *The Ego and the Id*) transform themselves – are 'sublimated' – into constitutive dimensions of the ego as identificatory ideals.[21] The envoy condenses all of these, celebrating an interchangeability of ego-ideals and objects of desire – a narcissistic poetics – whose homoerotic residues are inscribed in the figures of Love and Jupiter/Ganymede. Finally, the envoy also echoes the apotheosis of the precursor poem that Canzone 23 'rewrites,' for the *Metamorphoses* concludes with an image of the poet as Ganymede carried aloft to immortal fame and glory: 'parte tamen meliore mei super alta perennis/astra ferar, nomenque erit indelebile nostrum' (XV, ll.875–6; 'Still in my better part I shall be borne immortal far beyond the lofty stars and I shall have an undying name,' p. 427). Thus, through what Barkan calls 'the cultural allegory for the historical confrontation of self and other' (*Transuming Passion,* p. 22), Petrarch allusively and rivalrously identifies with Ovid, concluding his metamorphosis poem, as the Latin poet does, with an assertion of eternal glory. At the same time, by identifying with Jupiter rather than Ganymede, Petrarch articulates a relation of desire between himself and the precursor poet.

Nancy Vickers's study of Canzone 23 has highlighted the ways Petrarch's poetics and the tradition of petrarchism that is its legacy nevertheless require the mediatory figure of the Lady whose parts – like the poet's rhymes – are repeatedly scattered and dispersed, in order to effect a consolidation of poetic subjectivity.[22] She focuses on the Diana-Actaeon episode in the poem as an emblematic allegory of sexual difference: the confrontation with Diana is another version of Freud's reading of Medusa's head, where the child's perception of the mother's 'castrated' body threatens his own with dismemberment.[23] Like Narcissus, Actaeon gazes at a mirror-image of himself in the hunter-goddess (Petrarch plays with the notion in his phrase, 'stetti a mirarla,' l. 153; '[I] stood to gaze on her'), but rather than an image, a simulacrum of himself, he confronts difference itself, in its absolute (and female) form.[24] While Giuseppe Mazzotta, in his analysis of another Diana-Actaeon encounter (Madrigal 52), reads Petrarch's poetics in terms of a reciprocal exchangeability between subject and object in the constitution of a cross-gendered or 'bisexual' subjectivity,[25] Vickers argues instead that Petrarch's poetic strategy constructs the threat of sexual difference in the body of the woman only to neutralize it by 'dismembering' and 'scattering' ('spargere') her parts:

> Petrarch's Actaeon, having read his Ovid, realizes what will ensue: his response to the threat of imminent dismemberment is the neutralization, through descriptive dismemberment, of the threat. He transforms the visible totality into scattered words, the body into signs; his description, at one remove from his experience, safely permits and perpetuates his fascination.[26]

Thus, although in the scene of the encounter the poet is diagetically transformed into a stag, his declaration, 'vero dirò' (l. 156, a modification of an earlier version of the poem which read 'narro' ['I tell'], the verb repeated by Diana twice in the Ovidian encounter) reinforces the notion that he has indeed triumphed over Diana's prohibition: '"nunc tibi me posito visam velamine narres,/sit poteris narrare, licet!"' (*Metamorphoses* III, ll. 192–3; 'Now you are free to tell that you have seen me all unrobed – if you can tell' p. 137).[27] The poet as Actaeon thus neutralizes the goddess – she is alone and does not speak – in order to represent her in his verse as descriptive spectacle.

Whereas the narcissistic subjectivity of the Petrarchan lyric would seem to articulate homoerotic relations of identification and desire, it does so in part by repeatedly invoking the body of the Lady as that which must be seen, silenced, fetishistically fragmented, and collapsed back into the poet's words, as the revisionist scene of Actaeon's encounter with Diana in Canzone 23 suggests. This is the strategy Petrarch popularizes for generations of lyric imitators, and it characterizes what Eve Sedgwick has termed 'homosociality' – a triangulated relation of eroticized and identificatory rivalry between men effected through 'women' as objects and signs of exchange.[28]

'Bodies fetishized by a poetic voice,' Vickers notes, 'logically do not have a voice of their own; the world of making words, of making texts, is not theirs' ('Diana Described,' p. 277). But if 'silencing Diana' is indeed an 'emblematic gesture' (p. 278) that effaces the difference of the feminine object and permits its rearticulation as a masculinized identificatory ideal ('lauro,' or fame), this nevertheless suggests the allegorical power of the Ovidian encounter, a power both Norman O. Brown and Barkan have explored at length.[29] Ann Jones comments that 'women poets, too, confronted the prestigious and multivalent system of figures for power, erotic encounter, and transformation supplied by Renaissance versions of Ovidian metamorphosis,' but focuses on the absence, for women poets, of Ovidian models of poetic power such as Orpheus.[30] The sixteenth-century French lyric poet Louise Labé, self-consciously reformulating a Petrarchan poetics based in classical myth, not only adopts Ovidian tropes of identification and desire to formulate a poetic subjectivity, but also takes up the Ovidian practice of ventriloquization most prominent in the epistolary *Heroïdes* (elegaic verses enunciated in the 'voices' of female characters) in her elegies. In redirecting the gendered positionalities of the lyric subject (presumably male), Labé un- or re-crosses the identificatory and desiring positions of the Petrarchan subject, and – in a 'perverse' yet common strategy of feminine textual identification – adopts the subjectivities of the already travestied female voices that speak in the Ovidian corpus.[31]

Labé's Sonnet 19 in particular takes up the myth of Diana and Actaeon to 'rewrite' the encounter through a series of transformative identifications that mimic both Petrarchan and Ovidian metamorphoses by displacing the poetic subject. In the first stanza, the 'je' ('I') of the narrative might be taken to be Actaeon:

> Diane estant en l'espesseur d'un bois,
> Apres avoir mainte beste assenee,
> Prenoit le frais, de Nynfes couronnee:
> J'allois resvant comme fay maintefois ...[32]

> While Diana, in the thick of the woods after having killed many beasts was taking shade, crowned by her nymphs, I was walking along dreaming as I do oftentimes ...

The scene is set: there is a moment of suspense as the mythic confrontation is promised and deferred. Labé's Diana is restored to her Ovidian context, surrounded by nymphs, and Actaeon too retains the absent-minded wandering of 'non certis passibus errans' (*Metamorphoses* III, ll. 175; 'wandering ... with unsure footsteps' p. 137), rather than the intentional deliberation of the Petrarchan gaze: 'Io perché d'altra vista non m'appago/stetti a mirarla' (Canzone 23, ll. 152–3; 'I, who am not appeased by any other sight, stood to gaze on her' p. 66). But in the second stanza, instead of staging the apotropaic confrontation with the deity, the subject is interpellated as one of Diana's followers, a 'nynfe,' who ought to be, but is not, 'vers Diane tournee' ('turned toward Diana'). At the end of the second stanza, another metamorphosis occurs, for the voice 'sees' that the wandering subject is without her bow and quiver, like Diana when she is caught in Actaeon's gaze ('ut vellet promptas habuisse sagittas,' III, l. 188; 'and though she would fain have had her arrows ready,' p. 137). The last two tercets of the poem intertwine subject and object, identification and desire, in a series of reversals whereby the poet occupies the position of either Actaeon or Diana the hunter aiming at a passing 'stag'; at which point the stag undergoes a reverse transformation into a man, collecting up the weapons and returning fire on the poet now metamorphosed, presumably, into prey.

Edith Joyce Benkov analyses the anti-Dianan rhetoric of the poem and its demythification of 'the woman-goddess of male-voiced poetic discourse' through the poet's transformation into a woman who is 'powerless to inflict ... wounds.'[33] She remarks that, at the end of the poem, the poet is 'like Actaeon ... beset by her own hunting instruments' (p. 29). But the metamorphoses, from Actaeon to nymph to goddess/Actaeon to Actaeon – and back to nymph again (to tell the tale), establish the mirroring of identities between Diana and Actaeon in such a way that the two become interchangeable and their fates reversible. Thus the poetic subject refuses the fixity of positions that would result in a triumph of one over the other in this allegory of identification and desire.

Elsewhere Louise Labé deploys the image of the wounding arrows to articulate the predicament of occupying both sides of the subject/object split but only one side of the sexual difference divide. In the first elegy, she writes:

> C'estoit mes yeus, dont tant faisois saillir
> De traits, à ceus qui trop me regardoient
> Et de mon arc assez ne se gardoient.
> Mais ces miens traits ces miens yeus me defirent,
> Et de vengeance estre exemple me firent. (ll. 28–32; p. 108)

It was my eyes, from which I made spring forth many arrows towards those who watched me too much and did not guard themselves enough from my

> bow. But those shafts of mine those eyes of mine undid me, And made of me an example of revenge.

The confusing syntax of the line where the arrows and eyes belonging to the Lady in turn undo her and transform her from lethal 'object' of the gaze to poet-lover who laments her condition of unrequited love, articulates the difficulty of a lyric poet simultaneously occupying both positions. The passage might even be said to demystify as blatant pretext the gendered split of the masculine poet-persona in this neoplatonic schema of what looks like a self-wounding. The trajectory of the desire described is a boomerang: the beautiful Lady (here both subject and object) shoots arrows from her eyes that then return to pierce those very same eyes. The 'point' of identification and desire is the end of a circular movement where source and end are one. In this passage, there is no agency for the return fire: the poet declares that her own arrows circle back around to wound her. Here, then, love becomes the lethal gaze – the homicidal mirror – of Narcissus and his image.

But Sonnet 19 transforms the fatal 'narcissistic' encounter between Diana and Actaeon into a witty poetic rejoinder deploying a courtly and neoplatonic conceit – the beloved's eyes that send wounding arrows into the lover – that ironically mimics both Ovidian metamorphosis and Petrarchan narcissism. By metamorphically inhabiting the subjectivity of both main characters in the drama, Labé not only demythifies the goddess but also, in Ovidian fashion, 'restores' to her a voice. The refusal to remain stably in either position – subject or object, goddess or voyeuristic poet – revives the reciprocity of identification entailed in the mutual gaze of the Ovidian encounter, and it also achieves Diana's objective to elude the shame of being caught in the gaze. Moreover, although the poetic narrative suggests the presence of Actaeon, he is never mentioned by name and he remains voiceless, not the Petrarchan poet who lives to tell the tale, but a mere 'passant' whose arrows inflict hundreds of wounds but, unlike Actaeon's hunting dogs, do not kill. Labé reanimates the Ovidian narrative through a gendered identification with the voice of the goddess, even as she, Diana-like, reduces the narcissistic status of the poet as Actaeon by silencing him.

In appropriating – or as Barkan calls it, transuming – a powerful Ovidian narrative of the lethal effects of identification ('sameness') and desire ('difference') and displacing its Petrarchan homosocial twist, Labé allegorically articulates the dilemma of the female poetic subject of the love lyric. Further, by 'removing' both Diana and Actaeon from the scene and staging, instead, an encounter between two nymphs (or rather two female 'voices'), Labé displaces the encounter itself so that it becomes the subject of indirect discourse. In so doing, she also displaces the strategies of voyeurism and fetishism that would make a woman – Lady or goddess – the mute object of lyrical description or the fragmented signs of a disavowed difference that, 'like poetry ... gains immortality at the price of vitality and history.'[34]

NOTES

1 Sigmund Freud, 'An Example of Psycho-analytic Work,' in *An Outline of Psychoanalysis*, trans. James Strachey (New York: Norton, 1969), p. 50.
2 Sigmund Freud, 'On Narcissism: An Introduction (1914),' in *General Psychological Theory*, ed. Philip Rieff (New York: Collier, 1963), pp. 68–9.
3 Sigmund Freud, *The Ego and the Id*, trans. Joan Rivière, ed. James Strachey (New York: Norton, 1960), p. 19.
4 Judith Butler, *The Psychic Life of Power: Theories in Subjection* (Stanford, CA: Stanford University Press, 1997), chapter 5, 'Melancholy Gender/Refused Identification,' pp. 132–50.
5 John Freccero, 'The Fig Tree and the Laurel: Petrarch's Poetics,' *Diacritics* 5.1 (1975): 34.
6 Nancy Vickers, 'Vital Signs: Petrarch and Popular Culture,' *Romanic Review* 79.1 (1988): 186.
7 François Rigolot, 'Quel "genre" d'amour pour Louise Labé?' *Poétique* 55 (1983): 304; the translation is mine.
8 See Nancy Vickers, 'Diana Described: Scattered Woman and Scattered Rhyme,' *Critical Inquiry* 8.2 (1981): 265–79.
9 See Freccero, 'The Fig Tree and the Laurel'; see also Robert Durling, *Petrarch's Lyric Poems: The Rime Sparse and Other Lyrics* (Cambridge, MA: Harvard University Press, 1976), esp. pp. 1–33.
10 Jonathan Culler, *The Pursuit of Signs: Semiotics, Literature, Deconstruction* (Ithaca, NY: Cornell University Press, 1981), p. 142.
11 For discussions about the continuities between desire and identification, see, among others, Eve Kosofsky Sedgwick, *Between Men: English Literature and Male Homosocial Desire* (New York: Columbia University Press, 1985); and Jonathan Dollimore, *Sexual Dissidence: Augustine to Wilde, Freud to Foucault* (Oxford: Clarendon Press, 1991). Judith Butler, in *Bodies that Matter: On the Discursive Limits of 'Sex'* (New York: Routledge, 1993), explicitly takes up the question of the relation between identification and desire in the context of

homosexuality: 'In psychoanalytic terms, the relation between gender and sexuality is in part negotiated through the question of the relationship between identification and desire. And here it becomes clear why refusing to draw lines of causal implication between these two domains is as important as keeping open an investigation of their complex interimplication ... The heterosexual logic that requires that identification and desire be mutually exclusive is one of the most reductive of heterosexism's psychological instruments ...' (p. 239).

12 See Butler, *Bodies that Matter*, p. 239, for a discussion of the heterosexual matrix.

13 Leonard Barkan, 'Diana and Actaeon: The Myth as Synthesis,' *English Literary Renaissance* 10.3 (1980): 318.

14 The narrative of the 'restoration' of a profane Ovid by a 'secular' Renaissance from the Christian Middle Ages risks being as purely ideological as the accusation of 'anachronism' launched by an enlightened secular modernity against a naïve 'dark ages.' Such an 'anti-moralization' bias is apparent in the special issue of *Cahiers de l'Europe Classique et Néo-Latine 1, Ovide en France dans la Renaissance* (Toulouse: Service des publications de l'Université de Toulouse-Le Mirail, 1981), but it is one that does not exempt the Renaissance: 'On peut s'étonner que pareilles erreurs aient été perpétuées jusqu'à la fin de la Renaissance: elles montrent, en tout cas, que la métamorphose des mentalités, la conversion d'une culture ne s'opérant que très lentement et debordent les cadres artificiels de la chronologie, en laissant subsister, abandonnées à une cohabitation monstrueuse, les formes étranges du passé' (pp. 33–4). In France, unallegorized editions of *The Metamorphoses* did not predominate until 1530; see Ann Moss, *Ovid in Renaissance France: A Survey of the Latin Editions of Ovid and Commentaries Printed in France before 1600* (London: The Warburg Institute, 1982). My point and – Barkan's too, perhaps – would be more that, rather than deploying a profane Ovid in the service of an enlightened secular modernity (or humanism), poets such as Petrarch deployed Ovidian narrative in the service of an idolatrous and deliberately perverse poetics.

15 Cf. Ovid, *Metamorphoses*, Books I–VIII, trans. Frank Justus Miller, rev. G.P. Goold (Cambridge, MA: Harvard University Press, 1916, repr. 1994), p. 157. All citations from Ovid will be taken from this edition. References are to book and line number. Durling, *Petrarch's Lyric Poems*, p. 112; all further citations and translations of Petrarch are from this edition.

16 Jacques Lacan, 'Le stade du miroir comme formateur de la fonction du Je telle qu'elle nous est révélée dans l'expérience psychanalytique,' in *Ecrits* (Paris: Seuil, 1966), pp. 93–100; see also *Ecrits: A Selection*, trans. Alan Sheri-

dan (New York: Norton, 1977), pp. 1–7. Lacan describes the mirror stage as an initial site of subject-formation akin to primary narcissism and the formation of the ego-deal, whereby the infant assumes an idealized image of itself as other thus involving, to a certain extent, a self-alienation. Lacan seems to be citing Narcissus's 'iste ego sum' when he writes, in the conclusion to his essay: 'la psychanalyse peut accompagner le patient jusqu'à la limite extatique du "*Tu es cela,*" où se révèle à lui le chiffre de sa destinée mortelle ...' (p. 100; 'psychoanalysis may accompany the patient to the ecstatic limit of the "*Thou art that,*" in which is revealed to him the cipher of his mortal destiny ...' p. 7). Jason Jacobs (University of California at Santa Cruz), in an unpublished paper, makes the case that 'Petrarch – and later on what one might call the Petrarchan mode – performs on the level of language what Lacan conceives of on the level of image and of space: the retroactive formation of an "I" via the misapprehension of something outside that "I", a self that comes into being by folding into itself its own projection' ('Two's Company, There's A Queer,' unpublished paper, graduate seminar, winter 1999, p. 4).

17 Leonard Barkan, *Transuming Passion: Ganymede and the Erotics of Humanism* (Stanford, CA: Stanford University Press, 1991), pp. 21–2. See also his *The Gods Made Flesh: Metamorphosis and the Pursuit of Paganism* (New Haven: Yale University Press, 1986).

18 See Barkan's chapter, 'Erotic Humanism,' for further discussion of the Renaissance association between figural language and perversity. See also Thomas Greene's discussion of early modern *imitatio* and cultural and historical identification and estrangement, especially in relation to Petrarch, in *The Light in Troy* (New Haven: Yale University Press, 1982).

19 Petrarch quotes the first line of Canzone 23 in Canzone 70 as the culminating verse in a poetic genealogy of predecessors, a kind of poetic *translatio imperii* that begins with Arnaut Daniel, then cites Guido Cavalcanti, Dante, Cino da Pistoia, and finally, Petrarch himself. See Durling, *Petrarch's Lyric Poems*, pp. 150–3.

20 Barkan, 'Diana and Acteon,' p. 335. Durling comments, 'Metamorphosis is ... a dominant idea in the *Rime sparse* ... Ovid is omnipresent' (*Petrarch's Lyric Poems*, pp. 26–7).

21 Freud, 'On Narcissism (1914),' p. 71, and *The Ego and the Id*, pp. 18–21. See, in this connection, Earl Jackson, Jr, *Strategies of Deviance: Studies in Gay Male Representation* (Bloomington: Indiana University Press, 1995), who argues that 'On Narcissism' 'presents two definitions of "narcissism": first, a range of identificatory operations that form and refigure the ego; and second, a classification of object-choice. The former offers a potentially compelling

descriptive model of the dynamic interchanges constituting psychosocial subject formations ... the latter is merely part of a two-term typology of sexual relations, and one which is thoroughly implicated in a gender-hierarchized value system' (p. 26). See esp. pp. 26–31 for his discussion of narcissism.

22 Vickers, 'Diana Described,' p. 272: 'If the speaker's "self" (his text, his "corpus") is to be unified, it would seem to require the repetition of her dismembered image.'

23 Vickers, 'Diana Described,' p. 273. See Freud, 'Medusa's Head (1922),' in *Sexuality and the Psychology of Love*, ed. Philip Rieff (New York: Collier Books, 1963), pp. 212–13. In the *Metamorphoses*, the threat is real and realized; later on in book III, Pentheus will be dismembered at the hands of his mother, while crying out: 'moveant animos Actaeonis umbrae!' (3, ll. 720; 'Let the ghost of Actaeon move your heart!' p. 174).

24 Vickers writes, 'The Actaeon-Diana story is one of identification and reversal ... it is a confrontation with difference where similarity might have been desired or expected. It is a glance into a mirror ... that produces an unlike and deeply threatening image' (p. 273). Barkan also describes the similarities between the story of Narcissus and the story of Actaeon and Diana in 'Diana and Actaeon,' p. 321. For a discussion of Boccaccio's use of Diana as a principle of resistant femininity, see, among others, Carla Freccero, 'From Amazon to Court Lady: Generic Hybridization in Boccaccio's *Teseida*,' *Comparative Literature Studies* 32.2 (1995): 226–43.

25 See Guiseppe Mazzotta, 'The *Canzoniere* and the Language of the Self,' in *Petrarch: Modern Critical Views*, ed. Harold Bloom (New York: Chelsea House, 1989): 66–7.

26 Vickers, 'Diana Described,' p. 273.

27 Vickers invokes this previous version of line 156 in Canzone 23 ('Diana Described,' p. 273); see Dennis Dutschke, *Francesco Petrarca, Canzone XXIII from First to Final Version* (Ravenna: Longo Editore, 1977), pp. 196–8.

28 Eve Kosofky Sedgwick, *Between Men: English Literature and Male Homosocial Desire* (New York: Columbia University Press, 1985), especially chapter 1: 'Gender Asymmetry and Erotic Triangles,' pp. 21–7. Vickers also studies this aspect of male homosociality in relation to lyric poetry in '"The blazon of sweet beauty's best": Shakespeare's *Lucrece*,' in *Shakespeare and the Question of Theory*, ed. Patricia Parker and Geoffrey Hartman (New York: Methuen, 1985), pp. 95–115. Claude Lévi-Strauss, in *The Elementary Structures of Kinship* (Boston: Beacon Press, 1969), pp. 478–97, discusses women as currency exchanged among men to cement relations of reciprocity; see also Gayle Rubin, 'The Traffic in Women: Notes on the "Political Economy" of Sex,' in

Toward an Anthropology of Women, ed. Rayna Reiter (New York: Monthly Review Press, 1975), pp. 157–210, for a feminist discussion of the psychoanalytic and social implications for feminism of this theory of exchange.

29 See Norman O. Brown, 'Metamorphoses II: Actaeon,' *American Poetry Review* 1 (1972): 38–40; see also Barkan, 'Diana and Actaeon.' Neither Brown nor Barkan, however, explores what power the narrative might have as an allegory for the female poet.

30 See Ann Jones, 'New Songs for the Swallow: Ovid's Philomela in Tullia d'Aragona and Gaspara Stampa,' in *Refiguring Woman: Perspectives on Gender and the Italian Renaissance*, ed. Marilyn Migiel and Juliana Schiesari (Ithaca: Cornell University Press, 1991): 263.

31 On Louise Labé's complex practices of gendering the lyric, see Rigolot, 'Quel "genre" d'amour pour Louise Labé?'; see also 'Gender vs. Sex Difference in Louise Labé's Grammar of Love,' in *Rewriting the Renaissance: The Discourses of Sexual Difference in Early Modern Europe*, ed. Margaret Ferguson et al. (Chicago: University of Chicago Press, 1986), pp. 287–98. On women poets in the Renaissance, Labé included, see also Ann Jones, *The Currency of Eros: Women's Love Lyric in Europe 1540–1620* (Bloomington: Indiana University Press, 1990).

32 Louise Labé, *Oeuvres Complètes: Sonnets, Élégies, Débat de Folie et d'Amour*, ed. François Rigolot (Paris: Garnier Flammarion, 1986), p. 131. All citations of Labé's poetry are taken from this edition; translations, unless otherwise indicated, are my own.

33 Edith Joyce Benkov, 'The Pantheon Revisited: Myth and Metaphor in Louise Labé,' *Classical and Modern Literature: A Quarterly* 5.1 (1984): 29.

34 Freccero, 'The Fig Tree and the Laurel,' p. 39.

Imagining Heterosexuality in the Epyllia

JIM ELLIS

In *Echoes of Desire: English Petrarchism and Its Counterdiscourses*, Heather Dubrow argues that petrarchism 'repeatedly challenges the boundaries between characteristics that might be considered masculine and feminine; whereas its counterdiscourses react to these challenges in many different ways, one of the most common and revealing is their attempt to reestablish gender distinctions.'[1] This is true to some degree of the epyllion, one of the genres that Dubrow identifies as a counterdiscourse to Petrarchism, and one which is very much interested in establishing clear guidelines for masculine and feminine behaviour. Written for the most part in the last decade of the sixteenth century, and generally produced within the milieu of the Inns of Court, the epyllia retell classical myths, usually taken from Ovid's *Metamorphoses*. As Clarke Hulse points out, they are Ovidian not just in their subject matter, but more importantly in their tone – in the ironic, studied amorality with which they retell stories of love and transformation, or what William Keach calls 'the Elizabethan epyllion's ironic self-consciousness.'[2] As Lynn Enterline argues, this is one of the key differences between Ovidian and Petrarchan poety[3] – the distance of the narrator from the desire in the poem, a point to which I will return. This distance is crucial to the gender distinctions that the poems attempt to reestablish, or more accurately, to establish: the poems through their reimagining of Ovid invent a kind of heterosexuality.

Like their source, the epyllia are involved in what might be called ironic aetiology, often featuring, in a semi-comic way, tales of how things came to be the way they are. The most frequent explanations concern men and women, and gender norms. The poems are stories of sexual difference, sexual desire, and gender protocol. Readers are taught, for example, 'That nimphs must yeeld, when faithfull lovers straie not' ('*Scillaes Metamorphosis*' envoy).[4] Chapman tells us that no does not mean no, and that when female minds 'Breake out in fury, they are certaine signes / Of their perswasions' (*The Divine Poem of Musaeus: Hero and Leander*, ll. 190–1). We learn that women are ruled by the moon, and 'That as of Planets shee most variable, / So of all creatures they most mutable' (*Endimion and Phoebe*, ll. 421–2). Within the poems characters are instructed on behaviour appropriate to their sex and to sex, and are schooled in the differences that mark out male and female: 'Wert thou a mayd, and I a man, Ile show thee, / With what a manly boldness I could woo thee' (*Salmacis and Hermaphroditus*, ll. 715–16), says the bold nymph Salmacis to the bashful Hermaphroditus. Venus says similarly to the reluctant Adonis:

> Would thou wert as I am, and I a man,
> My heart as whole as thine, thy heart my wound:
> For one sweet look thy help I would assure thee.[5]

One of the functions of all of the aetiological digressions is presumably to naturalize these gender prescriptions. Nonetheless, the genre's obsession with offering these prescriptions undercuts this naturalizing process, implicitly demonstrating precisely the opposite, that gender norms are cultural and must be learned.

Although nominally about love affairs between gods and mortals, the epyllia are often as much about rhetoric as anything else. If nothing else, they are elaborate demonstrations of the poet's ability to embellish a mythic narrative. Elizabeth Donno explains this phenomenon as a simple joy in creation: 'This delight in the *artificial* explains why the writers of the epyllia frequently use only the core of a myth for their story line and why the narrative is the least important element. They attend rather to the embroidering and ornamenting of their poems with all the power of rhetorical devices and ingenious invention.'[6] This is certainly an accurate reflection of the wildly digressive and copious style of the epyllia, although it might be noted that there are other reasons than sheer joy in creation for displays of rhetorical command and ingenuity, especially within a humanistic educational system where rhetoric was the foundation of all further study and under a government increasingly reliant on a bureaucracy trained in rhetorical technique.

Rhetoric figures in the genre in a number of ways. In addition to being a display of an ambitious young poet's skill, the poems often portray a youth developing an increasing ability for rhetoric and acquiring an appreciation for its power, as we can see when Hero asks the 'bold sharp sophister' Leander: 'Who taught thee Rhethoricke to deceive a Maid?' (l. 338). Beyond this typical narrative of education, however, there is the general tendency of everyone in these poems to display polished rhetorical skills, so that the poems are often little more than lengthy debates about the pursuit of one's desire and, not coincidentally, displays of the poet's craft. A. Leigh DeNeef has recently argued, for example, that R.B.'s *Orpheus His Journey to Hell* works principally as a compendious catalogue of contemporary poetic and rhetorical genres and a demonstration of the poet's ability to effectively employ them.[7]

These poems were for the most part written by young poets pursuing an education (or simply connections) at either the universities or, more often, the Inns of Court. The Inns of Court were the prime site in England for learning rhetorical and oratorical skills. Young men on the rise engaged in mock combats, sparring over real and imagined points of law, just as the characters in the epyllia offer elaborate and legalistic disquisitions in support of their desire. Wilfred Prest argues that 'by the beginning of Elizabeth's reign, the law had virtually replaced the church as the career open to talents, the ladder on which able young men could climb to power and riches.'[8] A modest example of such a career is that of Justice Shallow in *Henry IV, Part 2,* who, waxing nostalgic about his youthful days at Clement's Inn, seems to have spent all of his time there drinking, fighting, and whoring. Nonetheless, as Falstaff bitterly observes, after sowing his wild oats in the city, Shallow returns to his country home: 'now is this Vice's dagger become a squire ... now he has lands and beefs.'[9] Shallow's experience is presumably typical of a large number of country gentleman who attended the Inns of Court to become JPs or other local administrators.

Philip J. Finkelpearl characterizes the Inns of Court as 'a finishing school,' populated largely by 'an inbred milieu of young men, mostly wealthy, whose orthodox ideals and ambitions mingled easily with licentious conduct (or the pretense of it) and whose fashions in clothes and literature were picked up and discarded overnight.'[10] Students attended the surrounding schools that taught fencing, dancing, and music, and were notoriously enthusiastic theatre-goers. The poets at the Inns were both sensitive to and at the mercy of social change, but at the same time relatively orthodox in their views. The poems themselves evoke a culture in transition, partially by evoking poetic clichés about mutability. As

Glaucus says to the poet, 'times change' (7.5): 'Take moist from sea, take colour from his kinde, / Before the world devoid of change thou finde' (5.5–6). Clark Hulse suggests that the epyllia 'was the medium by which the poet could transform himself from an ephebe to a high priest. It was a genre for young poets ceasing to be young, a form somewhere above the pastoral or sonnet and below the epic, the transition between the two in the *gradus Vergilianus.*'[11] The writing of an epyllion thus both suggests a transition and represents one in the career of the poet. These tales of metamorphosis were written by and for ambitious young men experiencing or perhaps desiring a metamorphosis, in a society that was itself undergoing change.

It is thus not accidental that the mythological stories that the genre retells are principally stories of the transformation of young men: stories, as Ovid says in Arthur Golding's translation, 'of shapes transformde to bodies straunge.'[12] The writers are interested in the phemonenon of change, however much they present their poems as simply witty and salacious excursus on the subject of desire. In fact, the poems often attempt to effect a kind of change in poetic conventions of desire by staging a rejection of Petrarchan conventions. When the genre is satiric, it is generally satirizing Petrarchan poetry, and it does this most often by associating it with immaturity, narcissism and occasionally effeminacy. The Petrarchan poet is shown to be in love with his own fancy, desiring desire, whereas the mature Ovidian poet wants a real, flesh and blood woman. Narcissus himself moralizes on this distinction: 'Had *Priapus Narcissus* place enjoy'd / He would a little more have done than toy'd.'[13] In staging this rejection of Petrarchan erotics as a part of the process of maturation, it can be argued that the poems are attempting to install a version of heterosexuality. I do not mean to suggest that the writers of the epyllia single-handedly worked to create heterosexuality, or a modern masculinity, merely that they participated in a shift that occurred over the course of the early modern period in England, when newer, more recognizable (from our perspective) versions of masculinity, heterosexuality, subjectivity, and selfhood came into being. In the epyllia, what this generally means is rejecting the compromising position of object of desire in favour of becoming the autonomous subject of desire, which the poems unsurprisingly associate with a mastery of rhetoric. In what follows, I will be exploring these issues through two Ovidian poems: Thomas Lodge's poem *Scillaes Metamorphosis,* generally acknowledged to be the first English epyllion, and an earlier poem by Thomas Peend, which seems to have significantly influenced the genre.

I

While Thomas Lodge's *Scillaes Metamorphosis* is the first example of the genre, Lodge clearly made use of Golding's translation of the *Metamorphoses,* and 'of even more importance, of a translation of the story of Salmacis-Hermaphroditus by Thomas Peend.'[14] In 1565 Peend published *The Pleasaunt Fable of Hermaphroditus and Salmacis,* as a way of compensating, he writes, for having had his translation of the *Metamorphoses* 'prevented' by the earlier publication of Golding's. Peend's poem follows Ovid more or less faithfully, and in the tradition of the medieval Ovid, he appends the tale with a moral. In order 'that the unlearned myght the better understand these' verses, Peend also includes a glossary of mythological names and their significance.

The tale of Hermaphroditus and Salmacis would be the subject of a later epyllion by Francis Beaumont in 1602, but the poem's influence on the genre goes beyond this. Most importantly, perhaps, it introduces what will be the most common couple of the genre – the aggressive female wooer and the beautiful but reluctant youth. In discussing Shakespeare's innovation of portraying a 'chaste, resistant Adonis,' Keach notes that 'Ovid himself provided the models for developing this conception in the tales of Hermaphroditus (*Metamorphoses* IV. ll. 285–388), Narcissus (*Metamorphoses* III. ll. 342–510), and Hippolytus (*Metamorphoses* XV. ll. 492–546). Like Shakespeare's Adonis, all of these figures are supremely beautiful young men full of self-love and self-ignorance who come to tragic ends.'[15] Hermaphroditus, along with Adonis, Leander, Endymion, and Narcissus, acts out one of the most recurrent narratives of the genre – an attractive youth who is metamorphosed through desire.

In Peend's poem, *The Pleasaunt Fable,* Hermaphroditus is the child of Mercury and Venus, 'for beauty farre excellyng all that erst before hym weare' (l. 2), surpassing, says the narrator, even the beauty of Ganymede, Narcissus, and Adonis. At the age of fifteen he leaves home and wanders to the hot land of Caria, where he is spied by the nymph Salmacis. She falls in love immediately and attempts to woo him, but he 'blush[es] as red as blood' (l. 69) at her advances and flees. Salmacis retreats, and then spies on the youth from a bush. He strips, cavorts in the fields, and then slowly enters the water. Overcome with desire, Salmacis stalks her prey, grabs him in the water, and begs the gods to unite them. They do, but not in the way she had in mind, and Hermaphroditus becomes a hermaphrodite:

But now, when that Hermaphrodite dyd see in water playne,
He entred lyke a man therin, and shulde come foorth agayne
But halfe a man. Hym selfe he loste. Hys fortune it was so. (ll. 158–60)

Curiously, although the pair are united, Salmacis seems to have disappeared entirely; as with many epyllia, the poem is really only interested in the fate of the youth. Hermaphroditus asks the gods to change the well so that it will have the same effect on whomever else enters it and the gods answer his prayer.

At the conclusion of the story, Peend offers a justification for retelling this 'tryflyng tale' of Ovid, saying that 'it shewes a worthy sence, if it be marked well' (ll. 167–8). He then shows the sense to us. For the person of Hermaphroditus, 'understand, such Youthes as yet be greene' (l. 171), who, as yet untouched by 'affection vyle' (l. 173), go out in the world 'To lerne and see the trades of men' (l. 179). The land Hermaphroditus travels to is 'the worlde where all temptations be' (l. 181). 'By Salmacis, intende eche vyce that moveth one to ill' (l. 183). When we surrender to such vices, 'We chaunge our nature cleane, being made effemynat' (l. 213):

And so it may now playne appere
  The Poet thus dyd tell.
As many as hereafter shall
  Once enter in thys well
Of vyce, he shalbe weakned so
  Hys nature sure he shall forgo. (ll. 217–19)

Having expounded the meaning of the myth, Peend goes on to give notable examples of lustful women, including such Elizabethan favourites as Echo, Medea, Dido, Helen, Hero, and Juliet.

The moral of the story that Peend offers is interesting for a number of reasons. One of the things that differentiates this poem from the epyllia of the 1590s is this need to moralize: the later poems will either abandon this tendency or parody it, adopting a distinctly Ovidian amorality that becomes a hallmark of the genre. However, because the poems tend to tell the same story, that of a youth metamorphosed by desire, the moral of the earlier poem can perhaps tell us something about the interest that this particular story had for both the writers and readers of the genre, since the constituency of all of the poems is the same. As Keach notes, 'almost all the authors of the Elizabethan epyllia except Shakespeare were at one time or another formally connected either with one of the Universities or with the Inns of Court, or both.'[16] This is also true of Peend, who Anthony Wood says studied at Oxford and who was a barrister in London. He signs the dedication of *Hermaphroditus*, 'from my Chamber over agaynst Sergeants Inne in Chancery lane' and a later work is signed from the Middle Temple (*DNB*). Bearing in mind the Inns of Court milieu, the poem's moral becomes only too obvious and appropriate: Hermaphroditus is the naïve youth from the country, newly arrived at the Inns to become a lawyer or a courtier and in danger of being overwhelmed by the alluring vices of the great city, 'the world where all temptations be' (l. 181). Insufficiently guarded against his own desires, his masculinity becomes hopelessly compromised or metamorphosed. The story of the 'green youth' from the country is a common enough narrative, but one which was frequently told about the young men of the Inns.

II

Lodge's *Scillaes Metamorphosis, Enterlaced with the unfortunate love of Glaucus* (1589) is even more explicitly directed to the young men of the Inns than Peend's poem. Lodge dedicates the work 'To his especiall good friend Master Rafe Crane, and the rest of his most entire well willers, the Gentlemen of the Inns of Court and Chauncerie' and signs himself 'Thomas Lodge of Lincolnes Inne, Gent.' This echoes the dedication of Lodge's *Alarum against Usurers* (1584), a pamphlet probably written around the same time to warn young gentlemen about various unscrupulous characters populating London. The title page of *Scillaes Metamorphosis*, in a perhaps ironic nod to the tradition of moralizing Ovid, declares it 'Verie fit for young Courtiers to peruse, and coy Dames to remember.' The chance of coy dames reading it had to have been remote, however; as Keach argues, 'Lodge's epyllion bears every mark of having originally been a private piece, probably written during the period 1584–1588 and circulated among his friends at Lincoln's Inn.'[17] The Inns were a resolutely all-male space.

Unlike Peend's poem, *Scillaes Metamorphosis* diverges substantially from its source in Ovid. In the *Metamorphoses*, the story begins with Scilla, who is walking naked along the shore one day when Glaucus spies her from the water. Alarmed by his strange shape, she flees in terror, but he calls to her and tells her the story of his transformation. He was originally a human fisherman, he says, who one day landed his catch on a strange stretch of land, and all of his fish revived and 'too seeward took theyr flyght' (XIII.1096). Curious, he tasted an herb that they had been lying on, and it made him forsake the land forever. The sea gods received him, and asked Oceanus and Thetis to make him immortal. As a result, his shape changed dramatically: he now has a great grisly beard and hair, and a fish's tail. He concludes his tale by plaintively asking Scilla,

> But what avayleth mee
> This goodly shape, and of the Goddes of sea too loved bee,
> Or for too be a God my self, if they delyght not thee? (XIII.1124–6)

In spite of this explanation, Scilla flees without saying anything, and Glaucus is enraged. He asks Circe to make Scilla fall in love with him by means of herbs (transformation by herbs being one common thread of the stories in this section of Ovid). Circe refuses since she has fallen in love with Glaucus, who now flees her. Determined to seek revenge, Circe goes to the water where Scilla normally bathes, and puts some 'jewce of venymed weedes' (14.64) in the water. Scilla enters the water, and her lower parts are transformed into barking dogs: 'Nought else was there than cruell curres from belly downe too ground' (14.75). In this form she wreaks havoc for awhile, until she is later turned to stone, becoming one half of the infamous marine hazard. For George Sandys, who as Leonard Barkan notes, 'summarizes and epitomizes, even plagiarizes a whole tradition of mythographic writings,'[18] the myth is about the perils of women:

> *Scylla* represents a Virgin; who as long as chast in thought, and in body unspotted, appears of an excellent beauty, attracting all eyes upon her, and wounding the Gods themselves with affection. But once polluted with the sorceries of *Circe*, that is, having rendred her maiden honour to bee deflowred by bewitching pleasure, she is transformed into an horrid monster. And not so only, but endeavours to shipwracke others (such is the envy of infamous women) upon those ruining rocks, and make them share in the same calamities.[19]

Sandys's moralization of Scilla comes very close to Peend's moralization of Salmacis. Both are 'infamous women' who seek to shipwreck the virtue of others.

In Lodge's poem, the transformation of Glaucus from human to sea-god is never remarked upon, and in this version Thetis is his mother. If there is to be a metamorphosis of Glaucus, it will not therefore be of a merely physical nature. Circe is entirely removed from the tale: instead of Glaucus imploring her for aid, Glaucus's mother intervenes, pleading with Venus and Cupid to make Scilla fall in love with her son. This is accomplished, and now Glaucus is given the chance to reciprocate and rejects Scilla, having been cured of his love by Cupid. Scilla flees in anguish and, followed by a whole crowd of onlookers, seeks refuge on the shores of Sicilia. Allegorical figures of Furie, Rage, Wan-hope, Dispaire, and Woe appear by her side, and Scilla is metamorphosed into a rock. In short, the story told by Ovid (and by Golding in his translation) is nothing like that told by Lodge.

Another substantial change Lodge makes is the addition of an English narrator. The poem is set near Oxford, 'within a thicket near to *Isis* floud' (1.2), which places the poem in an institutional setting mirroring that of the poem's circulation. The narrator is clearly a student of the university, and so he acts as something of an identificatory relay between the young gentlemen of the Inns and the sea-god who becomes his companion. This relay will become crucial for the metamorphosis which the poem, through its lessons, proposes for the reader. The poem begins with the narrator 'walking alone (all onely full of greife)' (1.1), when he is surprised by the appearance from the waves of the sea-god Glaucus. At this point in the poem, then, the narrator fills the position of surprised auditor that was occupied in Ovid by Scilla. Like the narrator, Glaucus is mourning an unsuccessful love affair. The two sit down beneath a willow tree, the god's head on the poet's knee, and offer competing tales of woe. Glaucus notes the narrator's education and his seeming failure to profit by it: 'Thy bookes haue schoold thee from this fond repent, / And thou canst talke by proofe of wandering pelfe' (4.3–4). The reference to the education of the youth is a common feature of the genre, which perhaps again indicates its primary audience. Glaucus goes on to point out the narrator's youthful naivete, in terms reminiscent of Peend's moral:

> Respect thy selfe, and thou shalt find it cleere,
> That infantlike thou art become a youth,
> And youth forespent a wretched age ensu'th (6.4–6)

Here as elsewhere in the genre, youth is figured as a potentially dangerous time of metamorphosis.

What are the models of transformation or metamorphosis offered by the poem? Since the original metamorphosis of Glaucus is left out, we are forced to look for other ways in which he (and possibly the narrator) are transformed. The most obvious answer is Glaucus's transformation from a spurned lover, bemoaning his rejection by his cruel mistress, to the disdainful and triumphant lover at the end, who cruelly delights in his former mistress's transformation. Like many of the epyllia that follow, the poem traces out a certain process, often figured as a maturation, whereby a youth who is initially associated with a Petrarchan script of desire triumphs over it. This is certainly the case with Glaucus. As Keach argues, his initial posturing (and the narrator's) is in many ways a parody of contemporary Petrarchanisms – the young man besotted with the cruel mistress, moaning over love's losses, writing songs and blazons idolizing and idealizing her.[20] The poems often suggest that such a relation to one's mistress is the product of immaturity, and part of the maturation process involves rejecting a fruitless enslavement to desire. The narrator of Marston's *Metamorphosis of Pigmalion's Image* remarks that

I oft have smil'd to see the foolery
Of some sweet Youths, who seriously protest
That Love respects not actuall Luxury
...
And therefore Ladies, thinke that they nere love you,
Who doe not unto more than kissing move you. (19.1–3, 20.5–6)

We will see this transformation taking place in Glaucus, as he moves from one scheme of desire to another.

This contrast between Petrarchan and Ovidian eroticism is made early in *Scillaes Metamorphosis*. The initial period of communal moaning and weeping between narrator and sea-god is interrupted by the 'sweet melodious noyse of musicke' (9.2) that accompanies the arrival of the river nymphs. They too trade stories of love, but these stories are Ovidian rather than Petrarchan, tales of the cruelty of desire (rather than of women) and full of punning stories about pricks in bushes and in 'Ladies bosomes' (15.6). The natural world responds in kind to their advance: 'The watrie world to touch their teates do tremble' (10.6), and the flowers seem to recall their former human states:

The flowres themselves when as the Nimphes gan vowe,
Gan vaile their crestes in honour of their names:

And smilde their sweete and woed with so much glee,
As if they said, sweet Nimph, come gather mee. (17.3–6)

Placing Ovidian eroticism in the poem in the natural world works, of course, to naturalize it, which stands in direct contrast to the bookish theories of love held by the narrator and Glaucus.

Petrarchan desire is characterized in the poem largely by disproportion. This is literalized in the physical comedy of the grotesque sea-god posing as a melancholy youth, his head balanced on the narrator's knee, sighing, weeping, and, several times, fainting. Some version of the line 'so yong, so lovely, fresh and faire' (75.4) is applied to him several times (35.4, 72.2), always inappropriately. Glaucus's rhetoric is marked by excess, and especially by water. He is forever weeping at the grandiloquence of his own rhetoric, which we might characterize as leaky. Hearing his tale 'the rockes will weepe whole springs to marke our losse' (19.3); 'The aire from Sea such streaming showres shall borrow / As earth to beare the brunt shall not be able' (29.3–4); his 'moanings are like water drops' (60.1); Glaucus weeps (stanzas 8, 56, 60, 68, 78), Thetis weeps (stanzas 2, 77, 80) shepherds weep (stanza 20), the nymphs weep (stanzas 20, 35, 71, 80), the narrator weeps (stanzas 1–3, 72, 73). All of the precedents that Glaucus gives for his situation are female (Venus [stanzas 21–3], Angelica [stanzas 24–6], and Lucina [stanza 27]), all of whom are pictured weeping.

Glaucus's Petrarchan rhetoric is thus implicitly connected with womanliness, especially as that is characterized in early modern rhetorical theory. Women, writes Patricia Parker, 'are figured in discussions of rhetoric in ways which evoke links with the "far-fetched," with uncontrollable and even indecent garrulity or speaking out, and with the "mooveable" transportability of certain tropes.'[21] This last characteristic, argues Parker, is connected with the 'extravagantly "mooveable" and talkative harlot,'[22] the woman who speaks in public and thus disrupts order and abandons modesty. This applies more to Scilla in the poem than Glaucus, although as we will see there is a certain transferability between these characters. While Scilla is never impugned within the poem, Lodge in his dedication refers to the poem as Scilla in ways that evoke the discourse of the common, public woman, passed from man to man. Her punishment at the end of the poem, as well as the palpable relief of the other characters, seems attributable to her dangerous and disorderly mobility.

As we have noted, the removal of Circe from the poem means that it is Thetis, rather than Glaucus himself, who intervenes to effect Glaucus's liberation and transformation. The resolution involves two phases. First Glaucus is cured by Cupid:

> And from his bowe a furious dart hee sent
> Into that wound which he had made before:
> That like Achilles sworde became the teint
> To cure the wound that it had carv'd before:
> And sodeinly the Sea-god started up:
> Revivde, relievd, and free from Fancies cup. (91.1–6)

Glaucus is cured by a generic drug, epic masculinity, that infuses him with activity and quells his windy rhetoric. The cure is both sudden and hilariously phallic: 'all aloft he shakes his bushie creast' (92.4), evoking the Ovidian sexuality of the flowers who earlier try to tempt the nymphs to take their crests in hand. The narrator also feels a 'sodein joy' (94.6) within his heart, suggesting that he has also been to some degree transformed. Aside from a new-found interest in sex with nymphs, the other major transformation in Glaucus is a shift in rhetorical method. Glaucus rarely speaks for the rest of the poem, and when he does, he is short, pithy, and direct.

The second transformation is directed at Scilla. Soon after Glaucus's transformation, Scilla floats onto the scene and 'coilie vaunst hir creast in open sight' (95.3). Scilla's mobility, along with her phallic crest-vaunting and her 'lawles heart' (97.6), all place her outside the realm of proper femininity. Cupid rectifies this by making her fall in love with Glaucus. In effect, what happens is the role of ridiculous Petrarchan lover is transferred from Glaucus to Scilla:

> Oh kisse no more kind Nimph, he likes no kindnes,
> Love sleepes in him, to flame within thy brest;
> Cleer'd are his eies, where thine are clad with blindnes;
> Free'd be his thoughts, where thine must taste unrest (103.1–4)

Glaucus now scorns and disdains, the two activities most frequently associated in the genre with the Petrarchan mistress, and Scilla becomes the wooer, the pursuer, the weeper and the fainter. Woman as pursuer is, of course, inherently ridiculous, a continuation of the comedies of inappropriateness connected earlier with Glaucus's physical grotesqueness. At the same time, it makes plain what was perhaps only implicit earlier in the poem, that Petrarchan desire is inherently womanish.

Scilla's punishment does, in the end, return her to the role of Petrarchan mistress, if obliquely. She had been the subject of blazons earlier in the poem, first at length by Glaucus (stanzas 48–54) and later briefly by the assembled crowd (stanza 97). Nancy J. Vickers has argued that the impulse behind the blazon is to transfer the punishment of Acteon to Diana, to render the beloved silent rather than the lover.[23] This seems to be the end result here. Rather than having her lower half transformed to hounds, Scilla is beset by personifications of her own psychic disintegration. It is this psychic disintegration that finally renders her both immobile and silent. Diana becomes Acteon, but in a way that leaves her a permanent memorial to 'coy nymphs' everywhere. But Scilla's transformation is also, we should remember, a warning about rhetoric, and the appropriateness or inappropriateness of certain modes of eroticism. Scilla stands not just for coy Petrarchan mistresses, but Petrarchan rhetoric in general, which is perhaps why the poem is 'very fit for young Courtiers to peruse' (as the title page says), young courtiers presumably being the most prone to Petrarchan rhetorical excess.

Operating alongside this critique of Petrarchan love poetry is another story of rhetoric. Midway through the poem Glaucus tells of his rejection by Scilla, after which he wandered the rivers and oceans of the world until he ended up in 'A fruitefull Ile begirt with Ocean streames' (65.6):

> And heere consort I now with haplesse men,
> Yeelding them comfort, (though my wound be cureless)
> Songs of remorse I warble now and then,
> Wherein I curse fond Love and Fortune durelesse (69.1–4)

The god's habit of singing to other hapless men his songs cursing Love and Fortune is reminiscent of another more important Ovidian singer, Orpheus. After losing Eurydice, Orpheus abandons the love of women, and dedicates himself to singing about love's disappointments. In R.B.'s *Orpheus His Journey to Hell*, for example, Orpheus similarly sings to the men of Thrace 'invective ditties' about 'unconstant Love' and the 'manie woes a womans beauty brings' (110.1–3). Moreover, in Lodge's poem both the god and the narrator have Orphic abilities. Glaucus asserts that on hearing of their woes, 'the rockes will weepe whole springs to marke our losse' (19.34). Later he tells the nymphs that 'Could my wit controule mine eyes offence: / You then should smile and

I should tell such stories, / As woods, and waves should triumph in our glories' (39.4–6). Not only is Glaucus a singer in this version, he is also, like Orpheus, a musician: 'How have the angrie windes growne calme for love, / When as these fingers did my harpe strings move?' (44.5–6).

The story of Orpheus is taken up at length in R.B.'s epyllion, but Orpheus had a far wider significance in the Middle Ages and the Renaissance than simply that of a character in the *Metamorphoses.* Orpheus was for early modern literary theorists the first poet, the originator of all poetic genres, and the model of the orator. The stories of Orpheus charming rocks and trees with his song was a tribute to the power of rhetoric that made him an obvious hero for an age that fetishized rhetoric as one of the foundations of civilization. Thomas Cain argues that the early modern humanists, 'find in Orpheus a convenient culture-hero triumphantly symbolizing the goals of their rhetorical programme.'[24] It should be remembered that the Inns of Court were one of the prime sites in England for the study of rhetoric, and so the students of the Inns would naturally see in Orpheus a model for their own aspirations as poets, orators, and legislators. That the Inns were an all-male space also resonates with Orpheus's career. Like Orpheus in the fields of Thrace, or Glaucus and the narrator on the banks of Isis's flood, the young men of the Inns to whom the poem is addressed inhabited a world of homosocial conversation.

III

Scillaes Metamorphosis ends with a warning to women who might desire a Petrarchan lover:

> Ladies he left me, trust me I missay not,
> But so he left me as he wild me tell you:
> That Nimphs must yeeld, when faithfull lovers straie not,
> Least through contempt, almightie love compell you
> With Scilla in the rockes to make your biding
> A cursed plague, for womens proud back-sliding (L'Envoy)

This, presumably, is the lesson fit for 'coy Dames to remember' that the title page promises. In relaying this message from sea-god to reader, the narrator shows that he too has been hit by the arrow of disdain. Like Glaucus, he has been transformed from a besotted Petrarchan lover in the opening stanzas to a lover who lays down the law to proud ladies.

As we have noted, the poem was not meant at least initially for coy Dames to read, so it is perhaps useful to isolate the lesson contained for the 'young Courtiers' of the Inns. Unlike many of the central figures in the genre, such as Adonis, Narcissus, and Hermaphroditus, Glaucus does not come to a wretched end. Nor does he face an aggressive female wooer, except when Scilla is shot with Cupid's arrow and by this time he is immune to her charms. Circe, the aggressive wooer in Ovid's version and a far more threatening figure than Scilla, is omitted entirely. Unlike the other male characters, Glaucus is not ultimately overcome by desire or a woman and therefore his transformation is enabling rather than debilitating. Scilla has also changed in this version, from the silent and terrified maiden of the *Metamorphoses*, to a proud and disdainful Petrarchan mistress: 'Scilla a Saint in looke, no Saint in scorning' (31.5). It might be argued that in these poems the aggressive female wooer is simply the flip side of the Petrarchan mistress. With the former, the youth is the helpless object of desire, with the latter, the youth is the slave to his own desire. In both cases, the youth, failing to escape, becomes like Hermaphroditus 'but halfe a man.' A whole man, argues the genre, is, like Glaucus or the narrator of *Pigmalions Image*, the subject rather than the object of desire.

To point out that the aggressive female wooer and the disdainful mistress are two sides of the same coin is perhaps to question the usual generalizations about the difference between Petrarchan and Ovidian women. Finkelpearl, for example, argues, 'With respect to sexual fulfillment, Ovidian poetry is quite unlike – one might almost say, it is opposed to – the tendency of 1590s Petrarchanism. Petrarchan ladies refuse and rebuff; Ovidian ladies like Venus and Hero often pursue.'[25] Keach concurs with this, arguing that the 'aggressive female wooer' of the epyllia functions 'as an anti-type of the chaste, idealized, cruelly reluctant mistress so prominent in Renaissance lyric and pastoral poetry.'[26] While it is true that the Ovidian figures have more spunk than their Petrarchan counterparts, ultimately the epyllia are really only interested in the effect this has on the male figure. Generally speaking, the women are silenced, humiliated, or abandoned by the end of the poem, as is the case with Venus, Hero, Scilla, and, arguably, Pigmalion's former statue.

At one level, the poems show the dangers for a male of being the object of desire, whether this is the desire of a god or a goddess, man or woman, and persistently attempt to reform him as the desiring subject. This we see in the narratives of the poems that feature the aggressive female, such as Shakespeare's *Venus and Adonis* or Thomas Edwards's *Cephalus and Procris.* It is at work in a different form in Marlowe's *Hero and Leander,* as Leander metamorphoses from a sexually ambiguous youth, desired by all, to a mature lover, possessing Hero instead of being possessed by her charms. The youth must reject the advances of the woman (or man or immortal) in order to become a man, or risk being trapped in an infantalizing, narcissistic relation, which is occasionally allegorized as a suspension of being: 'I have heard it is a life in death' says Adonis of love, which is an accurate enough description of the fate of Endymion in Michael Drayton's *Endimion and Phoebe: Ideas Latmus.* Phoebe

> layd Endimion on a grassy bed,
> With sommers Arras ritchly over-spred,
> Where from her sacred Mantion next above,
> She might descend and sport her with her love,
> Which thirty yeeres the Sheepheards safely kept,
> Who in her bosom soft and soundly slept. (983–8)

When we remember the importance in the genre of the rejection of Petrarchan erotics, we can see perhaps that at another level what the poems are protesting is a failure of the male subject to be in control of his own desire, which Dubrow argues in the Petrarchan scenario often involves a loss of agency or a blurring of the boundary between subject and object.[27] To be infatuated by the cruelly unresponsive woman is to be slave to one's own desire, which offends the integrity and autonomy of the self.

At still another level, this protest against subjection is enacted by the very choice of Ovidian erotics. In her discussion of Petrarch's use of Ovid, Lynn Enterline argues that 'Petrarch weaves a new, suffering "voice" by directing Ovidian irony against himself. In the *Canzoniere* a distance seems to surface *within* the poetic subject, pitting the self against itself, rather than, as in Ovid, *between* the narrating subject and his erotic stories.'[28] Enterline argues that 'Petrarch's specifically autobiographical version of Ovidian stories paradoxically produces a discourse of the self in love that looks forward to the alienated linguistic subject, and the story of its desire' (p. 122). If Petrarchan erotics in some way acknowledges the alienated subject of language, the Ovidian poetry of the 1590s might be seen as an attempt to deny this alienation by asserting the subject's mastery over language, which it partially acts out in the genre's bravura displays of rhetorical skill. More importantly, however, Ovidian erotics installs a distance between the subject and its desire, one which allows one to manage it. Or, to put it another way, Ovidian irony works to stave off any threat that desire might pose to the borders of the self. Here the role of the Ovidian narrator becomes crucial: the Ovidian narrator, much like Ovid himself in his poetry, is distanced, ironic, experienced. Dubrow notes that the Petrarchan lover is often in a position of subordination, a subordination that troubles both the line between the sexes and the line between self and other. Whereas critics of Petrarchan poetry have argued that the Petrarchan poet achieves mastery through a repetition of defeat,[29] here the Ovidian narrator goes one better, implicitly retelling stories of his own erotic misadventures from a position of complete mastery, since they are displaced onto other bodies. The Ovidian narrator is thus also Orphic, looking back on lost desire and converting it into rhetorical mastery.

This position of mastery is emphasized by a more fundamental circuit of desire that the poems trace out, between narrator and reader, which often involves the narrator teasing the audience from a position of knowing: 'Who knows not what ensues?' Marston's narrator coyly asks when Pigmalion and his statue consumate their passion; 'O pardon me, / Yee gaping ears that swallow up my lines' (38.1–2). The reader is here implicitly feminized, as the narrator becomes the ultimate Lacanian Subject-who-is-presumed-to-know. A similar scenario is at work in *Scillaes Metamorphosis*, where the narrator becomes the knowing relay between erotic experience and poetic audience, and where the final lesson is delivered to 'ladies,' in spite of the fact that the initial audience was completely male. If these poems follow the Renaissance habit of presenting models of behaviour to the reader, it is not any particular character in the poems that is to be emulated, but rather the narrator's knowing voice that is the ultimate model for the reader – a position of unassailable mastery and masculinity.

IV

Although the poems tend to stage the rejection of Petrarchan erotics for Ovidian as a process of maturation and thus as a natural progression, we can see the amount of labour required for this maturation signalled in *Scillaes Metamorphosis*. The nymphs, Glaucus's mother Thetis, Venus, and Cupid all have to intervene to bring about this change. It might also be observed that the maturation or heterosexualization of desire is undercut by the homosocial scenario of the situation or telling of the poem. It is two men, rather than a heterosexual couple, who are united by the telling of the story (although not the story itself). Outside the poem this is mirrored by the dedication by Lodge 'To his especiall good friend Master Rafe Crane.' This brings up a rather obvious complication: if the poems are working to construct a heterosexual masculinity, what does it mean that the poem takes place with the god's head in the poet's lap? Why is the eligible female spurned and chained to a rock? Doesn't this rather complicate the heterosexuality? I made the point earlier that rather too much was made about the differences between Ovidian and Petrarchan mistresses: both are props for the construction of differing forms of masculine subjects. What I want to argue for the rest of the paper is a parallel point about heterosexuality: that heterosexuality has very little to do with women.

In her much-debated essay 'Women on the Market,' Luce Irigaray makes essentially this same point: 'Reigning everywhere, although prohibited in practice, hom(m)o-sexuality is played out through the bodies of women, matter, or sign, and heterosexuality has been up to now just an alibi for the smooth working of man's relations with himself, of relations among men.'[30] Irigaray's argument about heterosexuality has unfortunately been overshadowed by her more provocative comments about what Eve Kosofsky Sedgwick would label homosociality. While theorists have focused on the homosocial, they have for the most part failed to investigate the nature and construction of heterosexuality. Irigaray's comments, however, parallel what Monique Wittig argues in *The Straight Mind*, that 'straight society is based on the necessity of the different/other at every level. It cannot work economically, symbolically, linguistically or politically without this concept. This necessity of the different/other is an ontological one for the whole conglomerate of sciences and disciplines that I call the straight mind.'[31] Wittig clarifies the import of the concept of the different/other by remarking, 'The concept of difference between the sexes ontologically constitutes women into different/others. Men are not different, whites are not different, nor are the masters. But the blacks, as well as the slaves, are.'[32] Judith Butler notes that for Wittig, 'the *relation* of heterosexuality ... is neither reciprocal nor binary in the usual sense; "sex" is always already female, and there is only one sex, the feminine.'[33]

Wittig's argument is valuable for pointing out the politics of difference, and showing the political nature of what is usually experienced as intensely personal, in particular, for showing that heterosexuality is not so much an experience of the passions as a mode of thought, that corresponds with modes of social organization and political subjection. Or, as Irigaray puts it more forcefully, 'heterosexuality is nothing but the assignment of economic roles.'[34] Wittig's argument for a transhistorical heterosexuality is not an instance of biological essentialism; it does not necessarily contradict the social constructionist arguments that gender and sexuality are socially constructed phenomena, although it does qualify them in an interesting way. At the very least, it shows that the ubiquity of heterosexuality as an institution is not simply an unfortunate coincidence. More importantly, it allows for a greater flexibility in identifying which practices and relations fall within the realm of the socially productive and thus within the realm of heterosexuality. For example, what has been called institutionalized homosexuality is not necessarily outside the sphere of heterosexuality; as Gerald Creet shows in his study of institutionalized homosexuality in Melanesia, practices generally designated homosexual can work entirely within the social order to enforce the subordination of women and younger males.[35] Within the early modern period, this is particularly evident in the codes surrounding male friendship, which arguably differs from sodomy only insofar as it respects the dominant order, the difference, as Mario DiGangi has recently argued, between orderly and disorderly forms of desire.[36] Male friendship was bound up in a system of mutual advantage and friends were assumed to be gentlemen. That is to say, early modern male friendship, however eroticized a relation, can hardly be seen as existing outside the dominant power structure of society and thus can usefully be labelled heterosexual. This is certainly the case with the two friends in *Scillaes Metamorphosis*, whose heterosexuality seems to comfortably coexist with, even depend upon, a circuit of desire between men.

When we remember Wittig's argument that heterosexuality is 'an ideological form that cannot be grasped in reality, except through its effects,'[37] we can begin to see that every society, or every renegotiation of society, must also involve a renegotiation of heterosexuality, especially if, as Wittig argues, the 'social contract and heterosexuality are two superimposable notions.'[38] And this, I would argue, is part of the project of the epyllia. Written in a period of societal change, by a group of writers who were arguably most attuned to these shifts, the epyllia educate their gentlemen readers about desire. The morals of failure or success at becoming an autonomous subject of desire are at the same time aligned to stories of rhetorical mastery, which for the period meant cultural mastery. By aligning a particular mode of sexuality with cultural agency, the epyllia attempt to install a new version of normative male sexuality which Wittig would identify as heterosexual.

NOTES

1 Heather Dubrow, *Echoes of Desire: English Petrarchism and its Counterdiscourses* (Ithaca: Cornell University Press, 1995), p. 11.
2 William Keach, *Elizabethan Erotic Narratives* (New Brunswick, NJ: Rutgers University Press, 1977), p. 119.
3 Lynn Enterline, '"Embodied Voices": Petrarch Reading (Himself Reading) Ovid,' in *Desire in the Renaissance*, ed. Valeria Finucci and Regina Schwartz (Princeton: Princeton University Press, 1994), pp. 120–45.
4 Unless otherwise indicated, epyllia referred to can be found in Elizabeth Story Donno, ed. *Elizabethan Minor Epics* (New York: Columbia University Press, 1963). References are to stanza and line number.
5 William Shakespeare, 'Venus and Adonis,' in *The Riverside Shakespeare*, ed. G. Blakemore Evans (Boston: Houghton Mifflin, 1974), ll. 369–71.
6 Donno, *Elizabethan Minor Epics*, p. 9.
7 A. Leigh DeNeef, 'The Poetics of Orpheus: The Text and a Study of *Orpheus His Journey to Hell* (1595),' *Studies in Philology* (1992): 20–70.
8 Wilfred R. Prest, *The Inns of Court under Elizabeth I and the Early Stuarts* (London: Longman, 1972), pp. 21–2.
9 William Shakespeare, *Henry IV, Part 2*, ed. A.R. Humphreys (London: Routledge, 1988), 3.2.313–14, 322.
10 Philip J. Finkelpearl, *John Marston of the Middle Temple* (Cambridge, MA: Harvard University Press, 1969), pp. 16, 61
11 Clark Hulse, *Metamorphic Verse: The Elizabethan Minor Epic* (Princeton: Princeton University Press, 1981), p. 12.
12 *Shakespeare's Ovid: Being Arthur Golding's Translation of the Metamorphoses* (1567), ed. W.H.D. Rouse (London: Centaur Press, 1961), Book I, line 1. All quotations from Ovid will be taken from this edition. All references to Ovid will be to book and line number.
13 Thomas Edwards, 'Narcissus' in *Poems by Thomas Edwards*, ed. W.E. Buckley (London: Roxburghe Club, 1882), pp. 35–64; stanza 14, ll. 6–7.
14 Wesley D. Rae, *Thomas Lodge* (New York: Twayne, 1967), p. 46.
15 Keach, *Elizabethan Erotic Narratives*, p. 56.
16 Ibid., p. 32.

17 Ibid., p. 36.

18 Leonard Barkan, 'Diana and Acteon: The Myth as Synthesis,' *English Literary Renaissance* 10 (1980): 328.

19 George Sandys, *Ovid's Metamorphosis Englished, Mythologized and Represented in Figures* (1632), ed. Karl K. Hulley and Stanley T. Vandersall (Lincoln: University of Nebraska Press, 1970), p. 645.

20 Keach, *Elizabethan Erotic Narratives*, p. 39.

21 Patricia Parker, *Literary Fat Ladies: Rhetoric, Gender, Property* (London: Methuen, 1987), p. 110.

22 Ibid., p. 107.

23 Nancy J. Vickers, 'Diana Described: Scattered Woman and Scattered Rhyme,' *Critical Inquiry* 8 (1981): 265–79.

24 Thomas H. Cain, 'Spenser and the Renaissance Orpheus,' *University of Toronto Quarterly* 89 (1971): 25.

25 Finkelpearl, *John Marston*, p. 101.

26 Keach, *Elizabethan Erotic Narratives*, p. 20.

27 Dubrow, *Echoes of Desire*, p. 37.

28 Enterline 'Embodied Voices,' p. 122.

29 See, for example, Ann Rosalind Jones and Peter Stallybrass, 'The Politics of *Astrophel and Stella*,' *Studies in English Literature* 24 (1984): 53–68; and Arthur Marotti, '"Love is not Love": Elizabethan Sonnet Sequences and the Social Order,' *ELH* 49 (1982): 396–428.

30 Luce Irigaray, *This Sex Which Is Not One*, trans. Catherine Porter (Ithaca, NY: Cornell University Press, 1985), p. 172.

31 Monique Wittig, *The Straight Mind and Other Essays*, trans. Louise Turcotte (Boston: Beacon Books, 1992), pp. 28–9.

32 Ibid., p. 29.

33 Judith Butler, *Gender Trouble: Feminism and the Subversion of Identity* (London: Routledge, 1989), p. 113.

34 Irigarary, *The Sex Which Is Not One*. p. 192.

35 Gerald W. Creet, 'Sexual Subordination: Institutionalized Homosexuality and Social Control in Melanesia,' in *Reclaiming Sodom*, ed. Jonathan Goldberg (London: Routledge, 1994), pp. 66–94.

36 Mario DiGangi, *The Homoerotics of Early Modern Drama* (Cambridge: Cambridge University Press, 1997), pp. 1–23.

37 Wittig, *The Straight Mind*, pp. 40–1.

38 Ibid., p. 40.

Inversion, Metamorphosis, and Sexual Difference: Female Same-Sex Desire in Ovid and Lyly

MARK DOOLEY

As a dramatist steeped in the humanism of the English Renaissance, John Lyly was well aware of his debt to the classical tradition. His grandfather, William Lily, was 'the author of a celebrated Latin grammar' and was made 'first High Master of St Paul's School in 1510.'[1] Lyly collaborated with both Colet and Erasmus on the Latin grammar, their aim being to 'take the pupils as quickly as possible to classical *literature* by cutting down to a minimum the rules that had to be learned.'[2] 'Lily's Grammar' remained a standard work down to the eighteenth century and surely played a part in developing John Lyly's 'intimate knowledge of Ovid which ... must have been partly acquired in the schoolroom, where Ovid was a favourite author.'[3] Recent critics of Lyly's work have emphasised its importance in bringing Ovid to the Renaissance stage and influencing the literature of the period more widely. Michael Pincombe acclaims Lyly as 'the writer who captured Ovid for his generation'[4] and Jonathan Bate concurs that 'Lyly ... became the first to introduce sustained Ovidianism into English drama.'[5]

In this essay, I wish to examine the ways in which John Lyly's play *Gallathea* (1584/5) employs several myths from Ovid's *Metamorphoses*, but particularly the Iphis and Ianthe myth, in order to explore female same-sex desire. I will argue that it is Lyly's use and, more importantly, transformation of Ovidian mythology that allows him to treat his subject in a far more radical way than has hitherto been recognized. Bate comments that '*Gallathea* ... is probably Lyly's best play; it certainly gives the best sense of his creative, transformational use of Ovid. It is not an overt dramatization of a single Ovidian story ... instead, it is stuffed with a rich variety of Ovidian matter.'[6] The myths of Hesione and Haebe, Ganymede, Pygmalion, Galathea, Proserpine, and Salmacis and Hermaphroditus have all been recognized as being integral to this play.[7] It is Lyly's adaptation of these myths in his own work which gives particular insight into the ways in which English Renaissance culture was attempting to develop its own understandings of the body. Texts, as new historicism has taught us, not only represent the culture from which they emerge but they play an active role in the shaping of culture. The Renaissance body, then, emerged at a historical interface where ancient authorities, revived in the Renaissance, met, and sometimes clashed with, new anatomical and medical discourses as well as with dramatic, legal, and religious discourses. An emphasis on a formalist, rather than a cultural, analysis of Lyly's employment of Ovidian mythology has resulted in critics such as Leonard Barkan seeing only a 'dramaturgical gaucherie' in Elizabethan dramatists who did not cover their tracks when employing *Metamorphoses* in their work.[8] As Barkan readily admits however, 'My account has paid less attention than is perhaps deserved to early Elizabethan traditions of comic stage metamorphosis.'[9] I will put forward the case here that not only is close study of such traditions deserved for its own sake, but that it exposes some crucially important new understandings of the ways in which the body and its desires were, and could, be understood in the Renaissance.

The narrative of *Gallathea* proceeds along the following lines. Tyterus opens the play by explaining to his daughter, Gallathea, that she must disguise herself as a boy in order to avoid being sacrificed to Neptune who, every five years, demands the fairest virgin of the village as recompense for an earlier challenge to his deity which was not committed by the villagers he terrorizes. In a parallel scene, Melebeus tells his daughter the same story and instructs her to disguise herself as he considers that she is the fairest virgin and is likely to be chosen. The now disguised girls escape to the forest (separately) to wait until the time for the sacrifice has passed. They meet and, each believing the other to be a boy, fall in love. In the meantime, Cupid is busy playing tricks on Diana's nymphs who scorn his power and he makes them fall in love with the 'boys' Gallathea and Phillida (now called Tyterus and Melebeus) whom Cupid knows to be the disguised girls. Diana's punishment of Cupid for this outrage against her deity leads to a clash between her and Venus (Cupid's mother), which is apparently resolved at the end of the play when the two plotlines come together. Diana manages to convince Neptune to forego future virgin sacrifices and Cupid and Venus are reunited. When Gallathea and Phillida discover for certain that they are both girls (though they have had their suspicions for some time) they refuse to give one another up despite the pressures put on them by the gods and their fathers. Venus, though, offers to turn one of them into a boy so that they can continue their love and, after an epilogue delivered by Gallathea, the play ends.

Though there is a great deal to be said about the sexual politics of *Gallathea* in general, I will focus here on the ways in which the end of the play positively encourages the continuation of the relationship between Gallathea and Phillida *as girls*. Jeff Shulman argues that Lyly 'relies on the *Metamorphoses* for substantial changes in dramatic technique that assist in arranging a ... satisfactory finale.'[10] For most critics of *Gallathea* that finale, satisfactory or not, is achieved in the sex-change of one of the girls, which echoes closely Catherine Belsey's reading of Shakespeare's comic finales where, she argues, 'the heroine abandons her disguise and dwindles into a wife. Closure clearly depends on closing off the glimpsed transgression and reinstating a *clearly defined* sexual difference.'[11] Valerie Traub, though stressing the importance of resisting a privileging of 'the final heterosexual teleology of these comedies'[12] sees the representation of female same-sex desire in these plays as 'a viable if ultimately untenable state.'[13] I would argue, however, that if attention is paid to the earlier drama a quite different picture emerges. Through the sex-change tantalizingly offered by Venus but deferred beyond the scope of the action of the play, Lyly is able to heighten recognition of female same-sex desire and makes a case for its viability and its tenability though at the same time exposing some of the anxieties surrounding female sexuality and bodies in the period.

The immediate source for the idea of the sex-change in *Gallathea* comes from the Iphis and Ianthe myth in Book IX of *Metamorphoses*. Ligdus and his wife Telethusa are expecting a baby, which Ligdus prays will be a boy. 'A girl is more of a burden, and fortune has not given me the means to support one ... if a girl is born, she must be put to death.'[14] The daughter that is born is named Iphis but on the advice of the goddess Io she is disguised by Telethusa and presented to her husband as a son. Iphis's father arranges a marriage between his 'son' and Ianthe and the two girls fall deeply in love though Iphis 'despaired of ever being able to enjoy [Ianthe].'[15] On the eve of the wedding, and in some desperation, Telethusa takes Iphis to the temple of Isis and prays for her assistance. On leaving the temple a fantastic metamorphosis occurs:

> Iphis accompanied her [mother] as she walked along, and moved with a longer stride than usual. Her face lost its fair complexion, her hair looked

> shorter, plain and simple in style, her features sharpened, and her strength increased. She showed more energy than a woman has – for she who had lately been a woman had become a man![16]

Crucially, then, a physical sex-change occurs and, to legitimize the wedding, Hymen is part of the assembled congregation in Ovid's myth. There are, however, several fundamental differences in Lyly's adaptation of the myth which raise important questions regarding the status of the Renaissance body's capacity for metamorphosis.

Debates raged in the early modern period about the ability of individuals to change their sex. Reginald Scot, for example, represents for Leonard Barkan the 'orthodox denial' of metamorphosis in his *Discoverie of Witchcraft* (1584) – a text contemporaneous with *Gallathea*. For Scot, anyone believing in the capacity for metamorphosis was 'without all doubt ... an infidell, and woorsse than a pagan.'[17] Though the arguments in support of the human, and more specifically the female, body's capacity for change have become well rehearsed, I think it will be useful here to outline some of them in order to assess their impact for my reading of the play. The 'one-sex' model discussed at length by Thomas Laqueur arises out of a reading of Aristotelian and Galenic understandings of the female body as an 'inverted' version of the male body. This logic of inversion results in Galen's belief that in women, 'that which would have become the scrotum ... was made into the substance of the uteri' and that she has all the generative parts that the man has but they 'could not because of the defect in the heat emerge and project on the outside.'[18] Critics have been keen to seize upon this model of 'differential homology' which, according to Stephen Greenblatt, gives rise in the period to the 'fascination with the possibility of sex-change – almost always from female to male, that is, from defective to perfect.'[19] However, the acceptance and repetition of this view has, in part, I will argue, created a critical commonplace which has imposed serious limitations on our ability to read female same-sex desire in early modern texts. Recent work by Janet Adelman has shown that even within vernacular medical works of the mid-sixteenth to early seventeenth centuries the idea of the one-sex model barely makes its presence felt. In her carefully historicized account, Adelman makes the case that by the time of John Banister's *The Historie of Man* (London, 1578), the 'transformations of gender that are local and contemporary in Montaigne and Pare are significant specifically as the sign of the far away and long ago; they testify to the strangeness of the remote, not to a current ruling of sexual homology.'[20] Lyly, I would argue, exploits the historical anachronism of the one-sex model in order to anatomize an emerging 'corporeality of deviance.'[21] The rush to accept the idea of the sex-change in *Gallathea* as actual or physical, which has occured in much criticism of the play, results in a reinscription of heterosexual norms which the play works hard to undermine. As Patricia Parker argues:

> it is important to interrogate the sheer repetition of the model of irreversibility as symptomatic and ideological rather than as a descriptive discourse, to focus in other words on the rhetoric of insistence rather than relying on such statements (or their exemplary anecdotes) as a basis on which to construct generalizations about gender or gender change in the period as a whole.[22]

The repetition of the move from a defective state to one of perfection implied in this model and, indeed, implied in Ovid's story, is exactly what Lyly avoids in his reworking of the myth in *Gallathea.* It is, therefore, astounding that so many critics simply accept that the sex-change offered by Venus happens in the same way as it does in Ovid's Iphis and Ianthe. Even a critic as subtle as Jonathan Bate to the particularities of Ovidian employment sees here a 'patterning myth ... explicitly invoked as a precedent for the resolution of *Gallathea,* and an Ovidian sex-change takes place within the drama.'[23] Phillipa Berry, too, sees Venus's 'resolution' as 'presumably [involving] the gift of a penis to a woman.'[24] In fact, no such sex-change takes place and Lyly goes out of his way to call into question whether the promised metamorphosis will ever occur. To return to where we started, with Lyly's education and familiarity with Ovid's work, it seems highly surprising that he appears to make a fundamental error in his reworking of the Ovidian myth. For my reading, however, this 'error' is, in fact, highly suggestive and raises serious questions about the validity of Venus's offer.

When the disguises of the two girls are revealed at the end of the play, after a very short period of apparent shock, the two girls insist that they will continue to love one another despite the formidable opposition of both Diana and Neptune. Diana argues that, 'Nowe things falling out as they doe, you must leaue these fond fond affections; nature will haue it so, necessitie must' (5.3.122–3).[25] Neptune calls their love, 'An idle choyce, strange, and foolish, for one Virgine to doate on another; / and to imagine a constant faith, where there can be no cause of affection. / Howe like you this Venus?' (5.3.128–30) Venus's response to Neptune's question is often overlooked yet it carries great significance: 'I like well and allow it,' she responds (5.3.131). Venus is quite clearly sanctioning the love between the two girls and disagrees profoundly with both Neptune's view that there can be no 'cause of affection' between them, and with Diana's assessment of their love as 'fond' and unnatural. Gallathea says she is willing to die if her love for Phillida is not 'vnspotted, begunne with trueth, continued wyth constancie, and not to be altered tyll death' and Phillida calls a curse on herself if her love for Gallathea is not equally true (5.3.133–7). It is at this point that Venus proclaims, 'Then shall it be seene, that I can turne one of them to / be a man, and that I will' Diana, herself a goddess of considerable power, asks Venus, 'Is it possible?' which, at least within the perameters of the play, raises anxieties about the viability of such a metamorphosis. Venus's somewhat pompous response to Diana, with whom she has been in constant competition, contains within it an intertextual crux which takes us back to Lyly's source in Ovid and should not be ignored. 'What is to Loue or the Mistrisse of Loue vnpossible? / Was it not Venus that did the like to Iphis and Ianthes?' (5.3.139–43) The answer to Venus's second question here is, of course, no! However, she quickly follows this question with three more in the same speech, which ensures that there is little chance to respond to her claim and, indeed, many critics have not. However, it was not Venus that 'did the like to Iphis' in Ovid's myth but Isis. Parker recognizes that 'the Iphis narrative [is] ... explicitly alluded to' in *Gallathea* but she does not concentrate on Lyly's highly suggestive reworking.[26] By allowing Venus to take the credit for a sex-change which she did not effect, on a Renaissance stage that had profound doubts about the possibility of such a metamorphosis, and in front of a highly educated audience who would have known their Ovid well, Lyly is *at least* placing a question mark over the status of the metamorphosis which Venus offers to 'resolve' the situation. For some critics, though, the play would not even make sense if Venus's promise was not fulfilled as, 'in an all-female cast [events] are brought to a happy conclusion in *the only way possible* – by sex-change or metamorphosis.'[27] It is my contention here that this is not the only way possible to read the end of the play nor is it desirable to see it as the only way possible. Lyly's reattribution of powers in his adaptation of his source in *Metamorphoses* creates a productive friction which is further heightened by another departure from the Ovidian myth.

At the wedding of Ovid's Iphis and Ianthe, the presence of Hymen, god of marriage, gives credence to the legitimacy of the event. His absence from Lyly's play could easily be overlooked as an unimportant departure from the source but, when seen alongside the questionable credibility of Venus's claim, it may be much more significant than it first seems. The absence of Hymen in Lyly's play keys into a contemporary debate about the status of virginity in early modern culture. According to Marie Loughlin there was a heated debate between anatomists and theorists of the body in the early modern period concerning the existence of the hymen as a guarantee of virginity. 'Ideology demands [the hymen's] material existence, because it is only its existence as a physical barrier that can mark the female body as passing into the sphere of marriage, from the possession of father to that of husband.'[28] Hymen's appearance at the end of *As You Like It* sets the patriarchal seal of approval on Rosalind and Orlando's wedding as he tells the Duke to 'receive thy daughter; / Hymen from heaven brought her, / Yea, brought her hither, / That thou mightst join her hand with his' (5.4.106–9).[29] If there were any doubt about the status of the cross-dressing bride here it is cleared up by Hymen's assertion that, 'I bar confusion.' (5.4.120). The question of Phillida and Gallathea's virginity, and therefore their 'importance ... for the functioning of patriarchal society' is a pressing issue throughout the play and Hymen's absence at the end raises doubts about the validity of their union.[30] Clearly, their virginal status is dependent upon what is defined as sex in a patriarchal society. Certainly, *Gallathea* does not appear to shy away from the suggestion that, in some way, these girls have had some experience of each others' bodies. As Theodora Jankowski puts it, they 'may, indeed, avoid male desire and male penile rupture of their hymens. But do they avoid desire altogether?'[31] In 3.2 of the play Phillida and Gallathea have strong suspicions about the 'truth' of their situation and, indeed, hint very strongly to each other that they are girls. 'Haue you euer a Sister?' asks Phillida. '[I]f I had but one, my brother must needs haue two; but I pray haue you euer a one?' replies Gallathea. 'My Father had but one daughter, and therefore I could haue no sister,' she is told and confirms her suspicions in the line, 'Aye me, he is as I am, for his speeches be as mine are' (3.2.36–41). Though there appears to be some clarity emerging here Phillida makes an invitation to Gallathea at the end of the scene which promises to clarify any remaining uncertainty. The invitation is phrased in such a way as to mark a shift away from an intellectual or psychological passivity and towards a reliance on action to clarify the situation and satisfy their growing desire for one another. 'Come let vs into the Groue, and *make much of one another*, / that cannot tel what to *think* of one another' (my emphasis 3.2.58–9) implores Phillida.

The significance of what is meant by 'make much of one another' is clearly open to question but it is suggestive of a need to actively produce a stable meaning for their situation and to achieve an understanding which involves, I would suggest, at least some level of sexual exploration. However, when Phillida and Gallathea next appear in 4.4, having presumably made much of one another, they both still think that the other may be a boy! The role of the boy player under the costume of the character is clearly significant but it is important not to simply fall back into reading the biological sex of the actor as an essential truth behind what are much more complex issues of representation. Phillida and Gallathea seek a linguistic marker of difference between them where they can find no physical marker: 'Seeing we are both boyes, and both louers, that our / affection may haue some showe, and seem as it were loue, let me / call thee Mistris,' Phillida asks. 'I accept that name, for diuers before haue cald me / Mistris,' Gallathea replies, to which Phillida reasonably responds, 'For what cause?' Punning on the term mistress and mysteries, Gallathea replies, 'Nay there lie the Mistrisse' (4.4.15–21). Both these girls have, I am arguing, explored each others' bodies by this stage of the play yet both are still fully able to believe that the other is a boy. As Kathleen McLuskie observes, 'The primary, biological distinction could not, of course, be represented on the stage';[32] yet after leaving the stage in order to 'make much of one another' Phillida still needs to ask Gallathea why others have called her 'Mistris' and, in so doing, asks her what it is that constitutes a woman. For Gallathea, the answer comes in the form of a pun and lies cloaked in mystery. What it is to be a woman, then, is a mystery in the sense that sexual difference remains unknowable to the girls as each has learned how to be a boy from another girl. (When she first sees Phillida in the woods Gallathea says, 'But whist! heere commeth a ladde: / I will learne of him how to behaue my selfe' [2.1.10–12]).

Robert Meyer argues that 'Venus picks up on the mistress-mystery idea ... and uses it to consent to the sex-change which makes amorous pleasure possible for Gallathea and Phillida.'[33] His conclusion, when seen alongside Ellen Caldwell's, shows the difficulty that many critics, even two with such differing perspectives on the play, have had in coming to terms with the possibility of a physical relationship between Phillida and Gallathea as women. Caldwell recognizes that Lyly 'favour[s] the steadfast love of two women.' However, this love, she argues, has as its emphasis 'the couple's spiritual, rather than physical compatibility.'[34] I wish now to examine the ways in which female same-sex desire in this play is represented as not only possible, but also as desirable for its own sake in the face of a stinging critique of the patriarchal, reproductive imperatives of heterosexual marriage.

Montaigne's story of Marie Germain, which has become the 'exemplary anecdote ... on which to construct generalizations about gender or gender change in the period'[35] has worked to close off some areas of inquiry into the female body and female same-sex desire in recent critical work as, like Ovid's Iphis and Ianthe, it ends in a physical metamorphosis which tends to emphasize the transformation to manhood as its central concern. As Katherine Park has recently shown, some early modern French women were so concerned not to become a 'popular tale' of gender transformation (like Marie Germain) by displaying any signs which could possibly be read as 'masculine' that they sought to 'police [their own] sexual boundaries' by seeking a 'clitoridectomy.'[36] This radical and life threatening procedure registers the extent to which the Renaissance 'rediscovery' of the clitoris in the mid-sixteenth century 'proved explosive, triggering a host of contemporary cultural concerns about female sexuality.'[37] Renaldus Colombus claimed in 1559 to have discovered the clitoris which, he argues, is the '"preeminent ... seat of woman's delight." Like a penis, 'if you touch it, you will find it rendered a little harder and oblong to such a degree that it shows itself as a sort of male member."[38] This deeply phallocentric description sees the woman yet again as a sort of inferior male with everything that he has but somehow less perfect. However, the name which Columbus gives the clitoris is suggestive for my reading of *Gallathea* which, as Phillipa Berry suggests, with 'the absence of any central male protagonists throws into especial relief the play's concern with female sexuality.'[39] Overlooking any woman's awareness of her own body, Columbus articulates his findings within a discourse of exploration and discovery and argues, 'Since no one has discovered these projections and their workings, if it be permissible to give names to things discovered by me, it [the clitoris] should be called the love or sweetness of *Venus*.'[40] The love between Phillida and Gallathea, which Venus 'like[s] well and allowe[s]' (5.3.131), is a love *between women*. Venus, it seems, is sanctioning a love which Neptune cannot comprehend; she does not accept his phallocentric view which sees a penis as the 'cause of affection.' Venus is tapping into male anxieties about female sexuality and is, in a sense, directing a knowing wink to the (female?) audience of the play at the expense of Neptune, who is clearly deeply anxious about the implications of allowing Phillida and Gallathea's relationship to develop. Neptune's insistence on the primary importance of the penis itself as the prerequisite for sexual relations is an attempt to reinscribe phallic sexuality as a model of perfection whilst attempting to dismiss a feminine sexuality reliant on the 'love or sweetness of Venus' as deficient. His need to privilege the penis might well be made more urgent by 'the anatomical discovery of the clitoris as a normal structure in women, rather than as an illness or anatomical peculiarity,' which 'suggested that many more women – indeed perhaps every woman – could potentially penetrate and give pleasure to another woman.'[41] There is an emerging understanding of the female body during this period which suggests that, even in phallocentrically determined terms, it was becoming increasingly less dependent, or subject to, the male body, which was struggling to maintain authority. *Gallathea,* I would argue, can be seen in many ways to be a gynocentric play – it draws on concerns which men clearly had in the period about women's bodies and their abilities to satisfy themselves and confirms the possibility of such self-sufficiency. However, in raising doubts about the need for physical metamorphosis in this relationship, it also goes beyond phallic understandings of female same-sex desire.

Parker argues that 'Ovid's Iphis is provided just in time with the consummating instrument of virility' but she sets this myth alongside a reading of Montaigne's *Essays* which, she emphasises, 'move from the transformation of Iphis to anecdotes that tell a different story – that of the failure of men on their wedding night to possess the use of this virile part.'[42] The *actual* supplementation of Iphis in Ovid's myth, then, is set against the *apparent* supplementation of one of the girls in Lyly's play and the failure of men to make effective use of their 'virile part.' The cultural anxiety surrounding impotence, which resonates throughout this play, raises further questions about whether this supplementation ever takes place and whether it would serve any useful function if it did.

At the beginning of *Gallathea* the two girls take on the names of their fathers to go with their disguises. The symbolic phallic power of the name of the father and the donning of male clothes leads to what Mark Breitenberg terms 'referential ambiguity,' which, in 'a culture in which identity is not, in theory, supposed to be mutable,' draws attention to 'a paradoxical reliance on outward signs to ensure stable gender identification.'[43] However, the cross-dressing of the girls serves as no real threat to patriarchy in itself as the disguises are patriarchally authorized. The total lack of interest shown by both Phillida and Gallathea in their fathers' wishes at the end of the play, however, exposes a real weakness in their authority. When the men attempt to intervene in Venus's plan by explaining its economic implications (Tyterus is concerned that his younger son will be disinherited if Gallathea is metamorphosed), the extent to which both men are, symbolically at least, impotent, becomes clear. When Venus asks the girls if they are content with her plan, Phillida confirms her assent but Melebeus intervenes: 'Soft Daughter, you must know whether I will haue you a Sonne' (5.3.147–8). His attempt to remind her of her daughterly duty falls on deaf ears; she does not respond at all. Melebeus and Tyterus fall into an argument between themselves about which girl should be transformed, which only has the effect of stressing even further their powerlessness in the situation! Moreover, the impotence of patriarchal power at the mortal level is replicated at the level of the gods.

Cupid, the ultimate representation of phallic power with his ever-piercing shafts, is punished by Diana for making her nymphs fall in love. She threatens, and delivers on her threats, to 'breake thy bowe, and burne thine arrowes, binde thy handes, clyp thy wings, and fetter thy feete ... I will teach thee what it is to displease Diana' (3.4.75–85). Cupid is left to lament to his mother, 'O Venus, if thou sawest Cupid as a captiue, bound to obey / that was wont to commaunde, fearing Ladies threates, that once / pearced their harts ...' (4.2.69–71) and appears a very sorry example of patriarchal authority. Neptune also, who has appeared several times throughout the course of the play to make great threats about how he intends to 'marre all' (2.2.24), is exposed as a mere braggart at the end of the play. Diana and Venus arrange a peace on their own terms, which they present to Neptune as a *fait accompli.* Despite his rantings all Neptune can offer as comment is, 'Well I am gladde you are agreed: / and saie that Neptune hath delt well wyth Beautie and Chastitie' (5.3.82–3). In fact, Neptune has 'dealt' with nothing. Venus and Diana have resolved their conflict and Venus is about to offer the resolution to the story. There is, on the part of Venus, I would suggest, a not so well concealed contempt for patriarchal authority. Jankowski reaches a similar conclusion:

> I would argue that Venus' cavalier attitude toward gender – a penis may be necessary to legitimize the union, but the organ here becomes an 'add-on' part, sort of like a better-fitting dildo – trivializes the whole notion of the traditional patriarchal marriage.[44]

The representation of men in this play, then, is hardly flattering and, indeed, one might well ask why either of these girls would wish to be turned into one. My own reading of this play is that there is in fact no such wish and Venus will not metamorphose *either* of the girls; she is merely pulling the wool over Neptune's eyes and framing the already existing love between the girls in such a way that Neptune can understand it. To return to my question regarding the necessity of such a transformation it would seem that at neither a symbolic nor a material level does such a necessity exist. As Traub has noted,

> male clothes worked as external projections, theatrical equivalents, of the cultural fantasy of the enlarged clitoris. Theatrical transvestism, in short, was also prosthetic; the donning of masculine dress enacts the logic of the supplement through the displacement of the body to the clothes.[45]

I do not want to simply replace the penis with the 'cultural fantasy of the enlarged clitoris' here but, at a symbolic level, the girls already appear to possess 'phallic' power and in this respect require nothing from Venus by way of supplementation. Moreover, there is no shortage of evidence from the period to show that women were able to marry and live wholly satisfactory and sexually fulfilling lives together.[46] It is this self-sufficiency which, I would argue, Venus attempts to disguise within her promise of a more traditional patriarchal marriage, in order to avoid invoking the wrath of a patriarchal power which already considered itself to be precariously balanced. Gallathea's willingness to follow Venus's advice is established much earlier on in the play when she follows Phillida into the woods and requests that, 'thou, / sweete Venus be my guide' (2.4.12–13) and Venus, like Isis in the Iphis and Ianthe myth, finds a way for Phillida and Gallathea to exist as women together in a hostile environment. Breitenberg argues that in Shakespeare's Sonnet 20, a 'playful tone' is employed to describe 'the all-important addition of a penis to what was formerly "nothing,"'[47] and this is clearly what Neptune thinks will have to happen before Phillida and Gallathea can consummate their relationship. Venus, well aware that this is not necessary, is more than willing to exploit Neptune's phallocentric (mis)understanding of feminine desire to her own ends. The sex-change which she promises, then, can, to a large degree, be seen as a product of male anxiety about women's potential sexual self-sufficiency. By promising to give one of the girls a penis, Venus is apparently reassuring patriarchal authority that a penis is, indeed, the prerequisite of any fulfilling sexual relationship. However, what we have seen during the course of the play is that those presumptively granted the 'privilege' of possessing a penis are, generally speaking, the least well-equipped to wield phallic power.

Thomas Nashe's poem 'The Choise of Valentines' (probably pre-1594) circulated in manuscript form (presumably amongst a male audience) and concerns the use of dildoes by women and the threat this poses to men. It embodies at its heart a contradiction which it seems not to recognize. Richard Hillman, commenting on the poem, argues that:

> we are shown the persona, struck to the quick of his masculine ego, constructing the dildo as a metonym for female sexual self-sufficiency, an alternative transcendental signifier to account for all behaviour that appears to break free from dependency upon men. The woman, in his eyes, enacts his castration by *having*, instead of merely *being*, the phallus.[48]

The dildo's greatest threat to patriarchy is perceived to come from its ability to interrupt the reproductive principle: 'Curse Eunuke dilldo, senceless, counterfet, / Who sooth maie fill, but neuer can begett.'[49] What is so threatening to patriarchy may, of course, be exactly what makes same-sex relationships between women so attractive in a period when sex between men and women carried with it such a real threat of death in childbirth for women. Park cites Brantome who 'specifically envisaged the possibility of women interested exclusively in sex with one another and "unwilling to suffer men."'[50] Both these examples register a male anxiety about the increasing possibility of a female sexuality which is independent of men and gives rise to a fear of impotency.

Lyly's reworking of his source material from Ovid – his misattribution of metamorphic powers to Venus instead of Isis, his refusal to stage the easily representable sex-change which Iphis undergoes, and the absence of Hymen from the end of the play – has significance for our understanding of female same-sex desire in the Renaissance theatre. Gallathea's epilogue in the play can be usefully contrasted with Rosalind's in *As You Like It* in order to highlight the way in which *Gallathea* is insistent to the end on the possibility of love between women, unlike *As You Like It* which situates such desire safely in the past. Rosalind's epilogue proceeds along the following lines:

> I charge
> you, O women, for the love you bear to men, to like as
> much of this play as please you. And I charge you,
> O men, for the love you bear to women – as I perceive

by your simpering none of you hates them – that
between you and the women the play may please. (Epilogue, 11–16)

As DiGangi rightly comments on the 'Ovidian marriage' represented in this play, 'Not even an appeal to the collapse of gender difference ... produced by the boy actor / Rosalind / Ganymede can deny that these words not only distinguish between real men and women playgoers but direct them into heteroerotic exchanges.'[51] Nothing could be further from the truth in Lyly's reworking of the Ovidian story for his play. Rosalind recognizes that 'It is not the fashion to see the / lady the epilogue' (Epilogue, 1–2) but it is Gallathea, still a woman, who delivers the epilogue in Lyly's play. She addresses not the men and women of the audience but the women only and her message is, 'Yeelde Ladies, yeeld to Loue Ladies, which lurketh vnder your / eye-lids whilst you sleepe, and plaieth with your hart strings whilst / you wake' (Epilogue, 5–7). Of course, Gallathea would be addressing an audience of courtly ladies, many of whom would spend much of their time in women-only spaces. The fact that it is not Cupid that delivers the epilogue is significant. He has attempted to encourage heteroerotic relations during the course of the play by making Diana's nymphs fall in love with what they think are boys. Any love encouraged by Cupid, though, is exposed as false and unnatural in this play whereas in contrast 'the love between [Phillida and Gallathea] is spontaneous, and, in that respect, "natural."'[52] Gallathea, then, who has only experienced homoerotic desire throughout the play and appears at the end as a woman who has confirmed her undying love for another of the same sex, tells the women of the audience to give themselves to love. For the audience to follow Gallathea's advice in a court that was, for the most part, hostile to the marriage of its ladies, would not prove easy. In his discussion of Lady Arbella Stuart, who found herself in an 'intolerable situation' regarding arrangements for her marriage, Stephen Orgel argues that 'it is hardly hyperbole to say that literary models offered her the only hope of release' and Lady Arbella apparently attempted an escape motivated by one such model.[53] I would argue that for the ladies of Queen Elizabeth's court, the literary model offered by Lyly's *Gallathea* might well have provided some alternative to both virginity and to marriage.

I have been keen here to maintain some sense of continuity in my discussion of gender and to avoid discussions of androgyny and hermaphrodism in the play.[54] It has been my contention that Lyly was able to recognize the limitations that physical metamorphoses would place on any exploration of female same-sex desire. To this end, Lyly adapts *Metamorphoses* as 'a model and a competitor for the problems of dramatic representation' and uses it as 'a kind of blueprint for theatre.'[55] Lyly's representation of the female body and its desires were, of course, shaped not only by classical texts such as Ovid's but also by emerging discourses circulating in Renaissance culture and I hope to have given some indication of the ways in which these might have influenced his work and, of course, our reading of it. However, it is important to recognize that Lyly's work in turn would shape Renaissance culture's awareness of the issues he represents. In *Gallathea* Lyly offers a radical alternative to heterosexual marriage by resisting the closure offered in his source. Instead, as Jankowski rightly observes, he allows Venus, the goddess of love, to establish 'a new sort of "marriage" that is designed to accommodate woman-woman desire and not a patriarchal inheritance scheme.'[56] Lyly may well have 'captured Ovid for his generation' but his concern was certainly not to moralize Ovid in the way that many of his counterparts did; rather, Lyly was concerned to radicalize the myths and to extract as much erotic potential from them as he possibly could.

NOTES

1 G.K. Hunter, *John Lyly: The Humanist as Courtier* (London: Routledge and Kegan Paul, 1962), pp. 18, 19.

2 Ibid., p. 19.

3 Ibid., p. 38.

4 Michael Pincombe, *The Plays of John Lyly: Eros and Eliza* (Manchester: Manchester University Press, 1996), p. ix.

5 Jonathan Bate, *Shakespeare and Ovid* (Oxford: Clarendon Press, 1993), p. 35.

6 Ibid., p. 36.

7 See Jeff Shulman, 'Ovidian Myth in Lyly's Courtship Comedies,' *Studies in English Literature 1500–1900* 25 (1985): 261, and Robert Meyer, '"Pleasure Reconciled to Virtue": The Mystery of Love in Lyly's *Gallathea*,' *Studies in English Literature 1500–1900* 21 (1981): 196, on Hesione and Haebe myths; Mario DiGangi, *The Homoerotics of Early Modern Drama* (Cambridge: Cambridge University Press, 1997), p. 36 on the Ganymede myth, and Joel B. Altman, *The Tudor Play of Mind* (Berkeley: University of California Press, 1978), pp. 210–11, and Philippa Berry, *Of Chastity and Power* (London and New York: Routledge, 1989), p. 125, on Pygmalion and Galathea myths.

8 Leonard Barkan, *The Gods Made Flesh: Metamorphosis and the Pursuit of Paganism* (New Haven: Yale University Press, 1986), p. 247.
9 Ibid., p. 354.
10 Shulman, 'Ovidian Myth in Lyly Courtship Comedies,' p. 261.
11 Catherine Belsey, 'Disrupting Sexual Difference: Meaning and Gender in the Comedies,' in *Alternative Shakespeares*, ed. John Drakakis (London: Methuen, 1985), pp. 187–8.
12 Valerie Traub, 'The (In)Significance of "Lesbian" Desire in Early Modern England,' in *Queering the Renaissance*, ed. Jonathan Goldberg (Durham and London: Duke University Press, 1994), p. 80.
13 Traub, 'The (In)Significance of "Lesbian" Desire,' p. 69.
14 Ovid, *Metamorphoses*, trans. Mary M. Innes (Harmondsworth: Penguin, 1955), IX, p. 221. All references will be to this edition. References are to book and page number.
15 Ibid., p. 222.
16 Ibid., p. 224.
17 See Barkan, *The Gods Made Flesh*, pp. 254–5.
18 See Galen, 'On the Usefulness of the Parts of the Body,' in *Renaissance Woman: Constructions of Femininity in England*, Kate Aughterson (London: Routledge, 1995), pp. 47–8.
19 Stephen Greenblatt, *Shakespearean Negotiations: The Circulation of Social Energy in Renaissance England* (Oxford: Clarendon Press, 1988), p. 81.
20 Janet Adelman, 'Making Defect Perfection: Shakespeare and the One-Sex Model,' in *Enacting Gender on the English Renaissance Stage*, ed. Viviana Comensoli and Anne Russell (Urbana: University of Illinois Press, 1999), p. 29.
21 Dympna Callaghan, *Shakespeare without Women* (London: Routledge, 2000), p. 32.
22 Patricia Parker, 'Gender Ideology, Gender Change: The Case of Marie Germaine,' *Critical Inquiry* 19.2 (1993): 340.
23 Bate, *Shakespeare and Ovid*, p. 37.
24 Berry, *Of Chastity and Power*, p. 125.
25 All references to *Gallathea* are from John Lyly, *The Complete Works*, vol. 2, ed. R. Warwick Bond (Oxford: Clarendon Press, 1902), pp. 416–72. References are to act, scene, and lines.
26 Parker, 'Gender Ideology, Gender Change,' p. 342.
27 Hunter, *John Lyly: The Humanist as Courtier*, p. 204 (my emphasis).
28 Marie H. Loughlin, *Hymeneutics: Interpreting Virginity on the Early Modern Stage* (Lewisburg: Bucknell University Press, and London: Associated University Presses, 1997), p. 32.

29 All references to this play are from William Shakespeare, *As You Like It*, ed. Alan Brissenden (Oxford and New York: Oxford University Press, 1994).

30 Theodora A. Jankowski, '"Where there can be no cause of affection": Redefining Virgins, Their Desires, and Their Pleasures in John Lyly's *Gallathea*,' in *Feminist Readings of Early Modern Culture: Emerging Subjects*, ed. Valerie Traub et al. (Cambridge: Cambridge University Press, 1996), p. 254.

31 Jankowski, 'Where there can be no cause of affection,' p. 259.

32 Kathleen McLuskie, 'The Act, the Role, and the Actor: Boy Actresses on the Elizabethan Stage,' *New Theatre Quarterly* 3 (1987): 125.

33 Meyer, 'Pleasure Reconciled to Virtue,' p. 200.

34 Ellen M. Caldwell, 'John Lyly's *Gallathea*: A New Rhetoric of Love for the Virgin Queen,' *English Literary Renaissance* 17 (1987): 33–4.

35 Parker, 'Gender ideology, Gender Change,' p. 340.

36 Katherine Park, 'The Rediscovery of the Clitoris: French Medicine and the Tribade, 1570–1620,' in *The Body in Parts: Fantasies of Corporeality in Early Modern Europe*, ed. David Hillman and Carla Mazzio (New York and London: Routledge), p. 183.

37 Ibid., p. 173.

38 See Thomas Laqueur, *Making Sex: Body and Gender from the Greeks to Freud* (Cambridge, MA and London: Harvard University Press, 1990), p. 64.

39 Berry, *Of Chastity and Power*, p. 125.

40 See Laqueur, *Making Sex*, p. 64 (my emphasis).

41 Park, 'The Rediscovery of the Clitoris,' p. 178.

42 Parker, 'Gender Ideology, Gender Change,' p. 343.

43 Mark Breitenberg, *Anxious Masculinity in Early Modern England* (Cambridge: Cambridge University Press, 1996), pp. 151–2.

44 Jankowski, 'Where there can be no cause of affection,' p. 267.

45 Traub, 'The (In)Significance of "Lesbian" Desire in Early Modern England,' pp. 69–70.

46 Both Greenblatt *Shakespearian Negotiations*, p. 66 (1988), and Traub 'The (In)Significance of "Lesbian" Desire in Early Modern England,' pp. 65–6 (1994), give examples of women who lived together as married couples.

47 Breitenberg, *Anxious Masculinity*, p. 156.

48 Richard Hillman, *Self-Speaking in Medieval and Early Modern English Drama: Subjectivity, Discourse and the Stage* (Basingstoke: Macmillan Press, 1997), p. 253.

49 Ibid., p. 252.

50 See Park, 'The Rediscovery of the Clitoris,' p. 186.

51 DiGangi, *The Homoerotics of Early Modern Drama*, p. 60.

52 Pincombe, *The Plays of John Lyly*, p. 140.

53 Stephen Orgel, *Impersonations: The Performance of Gender in Shakespeare's England* (Cambridge: Cambridge University Press, 1996), p. 115.

54 For an impressive account of these concepts in *Gallathea* see Grace Tiffany, *Erotic Beasts and Social Monsters: Shakespeare, Jonson, and Comic Androgyny* (Newark: University of Delaware Press, and London: Associated University Presses, 1995), pp. 49–54.

55 Barkan, *The Gods Made Flesh*, p. 247.

56 Jankowski, 'Where there can be no cause of affection,' p. 267.

A Garden of Her Own: Marvell's Nymph and the Order of Nature

MORGAN HOLMES

One of the most common approaches to Andrew Marvell's poetry has been to illuminate the ways in which his texts shadow political and religious controversies. This quest for historical specificity has, however, tended to draw attention away from less topical concerns, such as Marvell's treatment of multiplicitous erotic desires and practices. In his Ovidian lament, *The Nymph Complaining for the Death of her Faun*, for instance, Marvell provocatively dishabituates an emergent heteronormative sex-gender system.[1] Marvell's touching monody transports readers to a sensual greenworld into which cruelty, death, and metamorphosis violently intrude. Narrated by a melancholy nymph, the poem describes how the nymph's former lover Sylvio had given her a fawn and then abruptly absconded. Consoling herself with this delicate being, she spent many happy days until 'wanton Troopers riding by' (1) slaughtered her companion. Jonathan Goldberg remarks that the nymph and fawn are 'two marginal figures, two figures of marginality, representing encroachments and extensions, and yet exclusions from some central norm.'[2] As I hope to show, this tale of 'marginal' creatures and their passions challenges a dishearteningly 'central norm' of Western culture – the exclusive virtue and naturalness of cross-gender sexuality.

While critics have noted some of the text's generic affinities with and specific allusions to Ovid's poetry, they have for the most part not considered the cultural labour that an Ovidian poetics of desire and sexuality enables Marvell to accomplish.[3] Pastoral Ovidianism amounts here to far more than learned allusiveness or stylistic sophistication; an exploration of this component also facilitates a rebuttal of Rosalie Colie's infantalizing interpretation of the nymph as someone trapped by a 'myopically self-regarding' vision. Jonathan Dollimore remarks that throughout virtually all of Western history 'Nature [has worked] as an ideological restriction on social choice.'[4] *The Nymph Complaining* demonstrates that the Ovidian body and its corpus of pleasures could be the staging ground for a culturally significant reimagining of naturalized gender, sexual ethics, and erotic choices.

Paul Hammond has recently published an account of Restoration pamphlet attacks against Marvell's own supposed homo-predilections (including one that suggests he was mounted by John Milton!).[5] He also discusses the strong current of homoeroticism in Marvell's poetry; for example, in *The Definition of Love, The Last Instructions to a Painter*, and *The Unfortunate Lover*. Whereas, however, Hammond focuses exclusively on male sexuality, I would argue that some of Marvell's most insightful representations of nonheteronormative erotics dissidently reinscribe the relative cultural and legal silences pertaining to passions between women. The purpose of this essay is to show that *The Nymph Complaining* engages an Ovidian spirit and repertoire to encode the love between the nymph and her fawn with a powerful strain of same-gender female eroticism, thereby temporarily sheltering 'lesbian' *eros* from cultural and legal proscription.[6]

In order to comprehend Marvell's dissident poetics it is important first to take stock of the early modern responses elicited by Ovid's writings and the contemporary cultural positioning of same-gender female erotics. The *Amores, Metamorphoses*, and other Ovidian texts represent existence as suffused by desires that are uneasily (and often not at all) kept at bay by laws and conventions. Reacting to Ovid's perceived threat to conventional morality, the Puritan gadfly Stephen Gosson castigated his *Ars Amatoria* as 'that trumpet of Baudrie.'[7] With sentiments such as 'I cannot rule myself, but where love please, / Am driven like a ship upon rough seas' (II.iv.7–8), and 'We skorne things lawfull, stolne sweetes we affect' (II.xix.3), it is little wonder that in 1599 Christopher Marlowe's translation of the *Amores* was banned and burned by England's jittery civic and ecclesiastical authorities.[8]

Alongside these violent responses a more subtle form of censorship was implemented through the edifying reading practice advocated by Arthur Golding in his 1567 Englishing of the *Metamorphoses*, a phenomenon that George Sandys intensified in his 1621, 1632, and 1640 translations. In his preface to the Earl of Leicester, Golding asserts that the *Metamorphoses* contain 'pitthye, apt and playne / Instructions which import the prayse of vertues and the shame / Of vices, with the due rewardes of eyther of the same.' In his second edition, Sandys similarly proffered voluminous exegeses of the tales' 'Philosophicall sense.' Ovid, he maintained, presents things 'as they should bee; agreeable to the high affections of the Soule, and more conducing to magnanimitie: juster then either men or Fortune, in the exalting of Vertue and suppressing of Vice.'[9]

For certain other people, though, the literary fruits of Ovid's 'ambitious ranging mind' (*Elegies* II.iv.48) provided a marvellous inspiration for contesting public criteria of virtue and naturalness. An ultrasensual Ovid came into his own with the vogue for amorous epyllia penned in the 1580s and 1590s. As Jonathan Bate points out, many English writers knew the *Elegies, Ars Amatoria, Heroides,* and, especially, the *Metamorphoses* best for their tumultuous treatments of desire and sexuality, particularly the inexorable movement from love to suffering. William Keach argues that Ovid's texts provided epyllion authors with models for penning a 'subversive erotic ambivalence'; that is, 'a constantly active and poised awareness that sexual love can be humorous, grotesque, and animal-like in its savagery as well as beautiful, emotionally compelling, and an essential part of what it means to be human.' If Lodge, Shakespeare, Marlowe, and their contemporaries can be regarded as having used Ovid's texts not as 'sources' but, as Bate terms it, 'precedents' for their own unorthodox art, a similar genealogy can be posited for Marvell's imitation of both Ovid and the Roman poet's earlier English incarnations.[10]

Jonathan Crewe notes that in Marvell's lyric the nymph occupies an 'uninhabitable' position between the human and the nonhuman, nature and culture; 'nymph,' Crewe continues, signifies a 'virtually unpossessible female sexuality.'[11] Rejigging his comments slightly, I would suggest that these ontological and sexual indeterminacies can be understood by attending to Marvell's expression of an 'uninhabitable' sexuality. The sexual politics of Marvell's Ovidian dissidence becomes clearer in light of Elizabeth Harvey's contention that the 'transvestite ventriloquism' of early modern complaint literature is especially complex in cases of culturally 'censored' same-gender female sexuality. In John Donne's 'lesbian' elegy 'Sapho to Philænis,' for instance, Harvey discerns a male author's 'intertextual rivalry' with Sappho's legendary status and voyeuristic domestication of both Ovid and female 'otherness.'[12] Valerie Traub points out that in the early modern literary record 'lesbian' desires and acts are characterized by a persistent 'invisibility' or 'discursive *silence*,' a phenomenon that she elsewhere relates to heteronormative strategies of abjection.[13] In *The Nymph Complaining*, meanwhile, Marvell's Ovidian poetics of desire and the body avoids a Sapphic confrontation and instead conveys the potentially dissident erotic alterity of usually voiceless and/or demonized passions between women.

Claude Summers notes, 'Homoeroticism in the Renaissance is always circumscribed by homophobia'; the period's affirmative literary representations of, for example, masculine *amor* (superbly documented by Bruce Smith) coexisted in an often uneasy tension with moral and legal condemnation. In seventeenth-century England, Jonathan Goldberg observes, any erotic act that was not associated with marriage and procreation was vulnerable to accusations of sodomy. A clear example of institutionalized opprobrium appears in Sir Edward Coke's *Third Part of the Institutes of the Laws of England*:

> Buggery is a detestable, and abominable sin, amongst Christians not to be named, committed by carnall knowledge against the ordinance of the Creator and order of nature, by mankind with mankind, or with brute beast, or by womankind with bruite [*sic*] beast ... the judgement in all cases of felony, is, that the person attainted be hanged by the neck, untill he, or she be dead. (58)

While Coke is able to imagine female bestiality (apparently in Henry VIII's day 'a great Lady had committed Buggery with a Baboon, and conceived by it' [59]), he seems unable or unwilling to wrap his mind around women who engage in same-gender sex.[14] Though it is likely impossible to prove that Marvell had in mind Edward Coke's prohibition against 'carnall knowledge ... by womankind with bruite beast,' his poem is, on the surface, a tale of cross-species erotics.[15] Drawing on and literalizing Ovidianism's acknowledgment of what Keach describes as 'the fundamentally animalistic dimension of sexual experience,' Marvell, I believe, ironically uses this story of bestial love as a vehicle with which to address culturally and legally occluded 'lesbian' sexuality.[16]

The conceptual impossibility of erotic relations between women surfaces in a tale from the *Metamorphoses* itself. Both the story and its seventeenth-century redaction help to clarify the moral context in which Marvell wrote as well as the potential instability of 'natural' gender and sexuality. Ovid recounts the love of Iphis (an androgynously named girl, attired as a boy) for 'yellow-trest' Ianthe (IX.420). Despite their physical and emotional similarity, Iphis despairs because 'a maid, a maid affects' (IX.421). For one woman to have sexual relations with another, Iphis laments, is completely out of the question:

> No Cow a Cow, no Mare a Mare pursues:
> But Harts their gentle Hindes, and Rammes their Ewes.
> So Birds together paire. Of all that move,
> No Female suffers for a Female love.
> O would I had no being! Yet, that all
> Abhord by Nature should in *Creet* befall. (IX.421)

Sexual love of one woman for another is 'Abhord by Nature'; and yet, as it stands, simply by existing Iphis's devotion gainsays the tenet that 'No Female suffers for a Female love.' If Iphis loves Ianthe, and Iphis is a creature of nature just like any other person, then the desires she possesses must also be considered natural, even if they are not bovine, equine, or avian. Indeed, Ovid ironically presents the resolution of this perceived conundrum as a decidedly *unnatural* intervention on the part of the goddess Isis, who miraculously intervenes to transform Iphis's sex: *et voilà*, 'For thou, of late a Wench, art now a Boy' (IX.422).

In the accompanying commentary, Sandys registers his anxiety over this tale's questioning of natural sexuality. Endeavouring to obscure the unnaturalness of Iphis's sex-change, Sandys argues that, considered through Christian exegesis, the metamorphosis proves the power of prayer and divine intervention; he also attempts to shore up Iphis's experience with numerous accounts of similar events in Roman and European history.[17] Sandys concludes that these examples all prove that it is 'preposterous in Nature' when 'men degenerate into effeminacy,' yet it is 'contrarily commendable, when women aspire to manly wisdome and fortitude' (p. 450), thus evading the initial issue of 'lesbian' erotics by deploying an only tangentially relevant bit of gender ideology. This Ovidian tale and its heavy-handed moralization can be understood as ethical (and perhaps textual) precedents for Marvell's consideration of same-gender female love. In *The Nymph Complaining*, Marvell draws on Ovid the erotic boundary-breaker in a way that challenges both Ovid's nullification of 'lesbian' passion as well as the homophobic early modern erasure of same-gender female eroticism.

The most famous of Marvell's accounts of a 'lesbian' paradise appears in his panegyric *Upon Appleton House*, in which a cloistered realm of sensual nuns collapses before heteronormative union and dynastic engineering.[18] *The Nymph Complaining*, meanwhile, lacks any sense that cross-gendered relations are satisfying or noble. Instead, Marvell inscribes a cross-species relationship with strong signs of same-gender *amor.* Rather ironically in this tale of feminine ardour, the nymph's erstwhile paramour, Sylvio, helps to establish a homoerotic Ovidian intertext for the poem. In Edmund Spenser's *Faerie Queene* we are told that Sylvanus – one of Sylvio's literary progenitors – is deeply in love with another male, Cyparissus.[19] Contributing a further homoerotic element is the fact that in Ovid's account the handsome lad Cyparissus was himself adored by the god Apollo (*Metamorphoses* X.456–7). Given the topical similarities between Ovid's version of Cyparissus's fatal sorrow for his dead deer (X.456–7) and Marvell's poem on the emotionally crushing death of a fawn, it would have been quite in keeping with contemporary habits of reading to have drawn connections amongst the various tales of Sylvanus, Cyparissus, Sylvio, the nymph, and her fawn.[20]

My interpretation of the poem as a plaint for fractured love between women contrasts with the heteronormative view commonly taken by other commentators, a gloss which depends on reading the fawn as male. Michael Craze, for instance, feels that the fawn is clearly 'a buck.' Yvonne Sandstroem contends that the nymph's fawn, 'the object of mourning,' is 'male'; for Sandstroem, Marvell's poem is 'an allegory in which the speaker is a wife mourning her dead "husband,"' the martyred King Charles I. In her study of the text's anti-Petrarchanism, Barbara Estrin also unaccountably heterosexualizes the narrative; for example, she claims that the 'nymph becomes first the mother in the family plot and then the lover in the courtship plot, as the fawn waxes from infant to man.'[21]

It seems to me that Paul Hammond also makes an unnecessary interpretive stretch when he argues that Marvell possibly 'adopt[ed] the female persona as a way of exploring the experience of being seduced and jilted by a male lover.'[22] But *The Nymph Complaining* is only minimally about being 'jilted' by a boyfriend – references to 'Unconstant *Sylvio*' (25) figure in only eleven of the poem's 122 lines. Less critical contortion is required if one leaves aside biographical mimesis and considers instead the possibility of desire circulating between two female, or at least feminine, creatures.

The intertextual heritage of *The Nymph Complaining* includes poems which help warrant such a reading. William Browne's early-seventeenth-century Ovidian romance *Britannia's Pastorals*, for example, includes a relationship that has been cited as inspiration for Marvell's poem; what has not been noted, though, is the story's female-female circulation of love.[23] In Book I, the maiden Fida befriends a 'seely timerous Deere' (I.iii.53) who is said to be 'like a woman ... fram'd by nature' (I.iv.65). Similar to the nymph and her fawn, Fida and the deer become inseparable companions:

Vpon a pallat shee [i.e., the deer] doth lye at night,
Neere *Fida's* bed, nor will shee from her sight:
Vpon her walkes shee all the day attends,
And by her side shee trips where ere she wends. (I.iii.54)

Tragedy befalls this loving couple, however, when 'Riot' appears on the landscape and, like the soldiers who slay Marvell's fawn, destroys the deer: 'But with his teeth rending her throate asunder, / Besprinckel'd with her bloud the greene grasse vnder' (I.iv.67).

Probably even more influential was Ovid's contribution to the complaint genre in his *Elegies* II.vi, which opens: 'The parrat from east *India* to me sent, / Is dead, al fowles her exequies frequent' (1–2). A groundswell of grief propels Ovid's poem as its speaker recalls the bird's dainty loveliness:

A little fild thee, and for love of talke,
Thy mouth to taste of many meates did balke.
Nuts were thy food, and Poppie causde thee sleepe,
Pure waters moisture thirst away did keepe. (29–32)

Several times identified as female, Corinna's parrot is said to have joined other loving birds in an afterlife that strongly resembles that enjoyed by Marvell's fawn. Ovid first:

Elisium hath a wood of holme trees black,
Whose earth doth not perpetuall greene-grasse lacke,
. . .
There harmelesse Swans feed all abroad the river,
There lives the *Phoenix* one alone bird ever,
There *Junoes* bird displayes his gorgious feather,
And loving Doves kisse eagerly together.
The Parrat into wood receiv'd with these,
Turnes all the goodly birdes to what she please. (49–50, 53–8)

Marvell's octosyllabic couplets seem to echo Ovid's lines:

> Now my Sweet Faun is vanish'd to
> Whether the Swans and Turtles go:
> In fair *Elizium* to endure,
> With milk-white Lambs, and Ermins pure. (105–8)

For the purposes of my argument, the primary importance of recognizing Marvell's flexible imitation of this Ovidian poem lies in establishing the feminine gender of the dead creature. Given Bate's theory of precedence in early modern Ovidianism, awareness of this textual relationship encourages a reading of the nymph's fawn as also female. In addition, Marvell might have picked up on a moment of homoerotic devotion in Ovid's mention of the 'Full concord' (13) which existed between the parrot and a 'friendly turtle-dove' (12), a partnership Ovid compares to that of two ancient Greeks: 'What *Pylades* did to *Orestes* prove, / Such to the parrat was the turtle dove' (15–16). The inviolable *amicitia* between these two men stands as a homoerotic precedent for the love between the parrot and the turtle-dove, and, by extension, the parrot and Corinna; in Marvell's refashioning of Ovid's elegy this analogy might well also inform the fawn/nymph relationship.[24]

Turning to *The Nymph Complaining* itself, we discover plenty of evidence for considering the fawn in feminine terms. While pronomial usage indicates the nymph is clearly female, the fawn is a grammatically ungendered creature. Marvell's references to the fawn as 'it' (or a version) twenty-six times indirectly draw attention to the creature's gender identity, suggesting at the very least that Marvell was trying to problematize heteronormative interpretations of the relationship. If Marvell had intended to heterosexualize the narrative he could easily have limned the fawn as male; yet, he actually takes pains to distance the nymph's partner from conventional masculinity. The nymph observes, 'Thy Love was far more better then / The love of false and cruel men' (53–4); if not like men's, then was the fawn's amorousness like women's? While its bestial character remains throughout, in the fawn's gentle behaviour and delicate appearance it also exhibits characteristics that seventeenth-century society commonly regarded as feminine.[25] The nymph recounts, for example, that

> It had so sweet a Breath! and oft
> I blush to se [*sic*] its foot more soft,

And white, (shall I say then my hand?)
NAY any ladies of the Land. (59–62)

Marvell's comparison of the fawn to the 'ladies of the Land' implies that the 'ladies' and the fawn share the same gender. Later in her monologue the nymph recounts that while still alive her fawn was accustomed 'its pure virgin Limbs to fold / In whitest sheets of Lillies cold' (89–90); even for early modern poetry, it would have been rather eccentric to characterize a man as possessing 'virgin Limbs' enfolded in an oasis of lilies.

The text's relation to Petrarchanism also encourages a same-gender female reading. At one point the nymph sighs that

when 't had left me far away,
'Twould stay, and run again, and stay.
For it was nimbler much than Hindes;
And trod, as on the four Winds. (67–70)

Not only does the nymph again compare her fawn to a female creature – 'Hindes' – but her words suggest a feminized poetic intertext, Thomas Wyatt's translation of Petrarch's canzone 190, 'Whoso list to hunt: I know where is an hind.' In both the Italian and English versions the deer's femininity is clear. A probable additional Marvellian echo of the Petrarchan beast appears in relation to the decision of Wyatt's speaker to 'leave off' his pursuit of the deer 'Sithens in a net I seek to hold the wind.'[26] Marvell's fawn, 'nimbler' even than Petrarch's 'Hindes,' similarly fleets upon the 'four Winds.'

On a behavioural level too, the fawn and nymph never engage in activities which, either literally or metaphorically, two female creatures could not perform together; in fact, their amorous interaction often strongly suggests same-gender dalliance. Marvell's poem begins with a bluntness that recalls the matter-of-fact opening of Ovid's complaint: 'The wanton Troopers riding by / Have shot my Faun and it will dye' (1–2). These lines plunge us immediately into a cruel Hobbesian realm in which there is no rhyme or reason beyond the kick that random violence presumably gives to evil men. It was miserable enough that Sylvio had abandoned her, but at least with the fawn by her side the nymph could discover unalloyed happiness:

Thenceforth I set my self to play

My solitary time away,
With this: and very well content,
Could so mine idle Life have spent. (37–40)

Colie misinterprets the joyous idyll when she writes, 'The girl, the garden, and the fawn all blend into one virginal scene, white, cold, and still.'[27] In reality, before the troopers burst in, merry games of running and hiding in an aesthetically delectable landscape mingled with moments of carefree, eroticized interaction:

Upon the Roses it would feed,
Until its Lips ev'n seem'd to bleed:
And then to me 'twould boldly trip,
And print those Roses on my Lip.
But all its chief delight was still
On Roses thus its self to fill:
. . .
Had it liv'd long, it would have been
Lillies without, Roses within. (83–8, 91–2)

The little fawn was insatiable; its 'chief delight' was feeding upon the nymph's abundant roses. In this passage the fawn's external lily-white appearance suggests feminine virtue and chastity, while the red roses 'within' signify a more earthly, embodied love.

Recalling that the rose has for centuries symbolized female sexuality in general and the vulva in particular furthers an appreciation of the union's homoeroticism. Anna Nardo has drawn attention to the oral quality of the passion Marvell imagines. This aspect of the poem also manifests what Traub describes (in reference to the 1651 'lesbian'-erotic opera *La Calisto*) as an 'oral economy of desire' between women that displaces a 'conventional phallic economy' with a vision of 'atemporal, nonteleological' sensuality.[28] By presenting us with a beautiful fawn composed of 'Lillies without, Roses within,' and by describing the kissing of a nymph's lips by others which have been dyed a bloody shade of red by sensuous roses, Marvell invites readers to consider a type of erotic practice that involves the genital pleasuring of one female creature by another. Noting the early modern connection between 'nymph' and female genitalia intensifies the eroticism of these bleeding and kissing lips. In his *Lexicon Graeco-Latinvm*, for instance, Ioannis Scapulae defined 'nymph' as 'pars in pudendo muliebri' (sig. Aa3^r). Thomas

Thomas's *Dictionarivm Lingvae Latinae et Anglicanae* similarly translates 'Nympha/æ' as, among other things, 'A little peece of flesh rising vp in the midst of a womans priuie part, which closeth the mouth of the neck, and driueth cold from it.' Aside from a few minor variations in spelling, this translation endured from the dictionary's first edition in 1587 to its last in 1644.[29]

Through sharing and ingesting the garden's roses, the nymph and fawn essentially become one. Such gladsome mutuality, though, could never survive the harshness of 'Ungentle men' (3). Transfixed by her painful memories, the nymph cries out:

> O help! O help! I see it faint:
> And dye as calmely as a Saint.
> See how it weeps. The Tears do come
> Sad, slowly dropping like a Gumme.
> So weeps the wounded Balsome: so
> The holy Frankincense doth flow.
> The brotherless *Heliades*
> Melt in such Amber Tears as these. (93–100)

Marvell's lines on the nymph's bereavement possess an erotic quality reminiscent of Crashavian liquid ecstasy. These passionate tears also lend force to the survival of a strong current of devotion between women. An Ovidian gloss on the 'brotherless Heliades' who 'Melt in ... Amber Tears' illuminates this transcendent solidarity. When Phaëthon was killed through rashness and ambition, his sisters, the Heliades, so desperately grieved that they were turned into poplars. Ovid relates in his *Metamorphoses* that 'From these cleere dropping trees, teares yearely flow; / They, hardned by the Sunne, to Amber grow' (II.364–5). These devotional tears are both produced by and voyage back to women; as precious amber they are like gifts of nature 'on the moisture-giving River spent, / To *Roman* Ladies' (II.366–7).

This circulation of beauty and pleasure within a purely female economy of love and sorrow prefigures the revelation that even in death the nymph and her fawn will be united in baroque devotional pathos. Switching her lamentation to the future tense, the nymph foretells that

> I in a golden Vial will
> Keep these two crystal Tears; and fill

It till it do o'reflow with mine;
Then place it in *Diana's* Shrine. (101–4)

The importance of this particular memorial can be grasped if we consider Marvell's endeavour to use Ovidianism in order to write against the grain of normative Petrarchan gender and sexual relations. Earlier in the poem the nymph had recalled Sylvio's taunting Petrarchan pastiche when he had first given the fawn as a gift: 'Said He, look how your Huntsman here / Hath taught a Faun to hunt his *Dear*' (31–2). Instead of allowing the hunter's voice and desires to dominate, however, Marvell gives linguistic control to Sylvio's sorely used 'dear.' Problematizing heteronormative love as a sport of entrapment, Marvell reinscribes a clichéd lyric metaphor by having the nymph consecrate her relationship with the fawn at the temple of another hunter, the goddess Diana; 'wanton' men are, thereby, excluded from an exclusively female *locus amoenus.* This sacred resting place is an apt home for their physical traces of desire because, of all the classical pantheon, Diana is the deity most capable of preserving women against 'ungentle men.' In addition, as Patricia Simons observes with regard to Italian Renaissance art, there is abundant pictorial evidence that Diana and her nymphs could offer women evocative images of same-gender erotic and spiritual bonds.[30] Marvell's *Nymph Complaining* is a poetic corollary to this phenomenon of female desire and attraction routed, in part, through Dianic solidarity and resistance.

The nymph's account draws to a close with an echo of Ovid's tale of Niobe's death and transformation. In Marvell's poem the nymph projects a marble statue of herself and one of her lover crafted of 'purest Alabaster': 'For I would have thine Image be / White as I can, thought not as Thee' (120–2). In the *Metamorphoses,* Ovid relates how Niobe's husband and children were slaughtered because she had refused to allow her people to worship the goddess Latona. Her entire family destroyed, Niobe metamorphosed into a statue. Like Marvell's nymph, however, 'She yet retaines her teares' which continue to flow from out the 'mourning marble' (VI.273–4). The nymph and Niobe are not exact equivalents; Niobe's family, after all, was wiped out by Apollo and his sister Diana, the same goddess to whom the nymph sacrifices her 'golden Vial' of tears. The similarity between the fate of the nymph and Niobe is best understood as Marvell's turning again to Ovid in order to emphasize the excruciating vulnerability of happiness and love to unforeseen disaster. In addition, the Niobe-like statues of the nymph and her fawn present aestheticized simulacra of their ruined passion; the full scope of their love exceeds all available representational possibilities. In Marvell's poem, 'lesbian' eroticism is glimpsed; through a savage subtraction, however, it returns again to silence and invisibility.[31]

In his exploration of early modern male homoerotics, Bruce Smith finds that poetry far more sensitively reflects the vast range of possible desires and experiences – the 'untidy facts of day-to-day life' – than do moral or legal pronouncements.[32] Roaming about in the green Ovidian shadows of the forest and mind, Marvell's nymph details pleasures and devotions that disrupt tidy heteronormative prescription; her complaint enigmatically conjures a paracivil zone wonderfully (albeit temporarily) free of sexual orthodoxy. The mutual love between nymph and fawn challenges the cultural and jural determination that male-female relations uniquely represent truth and beauty. Nature, the poem reports, cannot be contained by prejudice. In the nymph's oft-quoted words:

> I have a Garden of my own,
> But so with Roses over grown,
> And Lilies, that you would it guess
> To be a little Wilderness. (71–4)

This garden is precisely the safe, secluded territory for which so much of Marvell's poetry yearns. The uninformed might 'guess' the nymph's private, unconventional garden 'To be a little Wilderness' in serious need of pruning and landscaping; to do so, however, would be to miss the fact that the nymph and her fawn revel in the 'over grown' invisible reaches of their erotic *hortus amoenus.* In a manner both memorable and affecting, the nymph's Ovidian lament provides a salutary reminder that human emotions and bodies are capable of a broader spectrum of pleasures than the straitened 'order of nature' defended by Coke, Sandys, and too many others of limited vision and sympathy.

NOTES

This essay was composed in Goran's inspiring Orphic shadow; *grazie ancora, amico.*

1 In both the title and body of the poem's first printed appearance in Marvell's posthumous *Miscellaneous Poems,* the nymph's partner is rendered as

'faun.' In his notes to *The Poems and Letters of Andrew Marvell*, vol. 1, 3rd ed. (Oxford: Oxford University Press, 1971), pp. 250–1 – which reproduces the poem's original seventeenth-century orthography – H.M. Margoliouth speaks of a 'fawn,' a practice I have retained. All quotations from Marvell's poems are from this edition and are cited parenthetically by line.

2 Jonathan Goldberg, *Voice Terminal Echo: Postmodernism and English Renaissance Texts* (London: Methuen, 1986), p. 16.

3 For notice of the poem's Ovidian elements, see Sarah Annes Brown, 'Ovid and Marvell's "The Nymph Complaining for the Death of her Faun,"' *Translation and Literature* 6 (1997), pp. 167–85; Don Cameron Allen, *Image and Meaning: Metaphoric Traditions in Renaissance Poetry*, rev. ed. (Baltimore: Johns Hopkins University Press, 1968), pp. 167, 169, 185; Goldberg, *Voice*, pp. 21, 36, 165 n.9; Nicholas Guild, 'Marvell's "The Nymph Complaining for the Death of Her Faun,"' *Modern Language Quarterly* 29 (1968): 388; Frank Kermode and Keith Walker, eds., *Andrew Marvell* (Oxford: Oxford University Press), p. 287n.; Edward Le Comte, 'Marvell's "The Nymph Complaining for the Death of Her Fawn,"' *Modern Philology* 50 (1952): 99; J.B. Leishman, *The Art of Marvell's Poetry* (London: Hutchinson, 1966), p. 156; and Graham Parry, 'What is Marvell's Nymph Complaining About?' *Critical Survey* 5 (1993): 244. To my knowledge, Paul Hammond is the only other critic who has noticed the intersection of Ovid (via the story of Narcissus) and homoeroticism in Marvell's *oeuvre*; see his 'Marvell's Sexuality,' *The Seventeenth Century* 11 (1996): 87–123.

4 Rosalie Colie, *'My Ecchoing Song': Andrew Marvell's Poetry of Criticism* (Princeton: Princeton University Press, 1970), pp. 87–9; Jonathan Dollimore, *Sexual Dissidence: Augustine to Wilde, Freud to Foucault* (Oxford: Oxford University Press, 1991), p. 114.

5 Prior to Hammond, a small clutch of earlier twentieth-century scholars also alluded to Marvell's amatory desires. Vita Sackville-West observes, 'In the whole of Marvell's own correspondence, as in all contemporary writings concerning him, there is no mention whatsoever of a wife; on the contrary, such allusions as were made to his private life, pointed to quite different conclusions' (*Andrew Marvell* [London: Faber and Faber, 1929], p. 23). Others have written enigmatically of the poet's 'private inadequacies' (A. Alvarez, Introduction to Andrew Marvell, *The Complete Poems*, ed. George de F. Lord [New York: Knopf-Everyman, 1993], p. xxiii) and 'embarrassment' at wanting to 'make love' with 'young men' while inebriated (William Empson, *Using Biography* [London: Chatto & Windus, 1984], p. 87).

6 My analysis does not exclude the many other interpretations which have been advanced. Rather, as is often the case in life, eroticism in Marvell's com-

plaint is best understood as intimately woven with a variety of personal, religious, political, and cultural issues.

7 Stephen Gosson, *The Schoole of Abuse*, facs. repr., in The Schoole of Abuse *by Stephen Gosson and* A Reply to Gosson's 'Schoole of Abuse' *by Thomas Lodge* (1579; New York: Garland Press, 1973), sig. A2r.

8 Ovid, *All Ovid's Elegies*, trans. Christopher Marlowe, in *The Complete Works of Christopher Marlowe*, vol. 1, ed. Roma Gill (Oxford: Oxford University Press, 1987), pp. 13–84; references are cited parenthetically by book, elegy, and line.

9 Arthur Golding, trans., *Ovid's Metamorphoses*, ed. John Frederick Nims (1567; New York: Macmillan, 1965), ll. 64–6; George Sandys, trans., *Ovid's Metamorphosis Englished, Mythologized, and Represented in Figures*, ed. Karl K. Hulley and Stanley T. Vandersall (1632; Lincoln: University of Nebraska Press, 1970), p. 8; all subsequent quotations from the *Metamorphoses* are from Sandys's edition and appear parenthetically by book and page number.

10 Jonathan Bate, *Shakespeare and Ovid* (Oxford: Oxford University Press, 1993), 15; William Keach, *Elizabethan Erotic Narratives: Irony and Pathos in the Ovidian Poetry of Shakespeare, Marlowe, and Their Contemporaries* (New Brunswick: Rutgers University Press, 1977), pp. xviii, 5; and Bate, *Shakespeare and Ovid*, p. 84.

11 Jonathan Crewe, 'The Garden State: Marvell's Poetics of Enclosure,' in *Enclosure Acts: Sexuality, Property, and Culture in Early Modern England*, ed. Richard Burt and John Michael Archer (Ithaca: Cornell University Press, 1994), p. 276.

12 Elizabeth Harvey, *Ventriloquized Voices: Feminist Theory and English Renaissance Texts* (London: Routledge, 1992), pp. 129–33.

13 Valerie Traub, 'The (In)significance of "Lesbian" Desire in Early Modern England,' in *Erotic Politics: Desire on the Renaissance Stage*, ed. Susan Zimmerman (New York: Routledge, 1992), p. 164; and Traub, 'The Perversion of "Lesbian" Desire,' *History Workshop Journal* 41 (1996): 19–49. For a discussion of poeticized 'lesbian' desire contemporary with Marvell, see Arlene Stiebel, 'Not Since Sappho: The Erotic in Poems of Katherine Phillips and Aphra Behn,' in *Homosexuality in Renaissance and Enlightenment England: Literary Representations in Historical Context*, ed. Claude Summers (New York: Haworth, 1992), pp. 153–71.

14 Claude Summers, rev. of Bruce Smith, *Homosexual Desire in Shakespeare's England: A Cultural Poetics*, in *The Journal of Homosexuality* 23 (1992): 122; Jonathan Goldberg, *Sodometries: Renaissance Texts, Modern Sexualities* (Stanford: Stanford University Press, 1992), pp. 18–20; and Edward Coke, *The Third Part of the Institutes of the Laws of England* (London: M. Flesher, 1644), pp. 58–9. On the legal proscription of homosexual acts between males in

early modern England, see Bruce Smith, *Homosexual Desire in Shakespeare's England: A Cultural Poetics* (Chicago: University of Chicago Press, 1991), pp. 41–53. Smith's discussion is especially important because it teases out the differences among the spirit, letter, and application of the law. By and large, I am most concerned with the moral dimension of non-normative erotics.

15 Given his keen interest and involvement in England's political life, the possibility that Marvell was aware of and responded to Coke's proscription cannot be dismissed. The chapter preceding the one in which Coke details the sin 'amongst Christian not to be named' is devoted to an explication of the law 'Of Deodands' (pp. 57–8); by coincidence or design, one of the most unusual words in *The Nymph Complaining* is 'deodand' (l. 17), which, curiously enough, there signifies the *reverse* of its common legal definition.

16 Keach, *Elizabethan Erotic Narratives*, p. 17.

17 Sandys's final example of a sex-changing woman is the famous French villager who, Ambroise Paré and Michel de Montaigne also report, transformed from 'Marie' to 'Germain' as a result of physical exertion. Sandys likely drew on Montaigne's account and the connection he draws to Ovid's Iphis ('Of the Force of the Imagination,' in *Montaigne's Essays*, vol. 1, trans. John Florio [London: Dent, 1910], pp. 93–4). On Marie's relation to the cultural constructedness of sex, see Thomas Laqueur, *Making Sex: Body and Gender from the Greeks to Freud* (Cambridge: Harvard University Press, 1990), pp. 122–30.

18 I have recently explored Marvell's treatment of same-gender female homoeroticism in *Upon Appleton House* in my book *Early Modern Metaphysical Literature: Nature, Custom and Strange Desires* (Basingstoke: Palgrave, and New York: St Martin's, 2001), pp. 69–88.

19 Edmund Spenser, *The Faerie Queene*, in *Edmund Spenser's Poetry*, 3rd ed., ed. Hugh Maclean and Anne Lake Prescott (New York: Norton, 1993), I.vi.17.

20 My interpretation of Sylvio's literary genealogy is not intended to exclude other possibilities; see, for instance, Parry's detection of correspondences between Sylvio and a similarly named huntsman in Guarini's *Il Pastor Fido* ('What is Marvell's Nymph Complaining About?' pp. 245–7).

21 Michael Craze, *The Life and Lyrics of Andrew Marvell* (London: Macmillan, 1979), p. 72; Yvonne L. Sandstroem, 'Marvell's "Nymph Complaining" as Historical Allegory,' *Studies in English Literature* 30 (1990): 95, 98; and Barbara Estrin, *Laura: Uncovering Gender and Genre in Wyatt, Donne, and Marvell* (Durham: Duke University Press, 1994), p. 110 (cf. pp. 104, 109, 112, 115).

22 Hammond, 'Marvell's Sexuality,' p. 110.

23 Margoliouth, *The Poems and Letters of Andrew Marvell*, p. 250n.; William

Browne, *Britannia's Pastorals* (1613–16; facs. Menston: Scolar Press, 1969); all references are cited parenthetically.

24 Richard Brathwait cites Pylades and Orestes in his encomium on loving friendship between men (*The English Gentleman* [1630; facs. Amsterdam: Theatrum Orbis Terrarum, 1975], p. 243).

25 Hammond, 'Marvell's Sexuality,' also acknowledges that the fawn possesses an 'androgynous beauty' (p. 110), but does not note that it tilts far more towards the feminine than the masculine.

26 Thomas Wyatt, 'Whoso list to hunt,' in *Collected Poems*, ed. Joost Daalder (London: Oxford University Press, 1975), p. 7, ll. 7–8.

27 Colie, '*My Ecchoing Song*,' p. 131.

28 Anna Nardo, *The Ludic Self in Seventeenth-Century English Literature* (Albany: SUNY Press, 1991), p. 113; Traub, 'Perversion,' p. 31.

29 Ioannis Scapulae, *Lexicon Graeco-Latinvm* (Basil: Sebastianvm Henricpetri, 1604), sig. Aa3r; Thomas Thomas, *Dictionarivm Lingvae Latinae et Anglicanae* (London: Richard Boyle, 1587), sv. 'Nympha/ae'; Randle Cotgrave in his *A Dictionarie of the French and English Tongves* (1611; facs. Menston: Scolar Press, 1968); and John Florio in his *Queen Anna's New World of Words* (1611; facs. Menston: Scolar Press, 1968) reiterate the association with female genitalia. See also Traub, 'Perversion,' p. 32.

30 Patricia Simons, 'Lesbian (In)Visibility in Italian Renaissance Culture: Diana and Other Cases of *donna con donna*,' *Journal of Homosexuality* 27 (1994): 81–122.

31 Le Comte ('Marvell's Nymph,' p. 99) argues for an association between Niobe and Cyparissus; this link adds to the poem's homoerotic intertextuality.

32 Smith, *Homosexual Desire in Shakespeare's England*, p. 56.

'Male deformities': Narcissus and the Reformation of Courtly Manners in *Cynthia's Revels*

MARIO DIGANGI

The analysis of homoeroticism in Ovidian myth has been, and continues to be, an important concern of lesbian and gay Renaissance scholarship.[1] Thanks to such work, we now possess a solid understanding of the multiple ways in which homoerotic myths – particularly those about Jupiter and Ganymede, Apollo and Hyacinthus, Diana and Callisto, and Orpheus – were interpreted, translated, and appropriated within early modern culture. Surprisingly, however, lesbian and gay Renaissance scholarship has generally neglected the Ovidian subject most commonly associated with homosexual desire in our own era: the myth of Narcissus, the lovely youth who scorns his suitors and consequently perishes from a futile desire for his own reflection. The familiar link between Narcissus and homosexual desire comes from Freudian theory, in which 'narcissism' describes the interruption of proper libidinal development supposedly characteristic of homosexual object-choice. Of course, early moderns could not understand the Narcissus myth as a parable of 'homosexuality,' since the idea of distinct sexual orientations emerged from nineteenth-century discourses. Homoeroticism does play a role in certain Renaissance versions of the Narcissus myth, however, and a historicist queer criticism is well positioned to explain the connection between self-love and same-sex desire in these premodern texts.[2]

In this essay I want to pursue such an analysis by focusing on Ben Jonson's early comedy *Cynthia's Revels* (1600), which offers particular insight into the social and political implications of the Narcissus myth for early modern English culture. Originally entered in the Stationer's Register as *Narcissus, or the fountain of self-love,* this quirky satire of courtly manners represents Jonson's 'only extended use of Ovidian material.'[3] Jonson's uncharacteristic recourse to Ovidian subjects in *Cynthia's Revels* suggests his recognition of the Narcissus myth's theatrical viability as a vehicle for satire. While Narcissus never appears as a character in the play, the Narcissus myth provides Jonson with vivid material for exposing the transgressive bodily practices of unauthorized courtiers, especially through the character of Amorphous ('the deformed'), whose affected manners violate orthodox prescriptions for male aristocratic comportment. The play's ridicule of courtly affectation thus accords with early modern interpretations of the Narcissus myth that primarily associate self-love not with homoerotic desire but with effeminate manners: a clear sign of social, economic, and political transgression. By contrast, the virtuously 'masculine' comportment of the true gentleman, according to a particular strain of early modern political ideology, justifies his status and exercise of power. Exposing illegitimate courtiers as effeminate narcissists, *Cynthia's Revels* reveals the importance of an ideology of 'civilized' masculinity to early-seventeenth-century constructions of political legitimacy.

By the time Jonson wrote *Cynthia's Revels*, the Narcissus myth had developed an extended, complex, cultural legacy. Traditional medieval and Renaissance moral commentaries on Ovid generally explained Narcissus's error as the 'folly of loving an image.'[4] Arthur Golding's influential 1567 translation of *The Metamorphoses*, for instance, moralizes the myth as a 'mirror' of vanity and pride: 'Narcissus is of scornfulnesse and pryde a myrror cleere, / Where beawties fading vanitie most playnly may appeere.'[5] For emblematist Geoffrey Whitney, Narcissus symbolizes the inflated self-esteem that afflicts people at all levels of society:

> Narcissus lovde, and liked so his shape,
> He died at lengthe with gazinge there uppon:
> Which shewes selfe love, from which there fewe can scape,
> A plague too rife: bewitcheth manie a one.
> The ritche, the pore, the learned, and the sotte,
> Offend therein: and yet they see it not.

Whereas Whitney chastises rich and poor alike, Thomas Palmer's emblem illustrating the 'force of selfe love' attacks the vanity of social climbers in particular. Palmer describes Narcissus as a 'pereles boy' not only because he is exceptionally beautiful but also because he ranks well below a peer in the social hierarchy he attempts to violate. According to Palmer, the punishment of Narcissus provides a stern warning for ambitious people who 'looke alofte, / while theye be in their ruffe.'[6]

Cynthia's Revels likewise introduces the Narcissus myth as an emblem of the socially transgressive effects of self-love. At the beginning of the play, we learn that Jove has commanded Mercury to restore to Echo her body and voice so that she might finally mourn Narcissus's death. Cursing the 'Fountain of Self-love' at which Narcissus died, Echo laments that

> self-love never yet could look on truth
> But with bleared beams; sleek flattery and she
> Are twin-born sisters, and so mix their eyes
> As if you sever one, the other dies.[7]

Echo's anatomy of narcissism, which affiliates self-love with the quintessential courtly vice of flattery, clearly applies to the social and political as well as the epistemological realm. The political threat posed by members of the gentry who harbour a 'self-conceived excellence' becomes apparent in the play's subsequent depiction of proud courtiers and ladies who chafe at Cynthia's preeminence (1.2.44). Echo's complaint touches also on the economic implications of the envy and greed that destroyed Narcissus when he

> with starved and covetous ignorance,
> Pined in continual eyeing that bright gem,
> The glance whereof to others had been more
> Than to [his] famished mind the wide world's store:
> 'So wretched is it to be merely rich.' (1.2.47–51)

Comparing him to a miser, Echo seems to contradict the Induction's earlier description of Narcissus as a 'pretty foolish gentleman [who] melted himself away' (45), a likely allusion to the phenomenon of gentlemen frittering away their estates through extravagant expenditure.[8] The contradiction is only apparent, however, since excessive hoarding and excessive spending can be considered equally wasteful financial practices based on an exaggerated sense of self-worth. Emphasizing the disastrous social, political, and economic consequences of self-love, Echo's complaint accords with traditional moral commentaries on the Narcissus myth.

However, what such moralizing commentary omits is Ovid's vivid account of the erotic conflict and confusion unleashed by Narcissus's vanity and proud denial of love. In *Cynthia's Revels* such complications arise as soon as Echo has finished her lament and, having again lost the power of speech, prepares to leave the scene. At this moment the courtier Amorphous enters and greets Echo. Offended by the apparent rudeness of Echo's curt replies, Amorphous insists that she has nothing to fear: 'I am neither your minotaur, nor your centaur, nor your satyr, nor your hyena, nor your babion, but your mere traveller, believe me' (1.3.3–6). Tellingly, Amorphous defensively dissociates himself from creatures (both mythical and real) notorious for their sexual and anatomical aberrations. Ovid explains that the minotaur, a 'Monster that did beare / The shape of man and Bull,' was the product of Pasiphae's 'filthie whoredom' (Ovid XII.225–6, 206), while the hyena experienced an annual change of sex: 'interchaungeable it one whyle dooth remayne / A female, and another whyle becommeth male againe' (Ovid XV.451–2). Though not literally deformed, Amorphous grotesquely calls attention to his body by proclaiming the excellence of his 'behaviours,' (24) 'garments,' (25) 'countenance,' (25) and 'gesture[s],' (29) and by boasting that his 'optics have drunk the spirit of beauty in some eight score and eighteen princes' courts,' (33–4) where he had been 'fortunate in the amours of three hundred forty and five ladies, all nobly, if not princely descended' (35–7). Greedily drinking from the Fountain of Self-love, Amorphous establishes himself as the exemplar of a prodigious narcissism.

A spectacularly performative character, Amorphous continues to manifest his social deformity as bodily deformity. To illustrate his mastery of impersonation, for instance, he contorts his face to imitate the characteristic visages of various social types: the 'plodding' merchant, 'methodical' student, 'menacing' soldier, 'labyrinthean' lawyer, and so on (2.3.20–7). As a gentleman, Amorphous debases himself by imitating the appearance of social inferiors like merchants and soldiers. His foolish manner of speech, moreover, provokes Mercury to ridicule him in terms of gender and status debasement: 'He speaks all cream, skimmed, and more affected than a dozen of waiting women' (2.3.81–2). Amorphous does not add up: the multiple knowledges, fashions, and skills he amasses through his travels and observations at court have nothing to stick to. A monstrous hybrid of the excessive – he speaks 'all cream,' like 'a dozen' women – and of the deficient – the cream is 'skimmed,' the women only 'waiting' – Amorphous becomes difficult to visualize as an actual stage character. As Mercury observes, he is 'so made out of the mixture and shreds of forms that himself is truly deformed' (2.3.77–8).

In *Cynthia's Revels*, the figure of Narcissus thereby functions not only as the social and moral prototype but also as the aesthetic antitype of the contemporary narcissist. Narcissus's legendary beauty throws into sharp relief the deformed mannerisms of courtiers like Amorphous. Jonson's satiric use of Narcissus in this regard can be illuminated by an allusion to Narcissus in Robert Burton's *Anatomy of Melancholy*. Burton writes that self-love proceeds from 'an over-weening conceit' of

> our excellent gifts and fortunes for which *Narcissus* like, we admire, flatter, and applaud our selves, and thinke all the world esteemes so of us; and as deformed women easily beleeve those that tell them they be faire, we are too credulous of our owne good parts & praises, too well perswaded of our selves ...[9]

Burton faults Narcissus for taking an excessive pride in his 'excellent gifts,' but it is the blind vanity of a 'deformed woman' that provides the most palpable demonstration of self-love. Both Jonson and Burton cite Narcissus as a social prototype and physical antitype of the deformed narcissist; however, Jonson associates narcissism with a particularly male rather than female bodily deformity. To be sure, narcissistic women do not escape censure in *Cynthia's Revels*. For instance, the lady Philautia ('self-love') 'admires not herself for any one particularity but for all' (2.4.33): she believes herself fair, witty, and an accomplished dancer. Nonetheless, Jonson reserves the 'deformed' name of Amorphous for a male character, and male bodies are especially noted for physical deformity throughout the play. In Crites's satiric catalogue of courtiers, various male 'forms' are held up for ridicule (3.4.10): the 'proud and spangled sir, / That looks three handfuls higher than his foretop' (3.4.12), the 'mincing marmoset / Made all of clothes and face' (3.4.22–3), the 'subtle Proteus' who 'can change and vary with all forms he sees' (3.4.42, 43), the 'neophyte glazing of his face, / Pruning his clothes, perfuming of his hair' (3.4.55–6), and so on. The inappropriate display of the male body in *Cynthia's Revels* epitomizes the delusions and follies of narcissism.

The deformity of male courtiers appears even more glaring when set against Jonson's decision to place Echo on the stage as a visually striking female presence, a 'dear spark of beauty' of noteworthy 'feature,' 'lineament,' and 'symmetry' (1.3.1, 12–13, 17–18). Materializing Echo as a dramatic character instead of a mere allusion, Jonson provides her with a body and a voice, the lack of which constitute the very essence of her legendary identity.[10] According to Ovid, the loquacious Echo prevented Juno from catching Jove in adulterous acts; discovering the ploy, Juno deprived the 'babling Nymph' of independent speech (3.443). For Golding, Echo's transformation illustrates the 'lewd behaviour of a bawd, and his due punishment' (Epistle 108). The impaired nymph completely deteriorates after failing to seduce Narcissus:

Through restlesse carke and care
Hir bodie pynes to skinne and bone, and waxeth wonderous bare.
The bloud doth vanish into ayre from out of all hir veynes,
And nought is left but voyce and bones: the voyce yet still remaynes:
Hir bones they say were turnde to stones. (3.493–7)

In *Cynthia's Revels,* Jonson inverts this metamorphosis, reforming Echo's vanished voice and bones through the 'articulate power' and 'corporal figure' of a boy actor (1.2.11,10). Given the extended banter about the attractiveness of the boy actors or 'fine ingles' in the Induction (152–3), Jonson's audience might have been led to an even sharper aesthetic appreciation of Echo, the first female character to appear in the play. Why, then, does Jonson put on stage two physically impressive female figures who would normally confound theatrical representation altogether – namely, Echo and Cynthia (a transparent allusion to Queen Elizabeth) – while denying stable embodiment to the play's central male figures – the absent Narcissus and the protean Amorphous?

To frame the matter in this way is to emphasize the play's ideological investment in defining and regulating the boundaries of the aristocratic male body. The proliferation of 'male deformities' at Cynthia's court directly engages early modern discourses regarding the public comportment and sartorial display appropriate to the gentleman (5.11.113). In a recent analysis of Renaissance courtesy books, David Kuchta argues that in the 'semiotic regime' of the early modern court 'the phenomenon of display itself was not gendered.' The courtier's gendering as 'masculine' or 'effeminate' was instead determined by the degree of correspondence between the clothes – arbitrary, conventional signifiers – and their wearer:

> Conspicuous consumption was considered a rightful and manly honor bestowed upon [the courtier] by his noble status and position at court. Rich clothes proclaimed high status. Conspicuous consumption made the social order conspicuous. Effeminacy, on the other hand, was the misuse of these arbitrary status symbols, and thus a threat to the social order by the base materiality of the nouveau riche.[11]

Displaying an attitude of 'carelessness' and 'moderation' about clothes, the masculine courtier complied with the 'social doctrine of conspicuous consumption' and the 'political doctrine of crown prerogative' that justified it. Effeminacy, on the other hand, implied an excessive preoccupation with or inappropriate deployment of fashion: 'dressing out of place, thus calling attention to one's dress in a kind of "womanish vanity."'[12]

In *Cynthia's Revels*, Amorphous is just such an effeminate courtier. He relies on 'outward and effeminate shades' (5.4.575) – clothes, phrases, gestures – to gain access to a court at which he has no legitimate place. Although there is no explicit indication in the play that he has sexual relations with men, his effeminacy also manifests as a violation of the ideal of intimate 'acquaintance' between gentlemen (1.4.66).[13] Having drunk from the Fountain of Self-love, Amorphous grows 'dotingly enamored' of himself and the reflection of himself he sees in another 'pretty formal young gallant,' the citizen's son Asotus (1.2.104, 1.4.30). Flattering Asotus, Amorphous perverts the Renaissance convention of the unique bond shared by gentleman friends: 'I think I shall affect you, sir ... your sweet disposition to travel, I assure you, hath made you another myself in mine eye, and struck me enamored of your beauties' (1.4.111, 119–21). Asotus, in turn, finds his new friend 'ravishing' (1.4.57).[14] 'I would I were the fairest lady of France for your sake, sir,' he assures him (1.4.122). But what could the fairest lady of France do for Amorphous that Asotus cannot – grant him sexual favours? Since his male anatomy is not itself an obstacle to sexual relations with Amorphous, it is more likely that Asotus fantasizes about having the power to validate Amorphous's social identity as a 'masculine' courtier. The power to authorize the identity and agency of the courtier belonged, however, to the monarch, who, as Kuchta explains, invested the arbitrary signifiers of high status with their political significations.[15] Flattery, ambition, and an illegitimate desire to appropriate Cynthia's political prerogative, not homoerotic desire per se, mark the friendship between Amorphous and Asotus as an effeminate rather than a masculine same-sex bond.

This point bears repeating, for even a critic as dedicated to historicizing effeminacy as Kuchta falls into anachronism when it comes to sexuality. As Kuchta shows, some Renaissance courtesy theorists associated the semiotic immoderation of the effeminate courtier with sexual inversion. Giovanni della Casa, for example, advises courtiers to avoid 'extremely fancy' garments resembling 'Ganymede's hose.'[16] From such advice Kuchta concludes that courtly masculinity 'was defined in opposition to a series of "wanton and sensual imperfections," which were themselves linked with materiality: prostitution, homosexuality, and effeminacy.'[17] The anachronistic use of the word 'homosexuality' in this passage implies that in the early modern period men who engaged in same-sex relations were universally regarded as indulging immoderate and effeminate passions. Yet Renaissance court culture was structured by the normative same-sex relations of friendship, patronage, and favouritism, in which the signs of homosocial masculinity might well have been indistinguishable from the signs of homoerotic desire.[18] Thus, when della Casa maligns gaudy apparel as 'Ganymede's hose,' he is interpreting Ganymede's sexual domination by Jove as a sign not of unmanly homosexuality, but of unmanly subservience, which the courtier must avoid. To put this another way, if a courtier's effeminate taste for Ganymede's hose bewrays 'wanton' erotic tendencies, it is not because he is 'homosexual,' but because his sartorial *faux pas* reveals his inadequate attainment of élite male subjectivity.

In coding the socially disruptive narcissism of illegitimate courtiers as effeminacy, *Cynthia's Revels* accords not only with conduct books but with literary adaptations of the Narcissus myth. A brief account of some of these adaptations will show that despite their differences, they typically portray self-love as a disturbance of proper masculine social protocols, not as a necessary consequence or correlative of homoerotic desire. In Arthur Golding's faithful translation of *The Metamorphoses*, men and women are equally susceptible to the feminine beauty of Narcissus:

> For when yeares three times five and one he fully lyved had,
> So that he seemde to stande beetwene the state of man and Lad,
> The hearts of divers trim yong men his beautie gan to move,
> And many a Ladie fresh and faire was taken in his love.
> But in that grace of Natures gift such passing pride did raigne,
> That to be toucht of man or Mayde he wholy did disdaine. (3.437–42)

If homoerotic desire represents a problem in this scenario, it is because Narcissus so capriciously rejects those men who experience the culturally commonplace allure of youthful male beauty. In *The Maid's Metamorphosis* (1600), an Ovidian comedy contemporary with *Cynthia's Revels*, the beautiful youth Hyacinth, unlike Narcissus, does not refuse the advances of a male admirer. Apollo regards his passionate desire for

Hyacinth as unremarkable in nature and as authorized by divine precedent:

There saw I that, wherein I gan to joy,
Amilchars sonne a gallant comely boy,
Hight (Hiacinth) full fifteene yeares of age.
Whome I intended to have made my Page,
And bare as great affection to the boy,
As ever Jove, in Ganimede did joy.[19]

Where Hyacinth reciprocates Apollo's affection, Narcissus scorns all his male suitors, one of whom angrily prays that Narcissus might also feel the pain of rejection. Consequently, in *The Metamorphoses*, Narcissus mistakes his own reflection in the water for the face of a beautiful, disdainful, young man: 'He would he had. For looke how oft I kisse the water under, / So oft againe with upwarde mouth he ryseth towarde mee, / A man would thinke to touch at least I should yet able bee' (3.565–7). Sterile self-love thus serves as an ironic punishment for Narcissus's vanity in *rejecting* a male lover, an implication ignored by those who have interpreted the myth as a condemnation of homosexuality.

Renaissance verse adaptations of the Narcissus myth generally follow Ovid (and Golding) in placing the source of transgression elsewhere than in same-sex desire. In *Narcissus Change* (1611), an elegy by Richard Brathwayte, homoerotic desire is certainly present. Narcissus appreciates the beauty of other men – 'Bright-eide Alexis is beyond compare' – and recounts their attraction to him – 'Damon hath told me oft, I was most faire.'[20] Narcissus's downfall ensues not from homoerotic desire, however, but from his view of himself as beyond the reach of all but an immortal lover:

Narcissus gemme, for who can ere compare
With the surpassing beautie of his face?
Which intermixed is with red most faire,
Resembling Io, whose admired grace
Strucke such a love in Jupiters high brest,
That he protested, he lov'd Io best. (sigs. D4v–D5)

Even as he compares himself favourably to the various women loved by Jupiter and Apollo, Narcissus seems unaware that these same gods, unlike himself, also deigned to take young men like Ganymede and Hyacinth as lovers. Ultimately punished for indulging 'soaring thoughts' of 'his owne beautie fitter for Gods then men' (sig. D7v), Narcissus might have avoided tragedy, Brathwayte implies, had he deemed his beauty fit for merely mortal men like Alexis and Damon. What the poem represents as transgressive and perilous, then, is not same-sex desire but a boundless ambition attributed to feminine vanity.

Thomas Edwards's poem *Narcissus* (1595) depicts male effeminacy as the fruit of pride, indolence, and acquisitiveness. Although Narcissus, who 'stood as nice as any she alive,' (p. 39) initially scorns his female suitors, their presents ultimately transform him:

I tooke the Jewels which faire Ladies sent me,
And manie pretie toies, which to advance
My future bane, unwillingly they meant me,
Their whole attire and choise suites not content me:
  But like a lover glad of each new toy,
  So I a woman turned from a boy.

Which once perform'd, how farre did I exceed
Those stately dames, in gesture, modest action,
Coy lookes, deep smiles, faining heroique deeds,
To bring them all under my owne subjection,
For as a woman tired in affection,
  Some new disport neare thought on is requir'd,
  So now I long'd to walke to be admir'd.[21] (p. 48)

Once turned into a woman, Narcissus takes a seemingly homoerotic pleasure in the company of other women – 'thus we like to wanton wenches were, / In severall sports best pleasing and delightfull' (p. 49). Consequently, he mistakes his reflection in the water for the face of an actual woman. In an astute analysis of this poem, Jonathan Gil Harris observes that the ostensibly 'heterosexual' attraction Narcissus feels for this female figure in the water would be more accurately described as homoerotic, since 'its origin and object [are] disclosed as male': Narcissus actually desires himself. Yet Harris's conclusion – that what generally passes for male heterosexual desire might be fundamentally motivated by male homosocial, homoerotic, or narcissistic energies – fails to account for the importance of *female* homoerotic desire in the poem's climactic scene.[22] Upon discovering his error, Narcissus chastises himself for a double absurdity, for not only has he become a woman, he has become a woman homoerotically attracted to her own image:

Fie wanton, fie, know'st not thou art a boy,
Or hath a womans weeds, thee sinful elfe,
Made willful like themselves, or how growen coy?
Wer't thou a woman, this is but a shaddo,
And seldome do their sex themselves undo. (p. 59)

To my mind, therefore, Edwards's poem seems concerned less to deconstruct male heteroerotic desire as fundamentally homoerotic than to explore a common cultural fantasy about women's power to emasculate men. Whatever the truth of the claim that women seldom 'undo' (i.e., sexually ruin) other women, the poem demonstrates how effectively they can undo men.

Finally, in *Narcissus*, a 'Twelfth Night Merriment' performed at Oxford in 1602, the story of Narcissus is mined for the comic potential of scenes of disorderly courtship – heteroerotic as well as homoerotic. The confusion begins when two country men, overcome by Narcissus's beauty, incompetently address him in the language of a Petrarchan blazon: 'O thou whose cheeks are like the skye so blewe, / Whose nose is rubye, of the sunnlike hue.'[23] Jonathan Sawday has described the blazon as a courtly homosocial competition in which the 'female body may have been the circulating token,' but 'male desire ... valorized the currency.'[24] An anomalously gendered 'token' body, Narcissus fails to understand his position within this entirely male circuit of exchange:

Nor sunne, nor moone, nor twinkling starre in skye,
Nor god, nor goddesse, nor yet nimphe am I,
And though my sweete face bee set out with rubye,
You misse your marke, I am a man as you bee. (354–7)

Undeterred, his suitors retort that like will to like: 'A man thou art, Narcisse, & soe are wee, / Then love thou us again as wee love thee' (366–7). Clearly, this seduction is absurdly ineffective not simply because it is homoerotic – in a subsequent scene Narcissus just as readily dismisses two female suitors – but because it enacts a status and gender burlesque of elevated courtship rhetoric. Here and elsewhere, the play generates 'merriment' from incongruous and inept seductions, culminating in Narcissus's hopeless wooing of the 'delicate pretty youth' he sees in the water (719).

Vanity, sensual dissipation, immoderate consumption, and rhetorical affectation: these are the 'male deformities' that Renaissance writers typically extrapolate from the Narcissus myth and that Jonson satirizes in the ill-mannered Amorphous. Yet the association of these social vices with Narcissus does not explain why their censure should occupy so much of Jonson's attention in *Cynthia's Revels*. What is at stake in the ridicule of courtly narcissism? Certainly, an increased preoccupation with refined courtly manners has been identified as one effect of 'the civilizing process' in Renaissance Europe. In her analysis of the literary developments that contributed to this process in England, Anna Bryson argues that while sixteenth-century courtesy theorists continued to 'assert the traditional values of lineage and valour,' they 'increasingly stressed that honour also adhered in personal, moral and intellectual qualities developed in a liberal education.' The sixteenth-century gentleman displayed his good manners as a 'visible embodiment and social "representation"' of his 'possession of inner virtues perfected by education.' To be sure, Jonson was greatly concerned with the relation between manners and morals, and, as Jonathan Haynes observes, plays like *Cynthia's Revels* are 'full of studies of social gestures, the small arts of everyday life.'[25]

Yet more is at stake in the play's 'visible embodiment' of bad manners than the satirical pleasure and moral satisfaction derived from exposing the folly of particularly affected courtiers. For the individual courtier also represents the court to the nation; he circulates as a visible sign of the social and economic interests being served at the political centre of the kingdom. Jonson says as much in his dedication of the play to the court:

> Thou art a bountiful and brave spring: and waterest all the noble plants of this island. In thee, the whole kingdom dresseth itself, and is ambitious to use thee as her glass. Beware, then, thou render men's figures truly, and teach them no less to hate their deformities than to love their forms: for, to grace there should come reverence; and no man can call that lovely which is not also venerable. It is not powdering, perfuming, and every day smelling of the tailor that converteth to a beautiful object: but a mind, shining through any suit, which needs no false light either of riches, or honours, to help it.

At once a 'bountiful and brave spring' for the nobility and a 'glass' for the kingdom, the court must present only truly virtuous 'figures' as models of behaviour. The true courtier appears 'lovely' not because of his rich 'suit' but because of the virtuous mind that shines through his graceful 'form.' By contrast, those courtiers obsessed with powdering and perfuming are 'deformities,' their riches and titles comparable to the 'false light' a merchant uses to mask defective goods. A court that countenances such deformity transforms itself from a pure 'fountain of manners' into a 'Spring of Self-love.'

This all seems blandly conventional. And yet, what Jonson here presents to the court as a moral imperative – i.e., '"Beware" any slippage in your duty to uphold truth and beauty' – can also be understood as the mystification of a political imperative – i.e., '"Beware" any slippage in ideological legitimacy that might come about from your failure to uphold the image of truth and beauty.' The countenancing of deformed courtiers, Jonson suggests, will deform the image of the court, thereby weakening one source of its power.

This political insight helps to explain why, at the close of the dedication, Jonson identifies himself as the court's 'servant, but not slave.' Offering the abject body of the slave as a metaphor for the crooked language of the sycophantic poet, Jonson evokes particular cultural assumptions about the social threat posed by physical deformity. These assumptions are perhaps most notoriously visible in Shakespeare's *The Tempest*, the Folio text of which refers to Caliban as a 'savage and deformed slave.' Within the play, moreover, Prospero considers Caliban 'as disproportioned in his manners / As in his shape.'[26] In *The Tempest*, the deformed body of the slave seems not only to symbolize but actually to generate his insubordinate manners. Mark Breitenberg's analysis of Renaissance melancholia supports the positing of such a causal relation between disorderly bodies and disorderly behaviours. According to Breitenberg, in the *Anatomy of Melancholy* Robert Burton counterposes the melancholic body to an 'idealized vision of the masculine body as well as a utopian political state' in which 'all members ... act properly in accordance with their assigned places and designated functions.' In the Renaissance epistemological system of universal correspondences, Breitenberg argues, the corporeal and the social are not merely analogous; they are '*a priori* linked and coterminous.' Therefore, a melancholic, effeminate, or otherwise unbalanced body might weaken the body politic.[27] In Jonson's terms, to be the court's servant is to bolster its authority; to be the court's slave is, Caliban-like, to undermine it.

Through its depiction of 'male deformities' at court, *Cynthia's Revels* reveals how the corporeal, the social, and the political functioned as parallel registers of ideological meaning in the early modern discourse of manners. Unless narcissistic courtiers like Amorphous can be reformed and properly 'incorporate[d]' into the social body (5.5.29), their deformed manners will continue to undermine Cynthia's authority and make her court comparable to

> a state ungoverned, without laws;
> Or a body made of nothing but diseases:
> The one, through impotency poor and wretched,
> The other, for the anarchy absurd. (5.5.30–3)

What disease is to the physical body and anarchy is to the political body, bad manners are to the social body. As Bryson observes,

> Nothing better illustrates the close connection between ideals of personal social conduct and the values of public order and hierarchy than the emergence of the word 'civility' in the specialised sense of good manners, at precisely the time when its use had become frequent in political discourse.[28]

To properly embody his élite status, the English gentleman had to eschew whatever 'uncivilized' manners might be associated with his social or political others. One mark of uncivilized people was habitual engagement in disorderly and deforming bodily practices. For example, sodomy, Robert Burton writes, was 'customary in old times with the Orientals, the Greeks without question, the Italians, Africans, Asiaticks ...'[29] Narcissists like Amorphous threaten the integrity of English nationalist ideology by introducing into the court the barbarous, enervating manners – Italian 'remnant[s]' (1.4.70), 'Spanish shrugs,' and 'French faces' (Palinode 1) – acquired from their travels to less 'civilized' (unlawful, unchaste, irreligious) foreign cultures.

To understand the early modern equation between civil manners and civil order should be to appreciate more fully the serious ideological work performed by *Cynthia's Revels*. In seventeenth-century England, as a rising merchant class was competing with the traditional landed aristocracy for economic, social, and political power, an ideology of civilized courtly manners served to justify the aristocracy's 'natural' fitness to rule. Presenting himself as the servant of the true aristocracy, Jonson delegitimizes those ill-mannered courtiers who undercut its representational strategies and thus demystify its exercise of power.

In the very process of reforming courtly deformities, however, Jonson paradoxically creates 'the narcissist': not the neurotic persona of psychoanalytic invention but a disorderly social type reflecting seventeenth-century anxieties about the power and reputation of the court. Such anxieties are hardly dispelled, I would argue, by the ritual purgation of narcissists that concludes *Cynthia's Revels*. In a gesture of comic resolution, the corrupted bodies of Amorphous and his fellow narcissists are finally banished from Cynthia's presence. Narcissus himself, of course, never even appears during the course of the play. However, the corrupting Fountain of Self-love, the emblematic source of narcissism introduced at the very beginning of the play, seems to be a permanent fixture at Cynthia's court, for no mention is made of its ultimate destruction or purification. For Jonson's audience, the survival of the symbolically dominant Fountain of Self-love might well have presaged that narcissistic manners would continue to deform the individual bodies of courtiers as well as the collective body of the court. With the benefit of historical hindsight, we can regard the Fountain's endurance as a sign of the ideological conflict over élite male comportment that would continue to be waged, in early modern England, as the legacy of Narcissus.

NOTES

I would like to thank Elliott Trice for his helpful critique of an early version of this essay, and audience members of the Columbia University Shakespeare Seminar for their questions and suggestions.

1 Discussions of Ovidian myth are central to the following studies of early modern homoeroticism: Leonard Barkan, *Transuming Passion: Ganymede and the Erotics of Humanism* (Stanford: Stanford University Press, 1991); Gregory W. Bredbeck, *Sodomy and Interpretation: Marlowe to Milton* (Ithaca: Cornell University Press, 1991); Bruce R. Smith, *Homosexual Desire in Shakespeare's England: A Cultural Poetics* (Chicago: University of Chicago Press, 1991), and 'Rape, Rap, Rupture, Rapture: R-Rated Futures on the Global Market,' *Textual Practice* 9 (1995): 421–44; Valerie Traub, 'The (In)Significance of "Lesbian" Desire in Early Modern England,' in *Erotic Politics: Desire on the Renaissance Stage*, ed. Susan Zimmerman (New York: Routledge, 1992), and 'The Perversion of Lesbian Desire,' *History Workshop Journal* 41 (1996): 19–50; and Mario DiGangi, *The Homoerotics of Early Modern Drama* (Cambridge: Cambridge University Press, 1997).

2 For different attempts to theorize 'narcissism' in relation to early modern homoeroticism see Valerie Traub, *Desire and Anxiety: Circulations of Sexuality in Shakespearean Drama* (New York: Routledge, 1992), p. 104; Paula Blank,

'Comparing Sappho to Philaenis: John Donne's "Homopoetics,"' *PMLA* 110 (1995): 358–68; and Lynn Enterline, *The Tears of Narcissus: Melancholia and Masculinity in Early Modern Writing* (Stanford: Stanford University Press, 1995).

3 Robert Wiltenburg, *Ben Jonson and Self-Love: The Subtlest Maze of All* (Columbia: University of Missouri Press, 1990), pp. 5–6.

4 Louise Vinge, *The Narcissus Theme in Western European Literature up to the Early 19th Century* (Lund: Gleerups, 1967), p. 76. On the Narcissus and Echo myth in *Cynthia's Revels* see Dewitt T. Starnes and Ernest William Talbert, *Classical Myth and Legend in Renaissance Dictionaries* (Westport, CT: Greenwood Press, 1955), pp. 188–212.

5 Arthur Golding, *Shakespeare's Ovid: Being Arthur Golding's Translation of the Metamorphoses*, ed. W.H.D. Rouse (Carbondale, IL: Southern Illinois University Press, 1961), Epistle 105–6. Subsequent references to Ovid will come from this edition, and will be cited by book and line numbers, parenthetically in the text.

6 Geoffrey Whitney, 'Amor Sui,' in *Whitney's 'Choice of Emblemes,'* ed. Henry Green (1586; repr. London, [n.p.] 1866), p. 149; Thomas Palmer, 'The force of selfe love,' in *The Emblems of Thomas Palmer: Two Hundred Poosees*, ed. John Manning (New York: AMS Press, 1988), pp. 18, 15–16. 'In their ruffe' signifies 'an exalted or elated state; elation, pride, vainglory' (*OED*, ruff sb. 6.2).

7 Ben Jonson, *Cynthia's Revels*, in *The Complete Plays of Ben Jonson*, ed. G.A. Wilkes, vol. 2 (Oxford: Clarendon Press, 1981), 1.1.100, 1.2.36–9. Subsequent references to the play will come from this edition and will be cited parenthetically in the text by act, scene, and line.

8 Jonathan Haynes, *The Social Relations of Jonson's Theater* (Cambridge: Cambridge University Press, 1992), pp. 51–68.

9 Robert Burton, *The Anatomy of Melancholy*, vol. 1, ed. Thomas C. Faulkner, Nicholas K. Kiessling, and Rhonda L. Blair, intro. J.B. Bamborough (Oxford: Clarendon Press, 1989), p. 294.

10 On the dramatic materialization of notorious figures see Linda Charnes, *Notorious Identity: Materializing the Subject in Shakespeare* (Cambridge: Harvard University Press, 1993), pp. 8–11.

11 David Kuchta, 'The Semiotics of Masculinity in Renaissance England,' in *Sexuality and Gender in Early Modern Europe: Institutions, Texts, Images*, ed. James Grantham Turner (Cambridge: Cambridge University Press, 1993), p. 241.

12 Kuchta, 'Semiotics of Masculinity,' pp. 244, 240, 238. Stephen Orgel, *Impersonations: The Performance of Gender in Shakespeare's England* (Cambridge: Cambridge University Press, 1996), defines 'effeminacy' (pp. 26–30) and discusses the difficulty of distinguishing 'masculine' from 'feminine' courtly attire (pp. 84–98).

13 See Jeffrey Masten, *Textual Intercourse: Collaboration, Authorship, and Sexualities in Renaissance Drama* (Cambridge: Cambridge University Press, 1997), pp. 28–37.

14 The word 'ravish' also contributes to the homoerotic sparring of the play's Induction, in which one of three boy players protests against being 'rape[d]' by the other two (ll.84, 88). See Kristen McDermott, '"He may be our father, perhaps": Paternity, Puppets, Boys, and *Bartholomew Fair*,' in *Critical Essays on Ben Jonson*, ed. Robert N. Watson (New York: G.K. Hall, 1997), pp. 60–81.

15 See Kuchta, 'Semiotics of Masculinity,' pp. 241–4.

16 Giovanni della Casa, *Galateo (1558)*, ed. Konrad Eisenbichler and Kenneth R. Bartlett (Toronto: University of Toronto Press, 1986), p. 54.

17 Kuchta, 'Semiotics of Masculinity,' p. 239. The inset citation comes from Robert Greene's 'A Quip for an Upstart Courtier.'

18 Masten, *Textual Intercourse*, pp. 28–37; and DiGangi, *Homoerotics*, pp. 134–41.

19 *The Maid's Metamorphosis*, ed. John S. Farmer, The Tudor Reprinted and Parallel Texts (1600; London: Hazell, Watson and Viney, 1908), sig. D2r.

20 Richard Brathwayte, *The Golden Fleece, Whereto Bee Annexed Two Elogies, Entitled Narcissus Change and Aesons Dotage* (London, 1611), sigs. D7v, D5v.

21 Thomas Edwards, *Cephalus and Procris. Narcissus*, ed. W.E. Buckley (London, 1882).

22 Jonathan Gil Harris, '"Narcissus in thy face": Roman Desire and the Difference it Fakes in *Antony and Cleopatra*,' *Shakespeare Quarterly* 45 (1994): 408–25, esp. 414.

23 *Narcissus: A Twelfe Night Merriment*, ed. Margaret L. Lee (London: David Nutt, n.d.) ll. 341–2. References are to line numbers.

24 Jonathan Sawday, *The Body Emblazoned: Dissection and the Human Body in Renaissance Culture* (New York: Routledge, 1995), p. 192.

25 For more on the history of manners in the early modern period, see Norbert Elias, *The Civilizing Process*, trans. Edmund Jephcott (Oxford: Blackwell, 1994); Anna Bryson, 'The Rhetoric of Status: Gesture, Demeanour and the Image of the Gentleman in Sixteenth- and Seventeenth-Century England,' in *Renaissance Bodies: The Human Figure in English Culture c. 1540–1660*, ed. Lucy Gent and Nigel Llewellyn (London: Reaktion Books, 1990), pp. 145–6; Haynes, *Social Relations*, pp. 46–7.

26 William Shakespeare, *The Tempest*, ed. Stephen Orgel (Oxford: Oxford University Press, 1987), 5.1.290–1.

27 Mark Breitenberg, *Anxious Masculinity in Early Modern England* (Cambridge: Cambridge University Press, 1992), pp. 38–9.

28 Bryson, 'The Rhetoric of Status,' p. 148.

29 Quoted in Breitenberg, *Anxious Masculinity*, p. 61.

Arms and the Women: The Ovidian Eroticism of Harington's Ariosto

IAN FREDERICK MOULTON

By any measure, Sir John Harington's Folio translation of Ariosto's *Orlando Furioso* is an impressive book. Ariosto's poem – the most popular European epic of the early sixteenth century – makes its first appearance 'in English Heroical Verse' in equally heroic format.[1] The length of the great poem, the breadth of the folio pages, the baroque splendour of the engraved illustrations all strongly assert the volume's cultural importance. Bound in calf and adorned with gold leaf (as is the copy currently in the Huntington Library),[2] the book itself becomes an epic object – weighty, elegant, substantial, robust. One might almost say virile, and indeed the 'masculine' authoritativeness of Harington's volume can be seen as an editorial response to the 'erring femininity' ascribed to many poetic texts in the rhetoric of the early modern period.[3]

Harington's editorial apparatus is as heroic as the text. Each canto of Ariosto's epic is preceded by a verse Argument and followed by a passage of commentary divided into four sections: Morall, Historie, Allegorie, and Allusion. As the mighty verse rolls onward, stanza by stanza, marginal glosses provide interpretive information and mark classical references. At the conclusion of the poem is 'A generall Allegorie of the whole,' followed by 'The life of Ariosto,' 'The Table of the booke,' a glossary of characters, and finally a list of the principal episodes in the poem.[4]

Given its authoritative weight, Harington's translation of the *Furioso* can tell us much about the cultural ambitions of epic poetry in late-sixteenth-century England – as a physical volume it is much more imposing than either the 1590 or the 1596 edition of Spenser's *Faerie Queene,* which are both quartos.[5] Scholars have long recognized the debt

Spenser owed to Ariosto in writing his epic; less well known is the relation of Ariosto to the most popular form of English narrative poetry in the early 1590s. Published in 1591 – one year after Spenser's first installment of *The Faerie Queene* – Harington's *Furioso* first circulated in the midst of the English vogue for brief Ovidian narrative poems, or epyllia. Popular Ovidian works such as Thomas Lodge's *Scylla's Metamorphosis* (1589), Shakespeare's *Venus and Adonis* (1593), and Marlowe's *Hero and Leander* (published 1598) are characterized by an ironic, playful approach to eroticism and gender identity which is not dissimilar from that of Ariosto's epic.[6] As we shall see, the Ovidian quality of Ariosto's eroticism is crucial to the history of the poem's reception in England. By placing Harington's translation of Ariosto in the context of English Ovidian erotic narrative, one becomes much more aware of the anxieties in late-sixteenth-century England surrounding erotic writing, especially debates over the place of eroticism in epic or heroic poetry.

At first glance, the works of Ovid may not seem the most obvious classical analogue to the *Furioso*. Ariosto's poem begins by suggesting its kinship to a quite different poetic model, announcing that (as Harington puts it), it will treat:

> Of Dames, of Knights, of armes, of loves delight,
> Of Curtesies, of high attempts ...[7]

It begins, that is, by radically rewriting that most famous of epic beginnings, Virgil's 'Arma virumque cano,' in which the writer of the *Aeneid* announces he will sing of 'Arms and the man.' While Ariosto too mentions arms and men in his first line, he begins not with 'Arma' but with 'Le donne,' not with weapons but with women. *Orlando Furioso* opens by stating that it will deal with both knights *and* ladies, both love and war – and thus, despite the poem's many allusions to the *Aeneid*, it takes a widely different view on the relationship of heroism and eroticism than that of the great Roman epic. Whereas the Virgilian epic hero must renounce effeminate love in order to devote himself to masculine conquest, Ariosto's heroes and heroines are both fighters and lovers.

In its approach to eroticism and in its conception of the relation between sexual activity and heroism, *Orlando Furioso* is analogous not to the *Aeneid*, but to the *Metamorphoses*.[8] It has always been recognized that Ariosto draws on the *Metamorphoses* for specific episodes (Ruggiero's rescue of Angelica in canto 10 is a reworking of the story of Perseus and Andromeda, for example).[9] But Ariosto's debt to Ovid is much more extensive. *Orlando Furioso* looks to Ovid for its narrative style which shifts unpredictably from story to story, for its multiplicity of plot and character, and for its philosophy of love and desire.[10]

In both the *Metamorphoses* and *Orlando Furioso* sexual passion is seen as chaotic and socially disruptive. Ovidian eroticism celebrates *raptus* – a violent and unpredictable encounter between human and divine which leads to unforeseen transformations. These transformations sometimes raise the human to the divine, but more often the change involves a descent in the Chain of Being – men and women become animals and plants and rocks. Io becomes a cow, Adonis a flower, Niobe a stone. Sexual desire often disrupts social order as well – sisters lust after brothers, patriarchs rape their wives' sisters, children betray their parents. Erotic conflict is crucial to this vision. Eroticism is not (as in neoplatonic theory) a manifestation of cosmic unifying forces; it is an eruption of chaos and madness. Significantly, in his description of the creation of the world in Book I of the *Metamorphoses,* Ovid declines to attribute the production of order out of chaos to cosmic love, as many neo-Platonists did. He pointedly leaves the identity of the divine organizing force unclear: 'quisquis fuit ille deorum' (1.32).

The Ovidian disruptiveness of *eros* in *Orlando Furioso* is so ubiquitous as to barely require demonstration – though one might begin with the title of the poem itself. Orlando's Fury is, of course, the madness of frustrated sexual passion. After pursuing the lovely Angelica from one side of the world to the other, in the central cantos of Ariosto's epic Orlando discovers that she loves another – she has, in fact run off with Medoro, a lowly soldier, never to return. As Harington's summary of the relevant canto puts it:

> Orlando falls starke mad, with sorrow taken,
> To heare his mistres hath him quite forsaken. (canto 23)

Striken with madness, Orlando runs amuck, robbing the Christian forces in the poem of their most powerful champion. The chaotic, disruptive nature of Orlando's passion is clear enough. But one should note that Angelica's own erotic desire for Medoro is also disruptive, not merely because it provokes Orlando's rage, but also because it cuts across lines of class and status – exotic Eastern princesses aren't supposed to run off and marry humble soldiers in shepherds' huts. Harington characterizes Angelica's affection for Medoro as 'folly and disorder' (canto 19. stanza 25), a moral judgment not found in the original text.

One of the ironies of Angelica's choice of Medoro is that she chooses at all, for in this epic of frustrated eros she is herself the ultimate *object* of desire. In the poem's opening canto, Angelica's headlong flight through the woods provides a resonant image of the work's central theme – that sexual desire is a mad, irrational pursuit. Even Harington, who finds little allegory in the first canto, concedes that here 'an allegorie may not unfitly be gathered ... [for] a strong horse, without rider or governour, is likened to the desire of man, that runnes furiously after Angelica, as if were after pleasure or honor, or whatsoever man doth most inordinately affect' (sig. A5r).

In Ariosto, such furious pursuits tend to be seen ironically, as comic but nonetheless fundamental features of foolish human existence. In late-sixteenth-century England, the view was not always so generous and Olympian. English moralists such as Stephen Gosson (*The Schole of Abuse*, 1579) had long attacked poetry as an effeminate pastime which would weaken English manhood, with dire consequences for English national defence. Gosson nostalgically imagines that while in 'auncient' days poetry used to strengthen patriarchal order by celebrating 'the notable exploytes of woorthy Captaines, the holesome councels of good fathers, and vertuous lives of predecessors' (sig. A7v), contemporary English poets are 'effeminate writers, unprofitable members, and utter enemies to virtue,' imbued with the Circean power to 'turne reasonable Creatures into brute Beasts' (sigs. A2v–A3). Sir Philip Sidney's *Apologie of Poetry* expends a good deal of energy to refute Gosson's view that poetry and martial heroism are fundamentally opposed.[11]

In the final decades of the sixteenth century, as England drifted into war with Spain, anxieties about the adequacy of national defence took on an urgency they had previously lacked. If English manhood was corrupted by effeminate toys, how could the nation prevail in its unequal struggle with Catholic Europe? In this context it is not surprising that foreign poetry seemed to pose a particular threat to national virtue. Though the pressing military threat came from Spain, anxieties about foreignness and foreign corruption in late-sixteenth-century England tended to focus on Italy, (as they would on France in later periods). Roger Ascham's thundering diatribe against 'Italianate Englishmen' in *The Scholemaster* (published 1570) was just the first and most famous of the many denunciations of Italian erotic and moral corruption in the period.[12] As the century drew to a close, notorious Italian writers such as Machiavelli and Aretino became bywords for disorder and amorality in England. Anti-Italian feeling often led to a reevaluation of classical

Rome: while Virgilian piety and stoicism were admired, Ovidian lasciviousness was at times harshly criticized.

And what of Ariosto? Is the *Furioso* a manly epic on the Roman model or an effeminate Italian romance? Is it decorously Virgilian or scandalously Ovidian? Despite the volume's authoritative weight, Harington himself is clearly concerned to defend his translation from charges of immorality. He prefaces his text with a thirteen-page 'Apologie of Poetrie,' which draws strongly on Sidney's more famous tract of the same name, a text Harington certainly knew in manuscript.[13] Like Sidney, Harington sees 'lightnes & wantoness' as one of the chief reproaches levelled against poetry. But while Sidney argued that 'Orlando Furioso, or honest King Arthur, will never displease a soldier,'[14] Harington admits that '*Cupido* is crept even into the Heroicall Poemes,' and concedes that if anything may 'truely be objected against [poetry] ... sure it is this lasciviousnesse' (sig. ¶5v). An attempt to prove Ariosto's virtue by invoking Virgilian precedent is similarly ambivalent. Harington begins by comparing the opening lines of the *Furioso* and the *Aeneid* (sig. ¶6r) – an exercise that, as we have seen, reveals as many differences as similarities. Then he ruins the point of his comparison by admitting that Virgil himself was a lascivious writer, citing the passage from the *Aeneid* on the love of Vulcan and Venus which so intrigued Montaigne (sig. ¶7r).[15]

Although Harington argues that the conversion to Christianity of the Saracen knight Ruggiero is ample proof of Ariosto's commitment to 'Christian exhortation, doctrine, & example,' he ultimately concedes that many have found *Orlando Furioso* 'too lascivious' (sig. ¶7r). Indeed he gives a list of the passages commentators have objected to:

> as in that of the baudy Frier, in *Alcina* and *Rogeros* copulation, in *Anselmus* his *Giptian*, in *Richiardetto* his metamorphosis, in mine hosts tale of *Astolfo* & some few places besides (sig. ¶7r)

and begs 'alas, if this be a fault, pardon him this one fault.'

Unable to provide a convincing and effective rebuttal to the charge of Ariosto's lasciviousness, Harington is reduced to accusing his critics of hypocrisy: 'Me thinks,' he writes,

> I see some of you searching already for these places in the booke, and you are halfe offended that I have not made some directions that you might finde out and read them immediatly. (sig. ¶7r)

But prurient readers need not blame Harington on this account. Besides his having drawn attention to the poem's lascivious passages in the list just quoted, directions to many of these episodes can indeed be found by consulting a table of 'The Principal Tales in *Orlando Furioso* that may be read by themselves,' located on the closing pages of the volume (sig. Oo3v). Indeed, if Harington himself had found these passages offensive, he could simply have omitted them from his text. His translation is somewhat abridged in any case, and he cheerfully defends his excision or abbreviation of Ariosto's praise of his Italian patrons – passages he characterizes with some justice as 'tediouse flatteries of persons that we never heard of' (sig.¶8r).[16]

As his befuddled 'Apologie' suggests, Harington can be a charmingly awkward rhetorician. But the confusions of the 'Apologie' should not simply be ascribed to Harington's eccentricities as an apologist. They also reflect larger cultural conflicts, conflicts revealed clearly when Harington imagines that his old Tutor,

> a grave and learned man, and one of a verie austere life, might say to me in like sort, was it for this that I read *Aristotle* and *Plato* to you, and instructed you so carefully both in Greek & Latin? to have you now become a translator of Italian toyes? (sig. ¶8v)

Harington's Ariosto thus finds itself situated on several fault-lines in early modern English culture – it is both Virgilian and Ovidian, both epic and romance, both a serious poem and an 'Italian toy.' Heroic poetry ought to uphold manly virtue; *Orlando Furioso* is full of Ovidian eroticism. Epic ought to recall the glories of classical Greece and Rome, not the supposed wantonness of contemporary Italy.

While there was great critical debate in late-sixteenth-century Italy over whether or not *Orlando Furioso* might properly be called an epic[17] (a debate whose greatest monument is Tasso's *Jerusalem Delivered*), in Italy Ariosto's great poem was seen almost from its first appearance as a classic of the language, worthy of exegesis in the same manner as classical epics. Thus, to a certain extent, the elaborate editorial apparatus of Harington's volume can be seen as emulating Continental practices. For purposes of comparison, one might consider a 1558 Venetian quarto edition of *Orlando Furioso* published by Vincenzio Velgrisio.[18] This volume includes not only the text of the poem, but also an essay on Ariosto's language , a glossary of difficult words (sigs. 2m4v–p3v), an index of characters (sigs. ***3–***4), a life of Ariosto (sigs. **1–**4v), two essays summarizing the changes made to the text by Ariosto since its first publication (sigs. l4–n4v; 2b5–c1v), an outline summary of the plot (sigs. 2d1–l4), and much else besides. Each canto is preceded by an 'argomento' in verse and in prose, and is followed by 'annotations' detailing both the moral significance and the classical sources of Ariosto's tales. Four different editors are named: Girolamo Ruscelli is credited with the annotations; Giovan Battista Pigna wrote the life of Ariosto; Nicolò Eugenico supplied the plot summary; and Simon Fornari added an essay entitled 'A Few Other Things to be Aware of in *Orlando Furioso*' (Alcune altre cose da avvertirsi nel Furioso) (sigs. 2m1v–m4). A Venetian octavo from 1597, also in the Huntington (shelfmark 388061), is similarly packed with interpretive material. A 'Life of Ariosto' reappears (sigs. a3–a5v) – this time by Simon Fornari – as well as 'New Allegories and Annotations' by Tomaso Porcacchi, and an essay on allusions to other authors by Lodovico Dolce (sigs. Ss6–end). Each canto is preceded by an 'argomento' in verse (different from those in the earlier volume) and followed, once again, by annotations.

Clearly the *Furioso* is a work which demands a certain amount of editorial apparatus. But in Italy it does not require an 'Apologie of Poetrie.'[19] Although the apparatus surrounding Harington's translation seems analogous to that of contemporary Italian editions, Ariosto's poem is presented to its English readers in the context of specifically English debates. While in Italy *Orlando Furioso* was seen as a classic to be elucidated, in England Ariosto's poem is perceived as troublingly foreign and its moral and cultural value is uncertain.

Such was not necessarily the case in other European countries. A Dutch translation of the *Furioso* published by D. Mertens in 1615 limits its editorial apparatus to brief epistles at the front and an index at the back of the volume. At no point does the volume warn the reader of any potential threat or respond to any perceived criticism.[20] A French prose translation by Gabriel Chappuys, published by P. Rigaud in Lyon in 1616 has nothing but praise for the poem and the author.[21] The epistle to the reader (sigs. *2r–*3r) is a conventional praise of the work, pointing out its inspiration in the works of both Ovid and Virgil, and noting some basic allegorical meanings. There is some concern that the poem may be considered trivial, but no concern about erotic corruption:

> I have here only to recommend this work to you, seeing that it is, in itself, more than commendable, for the authority and knowledge ['scavoir'] of its author, Lodovico Ariosto, a poet, as everyone knows, among the finest and

> most excellent that Italy has produced. As for his inventiveness, it is such that everyone finds it admirable; his style is so pleasant, his verse so flowing, that it is a great pleasure for those who understand Italian. But all this is little in comparison to the meaning which is contained in his poem, which on the face of it seems vulgar and fantastic ('vile & fabuleuse') despite its infinity of beautiful phrases, which are like carnations and gorgeous flowers beautifying a bed or parterre in a garden.
>
> (sig. *2r – my translation)

Two editions of the sixteenth-century Spanish translation of the poem by Don Hieronimo de Urrea are similarly devoid of any sense that Ariosto's lewdness constitutes some sort of social threat, though they do delete three stanzas from the canto 34 because they deal lightly with theological matters and 'although they are ingenious, they might not be accepted in Spain' (sig. A4r – my translation).[22]

As these examples suggest, European editions of the *Furioso* do not reflect concerns about the moral status of poetry in the way that Harington's edition does. Anxiety about the morality of poetry abounds, however, in English translations of Ovid's *Metamorphoses.* While Ovid's authority was taken for granted by Latin readers, Ovid in English was a different matter. Just as the editorial apparatus of Harington's *Orlando* reveals a concern about the morality of Italian toys, so too the English translations of the *Metamorphoses* by Golding (1567)[23] and Sandys (1626)[24] demonstrate a concern about how Ovid will be read by vernacular readers. Like Harington's Ariosto, both Golding and Sandys give their English readers instructions on how to interpret the eroticism and lasciviousness of the foreign texts they present to native readers.

Golding's 1567 *Metamorphoses,* the first published English translation, showcases its ambivalence on its title page, announcing that the poem is 'A worke very pleasaunt and delectable,' but cautioning the reader that

> With skill, heede, and judgement, this worke must be read,
> For else to the Reader it standes in small stead.[25]

Golding's concern that the native English reader not misconstrue the meaning of the volume is also apparent in the verse epistle 'To the Reader' which precedes the poem (sigs. A1r–A4r). He proclaims the immorality of the tales he has translated, warning that 'all theyr Goddes with whoordome, theft, or murder blotted bee' (sig. A1r). He insists that these immoral pagan deities must be read as allegories – an approach to reading Ovid with a distinguished history in Christian Europe – though Golding's suggestions for likely allegorical readings once again point to his concerns about moral corruption and social disorder: Apollo represents 'young and lusty brutes,' Venus denotes 'such as of the fleshe too filthie lust are bent' and 'By Bacchus all the meaner trades and handycraftes are ment' (sig. A1v). Golding demands a comprehensive reading strategy which will ensure that Ovid's lascivious tales will prove morally beneficial:

> But if we suffer fleshly lustes as lawlesse Lordes too reigne,
> Than are we beastes, wee are no men, wee have our name in vaine.
> ...
> This surely did the Poets meene when in such sundry wyse
> The pleasant tales of turned shapes they studyed too devyse. (sig. A2r)

Golding criticizes both 'naughtie' readers who, reading tales of vice, 'dooth take occasion ... like vices to ensew' and censorious readers who, 'more severe than wisdome doth requyre,' will respond to the volume's seeming exaltation of vice by condemning and burning the book (sig. A3). For Golding, both of these extreme reactions to the text result from superficial readings which do not touch the deeper truths revealed by Ovid.

Such shallow and intemperate readers are implicitly contrasted to Robert, Earl of Leicester, the volume's dedicatee, to whom Golding addresses a second verse epistle.[26] The epistle to Leicester is more sophisticated than that to the Reader and deals with philosophical issues such as reincarnation and the relation of form to matter. The tone here is less anxious than in the address to the general reader; presumably one ought to have full confidence in Leicester's ability to read wisely. And yet, here too, Golding frets that Ovid's eroticism will be misunderstood. He provides a long list of simple allegorical interpretations for all the poem's major episodes and he stresses their value as cautionary tales:

> The piteous tale of Pyramus and Thisbee doth conteine
> The headie force of frentick love whose end is wo and payne.
> The snares of Mars and Venus shew that tyme will bring to lyght
> The secret sinnes that folk commit in corners or by nyght.
> Hermaphrodite and Salmacis declare that idlenesse
> Is cheefest nurce and cherisher of all volupteousnesse

And that voluptuous lyfe breedes sin: which linking all toogither
Make men to be effeminate, unweeldy, weake, and lither. (sig. a3r)

As if it were not enough that Ovid provides a useful warning against effeminate lust, Golding also explains to Leicester in some detail that the *Metamorphoses* was inspired by the five books of Moses and that Ovid's descriptions of the creation and Deucalion's flood are in substantial agreement with Genesis (sigs. b1v–b3r). Of course, someone as learned as the Earl ought to be clever enough to see all this for himself, and Golding begins to sense the awkwardness of his defence of the poem's virtue: 'But why seeme I theis doubts to cast ... / ... as if that they / who doo excell in wisdome and in lerning, would not wey / a wyse and lerned woorke aryght?' (sig. b4r). Why indeed? Perhaps the answer lies in the fact that Golding is well aware that, once printed, his epistle to Leicester will be read not only by the Earl, but by a broad audience many of whom are likely to lack Leicester's classical education, aristocratic breeding, and reputed sagacity. Like Harington's Ariosto, Golding's Ovid reveals deep ambivalence about bringing erotic foreign poetry to a native and unlearned book-buying public.

Published fifty years after Golding, and thirty-five years after Harington's Ariosto, Sandys's 1626 translation of the *Metamorphoses* is even more elaborate in its concern that vernacular readers not be corrupted by this potentially immoral text. Sandys's volume opens with a brief poem explicating the 'Argument of this Worke' which portrays *eros* as a cosmically unifying force in neoplatonic terms conspicuously absent from the *Metamorphoses* itself:

FIRE, AIRE, EARTH, WATER, all the Opposites
That strove in *Chaos*, powrefull LOVE unites; (sig. a1v)

This is followed by another, shorter poem which asserts that Ovid's tales of passion should be read as cautionary tales, and concludes that the work as a whole 'fitly mingl[es] Profit with Delight.' Not only does Sandys insist on the allegorical and moral import of the *Metamorphoses*, he also includes a prefatory prose essay entitled 'Ovid Defended.'[27] In this tract Sandys enlists a wide array of classical and Christian authorities, including – among others – Seneca, Quintillian, Tacitus, Martial, St Jerome, St Augustine, Erasmus, and Julius Caesar Scaliger, to argue that Ovid is a moralist, not a wanton frivolous writer of lascivious tales. Such a defence is necessary, Sandys claims,

> Since divers, onely wittie in reproving, have profaned our Poet with their fastidious censures: we, to vindicate his worth from detraction, and prevent prejudicacie, have here revived a few of those infinite testimonies, which the cleerest judgements of all Ages have given him.

One would think such a torrent of testimony would be enough to quell all debate, but the 'Life of Ovid' (sigs. a4–b3r) which precedes the Defence demonstrates once again the ambivalence surrounding Ovid and Ovidian eroticism in early modern England. Here Sandys attests to the upstanding nature of Ovid's life and character:

> He was of a meane stature, slender of body, spare of diet; and, if not too amorous, every way temperate. He drunk no wine but what was much alayed with water: An Abhorrer of unnatural Lusts, from which it should seem that age was not innocent: neat in apparell; of a free, affable, and courtly behaviour; whereby hee acquired the friendship of many, such as were great in learning and nobilitie ... and so honoured by divers, that they wore his picture in rings cut in precious stones. A great Admirer, & as much admired, of the excellent Poets of those times, with whom he was most familiar and intimate.' (sig. a4v)

In other words, despite his many male friends and intimacy with poets, Ovid was no sodomite. Unfortunately the known facts of Ovid's life do not entirely support this portrait of abstemious chastity. As Sandys admits, he was married three times and divorced at least once. More seriously, of course, Ovid was banished by Augustus, either for his lascivious poetry or, as Sandys puts it, 'for his too much familiaritie with Julia the daughter of Augustus.' Sandys even suggests that Ovid might have 'seene the incest of Caesar,' preferring this implication of actual involvement in illicit sexuality to the imputation that Ovid was punished for the immorality of his writings.

That concern over the corrupting lasciviousness of Ovid's poetry was directed primarily at the spread of printed texts *in English* is clearly revealed by a comparison of Golding's and Sandys's English translations with Latin editions of the *Metamorphoses* printed in England in the same period. Latin texts, while equipped with a modest amount of editorial apparatus, do not tend to feature 'Defences of Ovid' and are less concerned to direct the reader to specific allegorical readings.[28] An English prose translation of Book I of the *Metamorphoses* published in 1618 for use in schools (British Library C. 57.c. 43) is similarly devoid of moralistic front matter, though it is clearly indicated that the text is to be used under the supervision of a schoolmaster, and refers teachers to educational handbooks which will explicate its proper use. Ovidian eroticism becomes dangerous when it circulates in the book market, not in school, and in English, not in Latin.

In contrast to this English anxiety about Ovid, sixteenth-century Italian translations of the *Metamorphoses* show little concern about defending the morality of the text or of the author. For example, while both the Italian translation of the *Metamorphoses* published in Venice in 1522 by Nicolo Zoppino[29] and a Venetian octavo edition of 1547[30] are filled with editorial comment explicating the poem's allegorical significance, neither contains any defence of the poet or sense that his work might be morally suspect. A 1578 edition of a translation by Giovanni Andrea dell'Anguillara published in Venice by C. Franceschini contains hardly any editorial apparatus at all.[31] The notion that Ovid's poem might constitute a threat to unsophisticated readers is similarly absent from editions of Lodovico Dolce's popular reworking of the *Metamorphoses*, entitled *Le transformationi*.[32] The short 'Life of Ovid' which appears in a 1568 edition of Dolce's work[33] is remarkably deadpan, especially in contrast to the earnest defence of the poet's virtue in Sandys's translation: 'He wrote three books on his love affairs ... in which he greatly demonstrated the sharpness of his wit ... In his elegies he was held to be somewhat lascivious ... Similarly, he wrote on the art of love and on its remedy, and also many other poems, among which they say was one on fishing' (sig. †3v – my translation).

Although anxiety about vernacular circulation of morally challenging foreign works of literature was common throughout Europe in the early modern period, the matter-of-fact tone characteristic of these Italian translations suggests that concern about the corrupting effects of Ovidian eroticism is a particularly English phenomenon. More work would be necessary to corroborate this observation in detail, but this brief comparison of the way erotic narrative poetry was presented to its sixteenth-century vernacular readers may serve to indicate the complexities of the issues involved and the necessity of paying attention to the material detail of books as well as the 'content' of texts. Clearly, reception history of texts must take into account generic considerations which go beyond specific authorship. To understand how Ovid was read one must also examine how Ariosto was read, for despite their many differences, the eroticism of their texts seems, in England, to have raised the same social concerns.

NOTES

1 The work's full title is *Orlando Furioso in English Heroical Verse,* by John Harington (London, 1591; *STC* 746). Subsequent references to this text are to signature numbers for editorial material, canto and stanza numbers for the text of the poem.
2 Huntington Library shelfmark 62722.
3 On the gendering of texts and authorship in Renaissance England see Wendy Wall, *The Imprint of Gender: Authorship and Publication in the English Renaissance* (Ithaca: Cornell University Press, 1993), esp. 173–88.
4 The editorial apparatus of Harington's translation remains the same in the 1607 and 1634 editions of the text; the 1634 edition adds ninety-one of Harington's epigrams at the end of the volume.
5 *STC* 23080–23082.
6 On erotic Ovidian narrative poems, see Jonathan Bate, *Shakespeare and Ovid* (Oxford: Clarendon Press, 1993); Clark Hulse, *Metamorphic Verse: The Elizabethan Minor Epic* (Princeton, NJ: Princeton University Press, 1981); and William Keach, *Elizabethan Erotic Narratives: Irony and Pathos in the Ovidian Poetry of Shakespeare, Marlowe, and Their Contemporaries* (New Brunswick, NJ: Rutgers University Press, 1977).
7 Le donne, i cavallier, l'arme, gli amori, le cortesie, l'audaci imprese ... (Canto 1. Stanza 1)
8 Patricia Parker, *Inescapable Romance: Studies in the Poetics of a Mode* (Princeton, NJ: Princeton University Press, 1979), pp. 41–3, provides an excellent discussion of Ariosto's 'erring' from his Virgilian model, and argues that Ovid, specifically in his treatment of Virgilian material in the *Metamorphoses,* provides Ariosto with a model for his relation to Virgil.
9 Cesare Segre, 'Un Repertorio linguistico e stilistico dell'Ariosto: la Commedia,' in his book, *Esperienze ariostesche* (Pisa: Nistri-Lischi, 1966), pp. 51–83, claims that Ariosto bases passages or episodes in *Orlando Furioso* on Ovid twenty-nine times, in comparison to six from Dante, for example. C.P. Brand, 'Ariosto's Ricciardetto and Fiordispina,' *Stimmen der Romania,* ed. Gerhard Schmidt and Manfred Tietz (Wiesbaden: B. Heyman Verlag, 1980), pp. 121–33, argues that the *Metamorphoses* offers a source for the motif of sexual transformation in Ariosto.
10 See Daniel Javitch, 'Rescuing Ovid from the Allegorizers,' *Comparative Literature* 30.2 (1978): 97–107; this article also appears in *Ariosto in America 1974,* ed. Aldo Scaglione (Ravenna: Longo Editore, 1974), pp. 85–98. See also Mary Kay Gamel Orlandi, 'Ovid True and False in Renaissance Poetry,' *Pacific Coast Philology* 13 (1978): 60–70; and Marianne Shapiro,

The Poetics of Ariosto (Detroit: Wayne State University Press, 1988), esp. p. 95.

11 Philip Sidney, *A Defence of Poetry*, ed. J.A. Van Dorsten (New York: Oxford University Press, 1966), esp. pp. 54–7.

12 Roger Ascham, *The Scholemaster* (1570), ed. Edward Arber (London: Constable and Co, 1870), pp. 71–86. For the development of Ascham's anti-Italian views in the various revisions of his text, see George B. Parks, 'The First Italianate Englishmen,' *Studies in the Renaissance* 8 (1961): 197–216, esp. 200–5. Other representative examples of anti-Italian rhetoric may be found in Thomas Nashe's *Pierce Penniless* (vol. 1, p. 186) and *The Unfortunate Traveller* (vol. 2, p. 301), in *The Works of Thomas Nashe*, 5 vols., ed. Ronald B. McKerrow, (1904–1910), rev. ed. (Oxford: Basil Blackwell, 1958). On the ambivalent role of Italy and Italian characters on the English Renaissance stage, see the essays collected in Michele Marrapodi et al., eds., *Shakespeare's Italy: Functions of Italian Locations in Renaissance Drama* (Manchester: Manchester University Press, 1997), especially Andreas Mahler, 'Italian Vices: Cross-cultural Constructions of Temptation and Desire in English Renaissance Drama,' pp. 49–68.

13 Harington refers his reader to Sidney's 'Apologie' (sig. ¶3r) although it was not printed until 1595, four years after Harington's own text.

14 Sidney, p. 56.

15 Montaigne's 'Essay on Some Verses of Virgil' is a *locus classicus* for early modern discussions of sexuality and gender. Michel de Montaigne, *The Complete Works of Montaigne: Essays, Travel, Journal, Letters*, ed. Donald M. Frame (Stanford: Stanford University Press, 1948), Book 3, Essay 5, 'Sur des vers de Virgile.' The passage in question is *Aeneid* Book 8, lines 387–404.

16 Such excisions arguably make the work more English by downplaying explicit praise of foreign rulers. Sixteenth-century Spanish translations of the *Furioso* make similar cuts (see note 22, below).

17 For a brief outline of this debate and the issues involved, see A. Bartlett Giamatti, *The Earthly Paradise and the Renaissance Epic* (New York: Norton, 1966), pp. 170–210.

18 A copy is in the Huntington Library, shelfmark 111054.

19 The amount of editorial apparatus in sixteenth-century Italian editions varies, though editions from later in the century generally have more material than earlier editions. None of the Italian texts I have examined, from tiny duodecimos to large folios, contains any defence of poetry, or warnings to the reader about the immorality of the text. Additional examples – all held in the collections of the Newberry Library – include the Giolito editions of 1544 and 1554 (Case Y712 .A 7054; Case Y712 .A 7055); the Figliuoli di Aldo

edition of 1545 (Wing ZP 535 .A 3627); the 1561 edition published by G. Rouillio (Case Y 712 .A 7056); the Vincenzo Valgrisi editions of 1565 and 1572 (Case Y 712 .A 70565; Case Y 712 .A 7057); the 1574 edition of D. & G.B. Guerra (Case Y 712 .A 70574); Camillo Franceschini's edition of 1577 (Case Y 712 .A 70577); and the Francesco di Franceschi edition of 1584, the source for the lavish engravings in Harington's translation (Wing ZP 535 .F 845).

20 A copy is in the Newberry Library, shelfmark Case Y 712 .A 7162.

21 A copy is in the Newberry Library, shelfmark Case Y 712 .A 7196.

22 The first was published by G. Roville of Lyon in 1556, the second in Venice, 'A la enseña dela salamandra,' in 1575. Copies of both are in the Newberry Library (shelfmarks Case Y 712 .A 7193 and Case Y 712 .A 7195). Stanzas 58, 59, and 80 are cut from canto 34 (here numbered 33; cantos 2 and 3 are conflated to remove excessive and confusing praise of the D'Este family). These excisions are announced in the epistle to the reader included in both editions.

23 *STC* 18956, a quarto in eights. Citations are from this edition. Golding's translation, *The xv. Bookes of P. Ouidius Naso, entytuled Metamorphosis* (London, 1567), was reprinted in 1575, 1584, 1587, 1593, 1603, and 1612 (*STC* 18957–62), after which it was superseded by Sandys's 1626 version.

24 Sandys's translation, *Ovid's Metamorphosis Englished, Mythologized, and Represented in Figures*, was originally published as a folio (*STC* 18964.) Citations are from this edition. Like Golding's earlier version, it was frequently reprinted: 1628, 1632 (with extensive apparatus added), 1638, 1640, etc.

25 This motto appears on the title page of all the early editions of Golding, including his 1565 translation of the first four books of the *Metamorphoses* (London, 1565; *STC* 18955) which preceded the translation of the full text.

26 In the 1567 and later editions the verse epistle to Leicester precedes that to the reader, but it was written later. Golding's 1565 translation of the first four books of the poem includes the epistle to the reader (sigs. *2r–*4v), but there is only a brief prose dedication to Leicester (sig. *1v).

27 This essay begins sig. b3v and runs for six unmarked pages (before sig. A at beginning of text).

28 See for example an octavo Latin edition of the *Metamorphoses*, published in Cambridge in 1584 (Huntington Library shelfmark 30747). Commentary follows each episode in the poem, and the volume opens with a dedicatory epistle, and concludes with an Index. There are some printed marginal notes. There is, however, no vita or apologia, though the volume does include Sabino's explanation of the utility, argument, and title of the work, as well as an essay from Natalis Comes on Fables. This volume is not dissimi-

lar to Continental Latin editions: Latin editions of the *Amores* published in Venice in 1518 (Huntington Library shelfmark 137908) and of the *Metamorphoses* published in Paris in 1529 (Huntington Library shelfmark 420583) are similarly without moralizing commentary, though both are well provided with editorial annotation.

29 A copy is in the Newberry Library, shelfmark Case Y 672 .O 9647.

30 A copy is in the Huntington Library, shelfmark 355652

31 A copy is in the Newberry Library, shelfmark Case Y 672 .O 9656.

32 Venice, Gabriel Giolito, 1555. A copy is in the Newberry Library, Case Y 672 .O 965.

33 Newberry Library Case Y 672 .O 9653, sigs. †3r–†4r.

PART II

Speech, Voice, and Embodiment

Localizing Disembodied Voice in Sandys's Englished 'Narcissus and Echo'

GINA BLOOM

In the preface to his 1632 translation of Ovid's *Metamorphoses*, George Sandys professes to be well aware of the ethical sensibility of his seventeenth-century readers. Dealing seriously with Ovid's mythography at a time when Ovid's popularity was waning or controversial amongst devout Christians,[1] Sandys carefully argues his case for the applicability of Ovid's stories to early modern mores, claiming that the stories give access to philosophical and moral truths despite having been narrated by a pagan writer. Participating in a long tradition of *Ovide moralisé*, Sandys foregrounds the instructional objective of his translation: 'For the Poet not onely renders things as they are; but what are not, as if they were, or rather as they should bee.'[2] This justification of 'the Poet['s]' artistic license seems directed towards the poetic practices of both Ovid and Sandys. Just as Ovid's poetry can bend the truth of 'things' in order to represent them 'as they are,' so Sandys's text is authorized to 'render ... things' as he, the poet, sees fit. Armed with the argument that poetry is always on some level a craft of translation, of re-presenting reality, Sandys defends his manipulation of Ovid's original: he explains that he has made Ovid's stories fitting and useful for seventeenth-century readers 'by polishing, altering, or restoring, the harsh, improper, or mistaken' (p. 9).

As Sandys constructs a space for editorial freedom in his translation and, as my essay will demonstrate, exercises that freedom liberally, his translation of Ovid's *Metamorphoses* offers scholars insight into (how Sandys construed) the moral fiber of early modern English society *vis à vis* Ovid. Which elements of Ovid's tales needed alteration in order to confer Sandys's 'vital moral message' to English readers? So that I may explore the strategies by which Sandys grapples with what would have been considered 'harsh, improper, or mistaken' in his sociohistorical context, I examine closely one of the Ovidian tales, 'Narcissus and Echo,' that Sandys 'polish[es], alter[s], and restore[s].' The 1632 edition of Sandys's *Metamorphoses* is a particularly useful text in which to examine these strategies at work, for Sandys appends to his translation of each of Ovid's books an extensive commentary section. My essay explores how Sandys's translation and commentary work in collaboration to 'English' Ovid's depiction of Echo – a figure who, with her powerful disembodied speech, challenges popular early modern views about human vocal communication and the agency of the voice.

As her name indicates, Echo's only mode of 'speech' is the repetition of the sounds of others; a reverberation by definition, her vocal sound is produced seemingly without her volition and irrespective of her body (as becomes evident when her body disintegrates later in the myth, leaving behind her echoic voice). Though disembodied and disconnected from her person, Echo's voice is rendered as able to express the nymph's desires. When Echo repeats the ends of Narcissus's words, her resonating language implies meanings alternative to the ones intended by Narcissus; despite her supposed inability to speak on her own accord, she articulates an erotic interest in the youth. Ovid's wittiest use of this echoic trope occurs when the lost Narcissus mistakes Echo's sounds for the voices of the friends he has been trying to locate:

> perstat et alternae deceptus imagine vocis
> 'huc coeamus' ait, nullique libentius umquam
> reponsura sono 'coeamus' rettulit Echo (III. 385–7)

> [He stands still, deceived by the answering voice, and 'Let us come together here,' he cries. Echo, never to answer other sound more gladly, cries, 'Let us come together.'][3]

For Echo's resounding response, 'coeamus,' to Narcissus's call 'huc coeamus,' Ovid plays with the Latin double meaning of *coetus* – 'to meet' and 'to have sexual intercourse.' From the perspective of the reader, the lost Narcissus requests a meeting, and the smitten Echo agrees to a copulation. When Ovid has Echo repeat back 'coeamus,' capitalizing on its sexual connotations, he not only enables her to express interest in erotic conversation with Narcissus but also suggests that this meaning was embedded in Narcissus's call. Echo, the poem goes on to show, believes that Narcissus reciprocates her affections: she is so convinced that Narcissus intended the sexual undertones of the word 'coeamus' that she rushes out of the forest and embraces him. Intention, Ovid's poem submits, matters little once language leaves the speaker's body and enters a communal realm where it is subject to reinterpretation. Echo's words are not mere reflections of Narcissus's speech; they are copies that alter the stability of the 'original' they supposedly mimic. In uncoupling meaning and intention, Ovid's poem offers the eerie possibility that echoic sound may be read as the nymph Echo's volitional speech.

Whereas Ovid's Latin poem merely *suggests* that echoic sound may be volitional speech, Sandys's translation is particularly invested in representing aural reverberations as Echo's self-expression. Perhaps most tellingly, Echo's first word in Sandys's translation is the pronoun 'I.' Ovid's Narcissus asks 'ecquis adest?' ('is anyone here?' [III. 380]) and Echo answers, 'adest' ('here'), but Sandys translates the lines as follows: 'The Boy, from his companions parted, said; / Is any nigh? I, *Eccho* answere made' (p. 137). By translating the Latin *adest* as 'nigh,' Sandys sets himself up for an echoic pun (aye/I) that personalizes Echo's response. Through her articulation of 'I,' Echo declares her personhood using the grammatical signifier of subjectivity. Sandys's choice of this particular translation is not a result of his formal constraints of rhymed couplets, as the 'nigh? I' appears in the middle of the line and has the same rhythmic effect as 'here, here' would have. Sandys, in other words, could have translated this exchange as 'here, here,' a direct translation which foregrounds the physical location of the subject.[4] Instead, he plays with the possibilities offered by the English language in much the same way as Ovid plays with the possibilities of Latin. Sandys could also have had Echo resound 'nigh,' Narcissus's exact word, and achieved the effect of Ovid's text; the word 'nigh' would still have given Echo a mysterious aural presence. But Echo's first word, though it sounds much like 'nigh,' is different both in textual appearance *and* in meaning. The effect of changing the word in appearance amplifies Echo's vocal independence, and the choice of 'I' as her first word emphasizes her status as a subject who, though unable to choose her words, constitutes her personhood through the words which are available to her. In Sandys's translation, Echo emerges as a locatable 'I' by using the very voice she has been denied.

The provocative pun is only one among a number of Sandys's enhancements to Ovid's original poem. Indeed, the format of the 1632 edition, with translation interspersed by commentary, provides its author with two spaces in which to pursue his revision of Ovid. The translation grants Echo grammatical and linguistic 'ownership' of the voice she produces, lending her a greater aura of personal expression and of intentional articulation than is posited in Ovid's original. However, as I will explore later in the essay, the commentary on this translation revokes the potentially human origins of echoic sound, defining echoes as mere aural curiosity.[5] The two strategies might at first glance seem incomprehensibly counterposed: where the translation goes to great lengths to personify echoic sound, contemporizing it with the speaking subject Echo, the commentary goes to equal lengths to disqualify echoic sound from categories of voice and speech. The first of these strategies, linking Echo's voice to her body, might lead us to contrast the dehumanizing, scientific commentary with a translation that seems proleptically 'feminist.' Judith de Luce's work on the silenced women of Ovid's *Metamorphoses* considers Echo a pathetic figure whose loss of speech signals her degradation into beastliness;[6] if we follow de Luce's argument, we may be tempted to applaud Sandys's translation for restoring 'human' identity to Ovid's vocally disabled nymph. But is an embodied, 'human' voice necessarily more potent and more effective than a disembodied one?

Kaja Silverman's work on embodiment and the voice leaves room for suspicion. In her account of the ideological and psychic forces that shape the representation of female voices in mainstream cinema, Silverman argues that the obsessive attempts on the part of Hollywood's male directors to 'synchronize' women's voices with their visual images reflects male anxieties about the impotence of filmic representation.[7] Silverman contends, moreover, that although the practice of 'marrying' sound and image grants interiority to female characters – bolstering their authenticity of character by naturalizing their capacity for speech – such interiority is far from liberating where female subjectivity is concerned. As the disembodied voice is given a 'definitive localization,' it 'loses power and authority.' A far more potent female voice, according to Silverman, is the one presented by feminist filmmakers, who blur or eliminate a 'corporeal assignation' for the cinematic female voice.[8]

Silverman's argument suggests, then, that there is much at stake in terms of the construction of female subjectivity and its relation to the female body in Sandys's localization of the disembodied voice, in his personification and humanization of echoic sound. With the capacity (intentional or not) to manipulate the disembodied voice, Ovid's Echo is able to inhabit what Silverman calls a space of 'enunciative authority' in the story. Like the male voice-offs (voices sounding from off-screen) of classical Hollywood films, the echoic, disembodied voice allows Ovid's Echo the 'invisibility, omniscience, and discursive power' that, according to Silverman, is never available to the female characters in classical films.[9] But like the Hollywood films that Silverman discusses, Sandys's poem evinces concern about the potential powers of this disembodied female voice. In fact, I would argue that when Sandys turns Echo's reverberating, disembodied sound into self-expression, he practises his own form of *synchronization*: in contrast to Ovid's original Latin poem, Sandys's Englished translation strives to set up a 'definitive localization' for echoic sound by representing it as intentional speech and emphasizing Echo's interiority. Rather than offering a 'feminist' revision of Ovid, then, Sandys directly undermines Ovid's more generous representation of female speech. In Ovid's narrative, Echo emerges as a subject not in spite of, but *because of* the indeterminate nature of her vocal power. The uncanny ability of echoic sound to construct linguistic meaning on the nymph's behalf enables Echo to announce her desires but to remain beyond the reach of censure. Sandys's text, by normalizing Echo's sound and realigning it with Echo's body, places echoic sound within the range of surveillance.

Whereas Silverman theorizes the anxieties of her artists through the discourse of psychoanalysis, for my reading of Sandys's practice of synchronization, I emphasize the historically-specific variables that shape representations of the female voice.[10] The eerie vocal power of Ovid's Echo would have been met with particular consternation by early modern audiences, many of whom embraced an ancient Aristotelian understanding of speech contrary to the view personified by Ovid's Echo and by the phenomenon of disembodied sound in general. Aristotle describes speech as the definitive trait of human identity: 'Voice,' he maintains, 'is a certain sound of an animate being'; it is the 'impact of air breathed on the so-called "windpipe," and is caused by the soul in these parts of the body.'[11] Voice, in essence, is the material manifestation of a conscious human subject, of the will of a sensible being. It is by the property of speech that humans can be identified. This Aristotelian understanding of speech was prevalent throughout the Tudor and Stuart periods, extending well into the late seventeenth century. Sermon writer William Gearing refers to Aristotelian speech philosophy when he opens *A Bridle for the Tongue or A Treatise of Ten Sins of the Tongue* (1663): 'As Man is a reasonable creature, so is speech given to him by God to express his reason ... Brute creatures can make a noise, but man only can articulate his voice.'[12] A half century earlier, music theorist John Dowland, translating Andreadis Ornithoparcus's *Micrologus* (1609), remarks that only 'sensible creatures' can articulate voice: 'A voyce therefore is a sound uttered from the mouth of a perfect creature.'[13] That is, vocal production becomes proof of a 'man's' perfection in the eyes of God and nature. Robert Robinson similarly reiterates the claim when he explains in his pronunciation manual (1617) that the primary cause of voice is spiritual: the 'Microcosmos of mans body' contains a mind that was created in 'God's image' and this mind is the cause of speech.[14]

The disembodied sound of an echo, a 'voice' which is not rooted in any clearly locatable subject, would be disconcerting to those who follow Aristotle, because echoic sound violates assumptions about the relation between speech and the human body, between voice and selfhood. If speech is the primary trait that defines 'humanness,' then how does one apprehend the message delivered by a voice that has no locatable origin at all, let alone no human one? Moreover, that such unconventional vocal power is depicted as belonging to a *female* figure would have compounded the shock value of Ovid's story for early modern readers. As many feminist scholars have pointed out, Sandys's contemporaries compulsively monitored, in order to restrict, female speech.[15] And how can one monitor a voice that does not emerge from a locatable body?

Ovid relieves the echo phenomenon of some of its eeriness by imagining that the sounds closely approximating human speech may be the vocal products of a human entity, but he allows his Echo figure to straddle the line between intentional 'human' speech and merely imitative, 'inhuman' sound. As Joseph Loewenstein writes, Ovid attempts through personification to 'regulate ... the threat to consciousness implicit in the phenomenon of echo,' but ultimately he 'restrains' this personification.[16] That is, although Ovid creates the character of Echo to depict more comfortably the strange echo phenomenon, the poem disarticulates the link between subjectivity and voice, between personhood and agency.

It is this uncertain, incomplete personification of echoic sound that proves for Sandys to be one of Ovid's 'harsh, improper, or mistaken' narrative elements. Where Ovid's poem revels in the indeterminate nature of the voice, Sandys's Englished edition clarifies and polices the line between human and inhuman sound. What Ovid leaves ambiguous, Sandys 'polishes,' in an effort to normalize the eerie vocality that Ovid's Echo possesses. Faced with the task of moralizing Ovid's example of echoic linguistic production, Sandys ultimately finds a way to uphold Aristotelian logic about the relation between voice and subjectivity – but not without implications for the representation of early modern gender systems. For when Sandys's translation anchors echoic sound more firmly to Echo's personage, it not only imbues the nymph with a sense of interiority but represents her as having access to conventional forms of vocal power. Sandys's expressive Echo does not conform neatly to the Renaissance ideal of mute womanhood. Caught between the exigencies of early modern voice philosophy and ideologies of gender, Sandys works hard elsewhere in the text to undermine the agency that his own translation grants Echo.

By paying attention to the details of Sandys's 'Englishing,' I counter two trends in scholarship on the translated Ovid. First, though many scholars read Ovid's *Metamorphoses* in translation, few account for the sociohistorical circumstances of a particular translation and the effect these have on the representation of Ovid's stories.[17] The importance of factoring in history is particularly evident in the case of the 'Narcissus and Echo' episode, for in an early modern culture so preoccupied with marking the boundaries of expression, especially where women are concerned, the figure of Ovid's Echo and her startling vocal capacity resonate deeply. Secondly, while the methodology and content of Sandys's commentary have received serious attention from scholars, the Englished translation has been seen as less worthy of analysis, perhaps because, in the words of Deborah Rubin, it is 'notably literal and unbiased' in comparison to other 'Englished' classics.[18] Rubin's characterization of Sandys's translation merits further investigation. Because the semantic range of Latin words and the language's flexible syntax are almost impossible to represent fully in English, Sandys makes translation choices in places where Ovid's text is more ambiguous. Whether they result from the demands of poetics (e.g., Sandys's scheme of rhymed couplets) or from the pressures of an ideological project (*Ovide moralisé*), these changes metamorphosize Ovidian representations of female vocal agency into a narrative that would be comprehended and accepted more readily by seventeenth-century readers.

Person-alizing Echo

Ovid narrates that Echo received her liminal vocality as a punishment from the goddess Juno, whom Echo had enraged. Before Echo earned her name, she was like all other nymphs, complete with body and self-expressive voice. On Jove's order, Echo would distract Jove's spouse Juno by engaging her in conversation, so that the goddess would not discover Jove's infidelity:

> fecerat hoc Iuno, quia, cum deprendere posset
> sub Iove saepe suo nymphas in monte iacentis,
> illa deam longo prudens sermone tenebat,
> dum fugerent nymphae. (III. 362–5)

> [Juno had made her thus; for often when she might have surprised the nymphs in company with her lord on the mountainsides, Echo cunningly held the goddess with her long speeches until the nymphs had fled].

When Juno becomes aware of Echo's trickery, she curses the loquacious nymph: 'huius ... linguae ... potestas / parva tibi dabitur vocisque brevissimus usus' ('that tongue of yours shall have its power curtailed and have the briefest use of speech' [III. 366]). Echo's tongue, the instrument that stands in for her vocal capacity, will no longer work as efficiently after Juno's punishment: Echo will be restricted from owning her speech and will now merely have *usus* (use) of it. The term *usus* emerges from an ancient discourse about property law which, among other things, explains the conditions under which one may profit from the use of property which belongs to another. As Echo has only 'use' of speech, she reaps the benefits of a property that is not hers; Narcissus's speech passes through her momentary possession, and she profits from it, even though she does not officially own it. Loewenstein points out, moreover, that the legal notion of utility from which the term *usus* arises, 'challenges the boundary between object and subject ... Usus is a Janus-concept at the limits of property, sometimes splitting an object's utility off from its essential status of being-owned, sometimes revising ownership.' As a *usable* property, Echo's speech stands on what Loewenstein calls 'a weird frontier.'[19] It is neither as an embodied feature which inherently belongs to her (as speech, per Aristotle, would otherwise be assumed to be); nor is it a movable property entirely separable from her. Echo's speech is a product or tool of which she – whether owner or vehicle – temporarily claims possession.

Even before Echo's punishment, Ovid's descriptions of her speech convey its instrumental nature through corresponding grammatical form – the ablative of means. When narrating the history behind Juno's anger at Echo – 'illa deam longo prudens sermone tenebat' ('She

[Echo] cunningly held the goddess by means of her long speeches') – Ovid represents Echo's lengthy speeches to Juno in the ablative, 'sermone,' distinguishing and separating the speech from the nominative agent Echo. Speaking, in the Ovidian original, is grammatically the *tool* which Echo, the agent, deploys skilfully to fool Juno. When Sandys translates this moment, he shifts Echo's 'discourses' into the nominative position, into the position of the subject: 'Her long discourses made the Goddess stay.' Discourses that once were employed by Ovid's Echo become, for Sandys, the primary agents of the sentence. This grammatical change, though it does not significantly change Ovid's meaning and conforms very closely to the original Latin, still alters the overall sense of this line and distinguishes Sandys from his predecessors. Arthur Golding, whose translation choices Sandys usually follows, retains Ovid's ablative construction, translating this phrase, 'This elfe would *with her tatling talke* detaine her [Juno] by the way.' The ablative appears as well in Thomas Howell's 1560 translation: 'This Eccho *wyth a tale*, the goddes kepte so longe.'[20] In Sandys the engaging discourses, rather than being the instruments that Echo *uses* to fool Juno, are metonymies for the nymph, indicating her power over Juno. When Sandys grants agency to 'her long discourses,' he grammatically (through the inclusion of the possessive pronoun 'her') yokes the speeches more closely to Echo; the foolery is performed by discourses that Echo inherently owns.

The significance of differences between Sandys's and Ovid's poetic choices become especially evident at the point in the narrative when Echo discovers Narcissus wandering in the forest and falls in love with him. While he tries to locate his friends with his voice, she is provided with phrases to articulate her interest in him. Ovid's language suggests that the words that Echo speaks in response are the combined result of her planning and good fortune. The Latin poem sets up these seemingly contradictory circumstances for echoic speech:

natura repugnat
nec sinit, incipiat, sed, quod sinit, illa parata est
exspectare sonos, ad quos sua verba remittat.
forte puer comitum sedectus ab agmine fido
dixerat: 'ecquis adest?' ... (III. 376–80)

[Her nature forbids [her expression of desire for him], nor does it permit her to begin, but as it permits, she is ready to await the sounds to which she may give back her own words. By chance the boy, separated from his faithful companions, cried out: 'is anyone there?']

Her nature forbids her from initiating speech, but '*illa parata est / exspectare sonos*,' she is ready to await the sounds. Ovid's Echo does not merely hope that Narcissus will provide her with the opportunity to speak; she prepares herself for the event, *expecting* that such an occasion will present itself. And it does in the very next line. In his typically ambiguous style, however, Ovid prefaces the fulfilment of Echo's expectations with the word *forte*, by chance. The effect of this combination of anticipation and surprising luck is that Echo is represented as both an agent of her own desires *and* a victim of destiny who happens to benefit from the cards (or, in this case, the words) fate deals her. When Sandys translates these lines, however, the latter characterization falls away as Sandys sets *forte* aside:

But, Nature no such liberty affords:
Begin she could not, yet full readily
To his expected speech she would reply.
The Boy, from his companions parted, said;
Is any nigh? (III. 379–83)

Omitting any translation of *forte*, Sandys's text moves directly from Echo's state of preparation to the conversation that allows her to fulfil her expectations. The effect of this absence, which differentiates Sandys from his predecessors,[21] is that Echo expects Narcissus to provide her with auspicious words, and he seems to speak at her passive bequest. Narcissus's initial words, the words which allow Sandys's Echo to announce her person ('I') narratively proceed not *forte*, 'by chance,' but as anticipated. Narcissus's 'nigh' is rendered as 'expected speech.' With less vacillation than Ovid, Sandys portrays Echo as exercising some measure of control over vocal expression and communication.

Echo's role in communication processes is figured as more active in Sandys than in Ovid. Ovid's Echo is defined as the eternal respondent, never initiating discourse but involuntarily reflecting its close: 'haec in fine loquendi / ingeminat voces auditaque verba reportat' ('she doubles the phrases at the end of a speech and returns the heard words' [III. 368–9]). Unable to do more than 'return' heard words, Echo's speech is always the borrowed property of another. When Ovid's Echo speaks she moves that property *back* (*re*portat) into the possession of its ostensible owner, the previous speaker. Some essence of this sense of movement *back* is retained in Sandys when he translates *reportat* as 'relates': 'she yet ingeminates / The last of sounds, and what she hears relates.' Sandys likely chooses this meaning to strike a rhyme with '*ingeminates*,' and his phraseology conveys the repetitious form of Echo's speech in accordance with Ovid's general description of her vocal posture. Yet in using the term 'relates,' Sandys's text delivers a slightly different sense of vocal property: as early as the fifteenth century, the term '*relate*' is 'to recount, narrate, tell, give an account of,' and this is still the primary meaning today.[22] To a greater extent than the speaker who *reportat* (the definition of which is 'to give back information' or, as in this case, words), the speaker who 'relates' participates in the conveyance of information; she does not merely act as a receptacle but actually shapes the story. The focus of Ovid's *reportat* is on the initial source of the information, and the speaker acts as siphon; the focus of Sandys's 'relate' is on the task of narration itself. Thus, in Sandys's description of Echo as one who 'relates,' she is less an 'aural mirror'[23] who returns what belongs to someone else, than a messenger who offers selected information to a present and eager listener.

By virtue of this word choice, Sandys's earliest introduction of Echo links her to a tradition of echoic gossips or personified rumours that famously exaggerate the accounts that they relate. We might recall the echoic rumour that Warwick describes in Shakespeare's *Henry IV*, Part Two, when he reassures the king that the enemy's numbers cannot be as large as they are rumoured to be, for 'Rumour doth double, like the voice and echo, / The numbers of the feared' (3.2.98–9).[24] While the echo of this line is summoned in order to pun on 'double,' the association of echoes with errant gossip was long-standing. As a producer of rumours, Warwick's Echo does more than just repeat news that reaches her; her repetition can manipulate information, or, like Rumour who opens *Henry IV*, even manufacture falsehoods. The more active participation of Sandys's Echo in shaping the words that reach her might be further noted in his translation of Ovid's phrase 'auditaque verba reportat' (and she returns heard words). When Sandys translates this phrase as 'and what she hears relates,' he not only alters the definition of *reportat*, as I have noted, but also turns the modifying participle 'audita' into the verb 'hear.' The words that Sandys's Echo ostensibly reiterates are taken in and incorporated by her hearing body, and only then are they converted into vocal articulations. In grammatical terms, Echo's body is thus the site of a *listening* as active as the process of speaking.

In sum, Sandys's translation renders Echo as agent of her own desires, practically accountable for the words that issue forth from her body. Though Sandys does not (and, by virtue of the genre of translation, cannot) go so far as Ben Jonson in restoring Echo with independent speech and a visually recognizable body,[25] his translation still accentuates the personification of Echo that is only ambiguously suggested in Ovid. As such, readers of Sandys's Englished translation would have encountered a depiction of voice in Ovid commensurate with Aristotle's – that is, a voice that is expressive of human consciousness and will. In the process of aligning Ovid's tale more closely with Aristotelian voice philosophy, however, Sandys's text comes into conflict with early modern concerns regarding gender and vocal expression. To be sure, Sandys's Echo ignores the Pauline strictures of chastity, silence, and obedience and seems to escape regimes of discipline to which early modern women – in fiction and in reality – were subject often. But before we leap to the conclusion that Sandys's text evidences proto-feminist commitments, it is important to note that the text frames this generous rereading of personalized voice not as Sandys's, but as Ovid's. The English words might be Sandys's, but the essence of Echo's story – Sandys, the translator, insists – belongs to the heathen Ovid. This distinction and its strategic purpose become more evident when we consider the contrast between the translation and the moralizing commentary that follows it. Having insisted in the translation upon Echo's personhood, Sandys's commentary reduces Echo to an inhuman phenomenon, with a 'debility' (p. 156) in speech and a notable lack of vocal control.

Only a Repercussion

Sandys's commentary is only one among a number of additions/improvements to the 1632 text, but it is certainly the most notable and is partly responsible for the author's popularity as an Ovid translator. Much as Arthur Golding had dominated the sixteenth century with the Englished *Metamorphoses* that Shakespeare reportedly consulted, so Sandys dominated English readings of Ovid's poem in the seventeenth, publishing at least eight editions of his full translation.[26] The 1632 edition was the most glamorous, accompanied by fifteen full pages of new illustrations depicting mythological figures (as well as the stunningly revised frontispiece), marginal glosses that highlight the names of the central characters of each story, and the extensive commentary, organized by narrative episode. The composition and placement of the commentary strongly suggest that readers of the 1632 edition would have attended as much (if not more) to the commentaries as to the translation itself: the commentary sections are equal in length, sometimes even longer, than the Englished poem, and they take the form of pedagogical/philosophical essays, placed conspicuously between translated books.

Sandys justifies his commentary as a necessity 'since divers place in our Author are otherwise impossible to be understood but by those who are well versed in the ancient Poets and Historians' (p. 9). Having traveled to various worldly destinations and having settled for some time in Virginia, Sandys is indeed 'well versed.' The commentary evinces not only its author's experiences as a traveler but also his encyclopedic knowledge of classical history and philosophy, of mythography, and of science. The sources Sandys cites, whether these are stories relayed from scholastic traditions or drawn from his own observations, assess the credibility of Ovid's myths by appealing to scientific or historical precedent.[27] The commentaries are thus a reference book of sorts and, because they are posited as an assortment of alternative views, their ideological stance is tricky to determine.

The format of the commentary, like contemporary commentaries, positions Sandys as a capacious collector, not selective editor, of historical opinion. He draws on various sources, rarely offering his overt views except when he affirms the moral message of each tale. Some might say that Sandys presents himself as a 'mere' echo in that he claims to repeat the reports of others without much mediation. However, it is clear that the commentary provides some forum for Sandys's reflections on, and corrections to, the content of Ovid's tales. In addition to delivering the ethical lesson of the stories, announced with introductions such as 'now to the moral' (p. 160), each commentary draws on a limited selection of sources among the vast array from which Sandys could cull. By the time Sandys compiled his commentary on 'Narcissus and Echo,' Echo had received centuries of attention from writers with diverse interests in her as a mythical figure, a literary trope, a metaphoric emblem, and, of course, as a natural phenomenon. The constitution of Sandys's reference collection – the choice of citations in addition to the way he presents these pieces of evidence – tells us a great deal about the lessons that this pedagogue wishes to convey.

In its discussion of Echo, Sandys's commentary relies predominantly on the discourse of science. Exploring at length the nature of echoes as acoustic phenomena, Sandys appeals to empirical observations to dispute the 'human' quality of Echo's sound. He maintains that an echo, though sometimes uttered 'without failing in one sillable' (p. 156) is not an original voice, and he emphasizes the source which creates the initial sound:

> Now *Eccho* signifies a resounding: which is only the repercussion of the voice, like the rebound of a ball, returning directly from whence it came: and that it *reports* not the whole sentence, is through the debility of the reverberation. (p. 156; second emphasis mine)

Here Echo is reduced to object-status, an 'it' that helps explain the operation of repercussive objects. Differentiated from expressive human speech or 'voice,' echoic sound is compared to a rebounding ball that has no control over its movements and, by its nature, can only return back to its place of origination. Where Sandys's translation had described an Echo who actively 'relates' what she hears, his commentary strictly interprets the verb *reportare* that Ovid had used to characterize Echo's voice. In the commentary, Echo returns the voice 'directly from whence it came'; she does not actively hear words, process the information, and relate what she chooses like a messenger, but 'reports' the heard words like a mindless resonator. Sandys carefully explains away any hint of Echo's vocal intentionality. Her auspicious reverberations of only the ends of sentences, which in his own translation had given Echo the opportunity to announce her subjectivity, are here figured as the result of faulty reverberation. By emphasizing the echo as a purely material phenomenon, the commentary disqualifies Echo's vocal production from the category of human speech.

Although elsewhere in his commentary on the *Metamorphoses*, Sandys incorporates both mythological and scientific findings, his commentary on Echo primarily cites natural philosophy. Elucidated thoroughly by the empirical criteria of the 'new' science, Echo, in the commentary, loses her peculiar vocal powers. The impact that this explanatory apparatus has on Sandys's presentation of Echo becomes clear when we consider how Sandys draws on Francis Bacon's scientific writings about Echo. Scholars have recognized that Sandys's 1632 edition registers the extent to which the poet was influenced by Bacon, especially by Bacon's mythography, *De Sapientia Veterum* (translated into English in 1619).[28] Yet references to *De Sapientia* are absent in Sandys's commentary on Echo. The allusions to Bacon that Sandys does include derive from Bacon's *Sylva Sylvarum* (1626), an assortment of empirical studies about the nature of sound. In several of the experiments that appear in *Sylva Sylvarum*, Bacon discusses echoes, distinguishing between simple echoes, what he calls 'reflexion iterant,' and echoes of echoes, or 'super-reflexion.' In order to explain an observation about 'super-reflexions' reported to have been heard in a chapel outside of Paris, Bacon draws a parallel between visual and aural reflection:

> Like to *Reflexions* in *Looking-glasses*; where if you place one *Glasse* before, and another behinde, you shall see the *Glasse* behinde with the *Image*, within the *Glasse* before; And againe, the *Glasse* before in that; and divers such *Super-Reflexions*, till the *species speciei* at last die. For it is every Returne weaker, and more shady. In the like manner, the *Voice* in that *Chappel*, createth *speciem speciei*, and maketh succeeding *Super-Reflexions;* For it melteth by degrees, and every *Reflexion* is weaker than the former.[29]

With his technical nomenclature and experimentally based logic, Bacon empties echoes of their eerie potential. Sound operates in predictable patterns, Bacon insists. And Sandys, who shares Bacon's language, shares his views as well. Sandys also refers to the chapel in Pavia where Lambinus heard 'not fewer then thirty' echoes answering one another, and comments: 'The image of the voice so often rendred, is as that of the face reflected from one glasse to another; melting by degrees, and every reflection more weake and shady then the former' (p. 156).[30] Sandys's appeal to Bacon's scientific explanations reduces Echo's liminal speech to predictable sound that, if given the time, will dissipate like the 'super-reflexions' at Pavia. Furthermore, the placement of this citation in a commentary on the 'Narcissus and Echo' myth associates Echo's aural reflections with the visual ones that mislead Narcissus. Through this analogy, Echo's presence is rendered as illusive and fictive as Narcissus's mirror image, and she is defined, like the mirror image, in relation to Narcissus, rather than as an entity all her own.

A markedly different sense of the nymph appears in Bacon's mythographic writings about echoes, which Sandys neglects to cite or mention. Bacon follows a different mythographic tradition, which couples the nymph not with Narcissus, but with Pan. In *De Sapientia Veterum*, Bacon explains that Pan desires Echo because she represents 'true philosophy,' the only thing that Pan (the World) lacks:

> that alone is true philosophy; which doth faithfully render the very words of the world, and is written no otherwise then the world doth dictate, it

> being nothing else but the image or reflection of it, not adding any thing of its owne, but onely iterates and resounds.[31]

In Baconian mythography, Echo symbolizes the purity of philosophical discourse, the most transcendent form of the human voice.[32] Bacon's laudatory views of Echo extend from the writings of Macrobius, who had depicted the nymph as the representative of the celestial realm. Why does Sandys, a known scholar of Bacon's *De Sapientia*, forego mention of this tradition of the praiseworthy Echo? Why does he restrict his Baconian allusions to Bacon's scientific explanations, and what are the repercussions of his choices?

One might argue that Sandys excludes the Baconian reading because Bacon's Echo is derived from a mythological tradition that differs significantly from Ovid's. The story of Pan and Echo switches the roles of pursuer and pursued: Pan is captivated by Echo's song and pursues her, unlike in Ovid's narrative where Echo desires and chases Narcissus. The Echo of the Pan-Echo story pines for no man and courageously fends off her pursuer. In one rendition of the narrative, Pan becomes so enraged with Echo's refusal to surrender her chastity that he calls on wild animals to tear her limbs apart; under the tutelage of the Muses and the nymphs, however, Echo's invisible, scattered body parts retain their ability to produce captivating music, keeping Pan in a state of frustrated desire.[33] This account of Echo as defender of chastity, ally of nymphs and Muses, and desirable representative of the celestial heavens underlies Baconian notions of Echo as the representative of philosophical discourse. One might reasonably maintain that it was not appropriate for an Ovid commentator to muddy his commentary with discussions derived from a different mythological genealogy.

Yet at least one other translator of and commentator on Ovid's 'Narcissus and Echo,' coincidentally publishing in the same year as Sandys's expanded edition, *did* draw on the tradition of celestial Echo in his commentary. Mythographer and rhetorician Henry Reynolds follows his translation of Ovid's narrative with a moralizing commentary in which he condemns Narcissus for not listening to Echo's 'Divine voice.' Citing Pythagoras's notion 'while the winds breathe, adore Ecco,' Reynolds reports that Echo has been considered the 'reflection of divine breath,' since the wind is 'the Symbole of the Breath of God.'[34] Reynold's inclusion of a reference to the tradition of celestial Echo and her relationship to Pan results in a commentary that celebrates the uncanny, disembodied nature of Echo's speech. Her sound is not a simple reverberation of human voices, but a celestial prophecy that imitates and thus articulates the voice of God. Engaged in the same project and published at the same time, Sandys's and Reynolds's perspectives on Echo could not be more different.

Rather than cite the tradition of celestial Echo, Sandys includes a translation of Ausonius's Epigram XXXII, where Echo speaks to a painter, calling herself 'a voice without a mind' and the mother of 'judgment blind.' In Ausonius's poem Echo taunts the painter about his artistic limitations through a monologue. She challenges the painter to try to represent the 'Daughter of aire and tongue,' and goads him: 'If therefore thou wilt paint me, paint a sound' (p. 157). Echoes, she reminds him, can be processed only as aural experiences, and visual productions, like paintings, can never fully portray an aural happening. Representing Echo is quite impossible, the poem (and Sandys by including it) suggests, for Echo has no existence outside of her medium of sound.

Defining Echo as 'mere' sound is not inherently a slight against the figure. In early modern English culture, the medium of sound was understood to be incredibly powerful – for some writers even more powerful than vision.[35] Bacon's *Sylva Sylvarum* asserts the primacy of hearing over sight, claiming that sounds would more directly and more materially affect the spirits of a listener than sights would affect a visual observer. In comparison to other forms of sensory perception, Bacon writes, '*Objects* of the *Eare*, do affect the *Spirits* (immediately) most with *Pleasure* and Offence ... So it is *Sound* alone, that doth immediately, and incorporeally, affect most.'[36] And Echo's sound is especially potent given its pervasive nature – she is not found in one place but is rather 'omnibus auditur' (heard by all [p. 401]). In the context of Sandys's commentary, however, Ausonius's poem *is* a disparagement of the vocal nymph. Elsewhere in this commentary, Sandys undermines the efficacy and the materiality of sound, questioning, contra Bacon, whether sound has any power at all. In commenting on the bodily decay of Echo, Sandys writes that Echo 'consumes to an unsubstantiall voice.' She 'converts into a sound; that is, into nothing' (p. 156). The syntax of the latter sentence implies not only that Echo's body becomes 'nothing,' but that sound in general is 'nothing.'

The sober scientific and historical reality about Echo related in Sandys's commentary, like the corporealization of Echo in the translation, curbs the potential power of the disembodied voice – the translation by embodying this speech, and the commentary by disqualifying it *as* speech. However, the significance of each part of the text as moral instruction for the reader is not equal in Sandys's rendering, for the translated poem belongs more directly to Ovid, with Sandys presented as 'only' a translator, whereas the commentary is compiled and composed by Sandys himself. The 1632 edition does not merely distinguish Ovidian fiction from early modern truth, as Deborah Rubin points out;[37] it asserts the preeminence of the latter and secures Echo's agency in the domain of the former. For the Echo that Sandys offers to early modern readers is either the expressive human agent created by the pagan Ovid or the 'modern' scientifically validated phenomenon presented by the Christian Sandys. By constructing for himself the dual role of commentator and translator, Sandys strategically dissociates himself from the empowered Echo who emerges from 'Ovid's' poem. By emphasizing Ovid's responsibility for narrating a story of Echo's vocal power and offering the commentary as a moral corrective, Sandys's edition protects its early modern readers from the uncanny agency that the echoic voice seems to possess in Ovid's poem.

Now to the Moral

Ovid's capacity to produce potentially subversive representations of mythic and historical women has been recognized by several feminist critics, some of whom discuss, as I have, the reactions of Renaissance male writers to Ovid's characterizations. The most innovative scholarship on Ovid's depictions of women has centred on Ovid's *Heroides,* a collection of epistles narratively figured as authored by famous women to their lovers. According to Elizabeth Harvey, Deborah Greenhut, and others, the *Heroides* are especially interesting in terms of how Ovid represents female speech. Harvey situates her treatment of the *Heroides* in the context of a discussion about ventriloquized voices, the trope whereby male writers impersonate the female voice. She argues that Ovid's ventriloquization of Sappho's voice in *Heroides* challenges 'the epic and patriarchal ethos of Augustan Rome.'[38] Though Ovid's ventriloquization is motivated by a need to master the poetic legacy of Sappho, this project of anxious appropriation is self-consciously explored in *Heroides XV*: 'In a sense, Sapphic and Ovidian signatures are superimposed on one another in a palimpsestic transparency, and the usurpation that has made Ovid's ventriloquized speech possible is thus thematized in the text.'[39] By calling attention to his ventriloquization, Ovid offers an unstable answer to the question, 'Who is speaking and to whom does speaking belong?'[40] Greenhut similarly links Ovid's self-conscious ambiguity with subversive representations of gender identity in the *Heroides.* Assessing the rhetorical skill of female speakers in Ovid's text, Greenhut argues that Ovid creates a vital and unmoralized link between eloquence and sexuality, envisioning that the speakers of the *Heroides* articulate desire without shame and fear of social repercussions.[41] Harvey and Greenhut both note that Ovid's representations of women would have been difficult for Renaissance writers to accept. And both demonstrate how later adaptations of Ovid's *Heroides* alter the original to comply more easily with early modern attitudes towards female speech, thereby revealing the historical conditions that shape literary production.

Although attuned to the usefulness of Ovid for feminist literary historiography, Harvey and Greenhut, like most feminist scholars, dismiss the extraordinary potential of the echoic voice that Ovid himself suggests in the *Metamorphoses.* When both of these insightful critics recall the trope of echoing, they articulate views that bear closer resemblance to Sandys's writings than to Ovid's.[42] In her definition of the male poet's 'ventriloquistic appropriation' of the female voice, Harvey distinguishes echoing from the more masterful theft or 'linguistic rape' that Ovid pursues: 'Ovid knew Sappho's poetry and his epistle is full of its echoes, but whereas "echo" suggests a disembodied voice capable only of repetition, Ovid's radical reinscription of Sappho bears the marks of sexual mastery and theft, ... displacing the authority of her words.'[43] Harvey distinguishes impotent echoing from Ovid's authoritative, even violent, reinscription of voice, thereby implying that echoes are inherently incapable of the kind of powerful appropriation of another discourse that Ovid accomplishes. Greenhut, discussing the figuration of female speech as echoic in early modern conduct books, writes that in rhetorical terms the echo 'assigns polite women's speech the quality of an abstract or a digest, whose only value is in its confirmation of the original, or authoritative, sound. An echo is not original, and what it expresses is subordinate to and dependent on the original sound.'[44] Importantly calling attention to the misogynist nature of these characterizations of female speech, Greenhut inadvertently reiterates conduct book definitions of echoic speech. While there is no doubt that early modern conduct books use the trope of echoing to divest female speech of its potential power, one need not simply conclude that echoic speech is *inherently* impotent as a model of effective voicing.

Perhaps the tendency for feminist critics to view the mythical Echo as purely a victim of misogynist silencing regimes, rather than as a potential challenge to them, follows from criticism's insufficient theorization of echoic voice tropes and from the narrow scope of historical work on voice in general.[45] Critical readings of Renaissance representations of female speech have generally focused on the way in which early modern conduct books prescribe women's morality through a conflation of silence and sexual continence.[46] While this focus has enabled critics to address the relation between enforced silence and the disciplined female subject, a tendency to focus on the speaker's body (the site of articulation) has limited scholarly recognition of the potential power of *dis*embodied voice. What kind of power can the voice have *after* it leaves the speaker's body, before it reaches a listener's ears? How can theorizing the disembodied voice lead scholars towards a more capacious definition of female agency? In posing these questions, I am struck by the way in which Ovid's text seems to anticipate Judith Butler's contentious claim that 'agency begins where sovereignty wanes.'[47] It is precisely the *dis*articulation of speech from the speaker that opens up a space for Ovid's Echo to express and perform her desire for Narcissus. Transactive and dialogic, echoic speech enjoys a liminal kind of agency that is difficult to track and thus impossible to restrain fully. If Ovid's Echo speaks inappropriately, expressing desires that should, according to some readers, be left unarticulated, then how can Echo be held accountable and ultimately punished? Echo cannot be blamed for words that are not 'her own.' Echo thus reaps the benefits of speech, while the male subject, Narcissus, is held (anxiously) accountable.[48]

This ambiguous and yet powerful relationship of speech to agency changes in Sandys's translation of Ovid's story. By personifying Echo's voice and yoking the 'unintentionally' spoken words to their female speaker, Sandys places Echo firmly within the conduct book tropology of the loquacious and lascivious woman. Sandys translates disembodied echoic sound into the wilful, immodest expressions of (yet another) lusty woman. Although he grants Echo self-expressive power through her voice, he casts that power as immoral, and specifically, as indicative of a *classical* immorality which he aims to correct through his modern, scientific commentary. A generation of feminist criticism has, like Sandys, dismissed Echo's example by reading echoic voice through a discourse of moral instruction. But I would argue that Ovid's Echo offers us a way to think beyond the confines of the prescriptive literature and to reassess the terms by which we study 'voice' as a theoretical, historical, and performative vehicle of female agency. Critics who recognize agency primarily in the form of outspoken female historical and literary figures risk dismissing alternative models of potent voicing. Other models of the relation between articulation and agency might have been available in early modern English culture, particularly to women, whose access to conventional forms of power was circumscribed by legal and social practices.[49] Ovid's Echo exemplifies one such model – at least until Sandys refigures her in his 1632 *Metamorphoses*, granting her interiority and, in effect, a voice of her own. That Sandys's text needs to normalize, in order to dismiss, Echo's unintentional but effective vocality indicates just how disconcerting Ovid's Echo was for some early moderns and, at the same time, how compelling her legacy can be for contemporary feminist theories of agency.

NOTES

I am grateful to Valerie Traub for support and insightful feedback on this project during all stages of its conception and production. My thanks as well to Linda Gregerson and Elise Frasier for carefully reading various drafts; P.A. Skantze, Michael Schoenfeldt, and Theresa Braunschneider for their responses to early versions; and to the staff at the Folger Library for assistance with materials related to this project.

1 Lee T. Pearcy, *The Mediated Muse: English Translations of Ovid, 1560–1700* (Hamden, CT: Archon Books, 1984), p. 62.
2 George Sandys, *Ovid's Metamorphosis: Englished, Mythologized, and Represented in Figures* (London, 1632), p. 8. Citations to this work in the body of my essay correspond to the modern reprinting of the 1632 edition, ed. Karl K. Hulley and Stanley T. Vandersall (Lincoln: University of Nebraska Press, 1970).
3 For my translations of the Latin, I have consulted and modified Frank Justus Miller's translation of Ovid's *Metamorphoses*. The Loeb Classical Library (Cambridge, MA: Harvard University Press, London: W. Heinemann, 1984). I am grateful to Joanna Alexander for her early help with Ovid's Latin. In the Latin original, references are to book and line number.
4 Sandys was not the first Ovid translator or the first seventeenth-century writer to recognize the pun on 'aye.' Golding had chosen a similar translation in his edition of the *Metamorphoses*, and Ben Jonson performed the same move in *Cynthia's Revels*. Whether Sandys was the originator of the pun, his use of it certainly characterizes Echo in a compelling manner. Other translators found creative English translations which do not include

the aye/I pun. Sandys's contemporary Henry Reynolds translates this moment, 'Heare I not one? quoth he; One, sayes the mayde:/ Framing a troth from the last word he sayd' in his translation affixed to *Mythomystes* (1632), (repr. Scolar Press, 1972), p. 91. Thomas Howell (1560) slightly less elegantly writes that Narcissus 'Dyd saye is anye here to whome, she answereth her a none' (sig. Aiiir).

5 The differences between the project of the translation and the project of the commentary have gone unnoticed in Sandys criticism. Even Pearcy, one of the few critics to address Sandys's ideological positioning in a book which is admirably attuned to translation theory, does not consider the differences between the translation and the commentary. Pearcy sets up the two parts as equal, and he draws from both for evidence of Sandys's ideas.

6 Judith de Luce, '"O for a Thousand Tongues to Sing": A Footnote on Metamorphosis, Silence, and Power,' in *Woman's Power, Man's Game: Essays on Classical Antiquity in Honor of Joy K. King*, ed. Mary DeForest (Wauconda, IL: Bolchazy-Carducci, 1993), pp. 305–21.

7 Kaja Silverman, *The Acoustic Mirror: The Female Voice in Psychoanalysis and Cinema.* Theories of Representation and Difference (Bloomington and Indianapolis: Indiana University Press, 1988), p. 164. On the role of sound-image synchronization in Hollywood films, see also Mary Ann Doane, 'The Voice in the Cinema: The Articulation of Body and Space,' *Yale French Studies* 60 (1980): 33–50. Doane argues that '[t]echnical advances in sound recording ... are aimed at ... concealing the work of the apparatus' (p. 35).

8 Silverman, *The Acoustic Mirror*, pp. 49, 165.

9 Ibid., p. 164

10 On the ways in which historical study and psychoanalytic investigation mutually inform one another, see Carla Mazzio and Douglas Trevor, eds., *Historicism, Psychoanalysis and Early Modern Culture* (New York: Routledge, 2000). The collection *Embodied Voices: Representing Female Vocality in Western Culture* (ed. Leslie C. Dunn and Nancy A. Jones [Cambridge: Cambridge University Press, 1994]) analyses representations of the female voice in an array of historical periods and contexts, and from a number of different critical perspectives.

11 Aristotle, *On the Soul*, trans. Hippocrates G. Apostle (Grinnell, IA: The Peripatetic Press, 1981), p. 34.

12 William Gearing, *A Bridle for the Tongue: or A Treatise of Ten Sins of the Tongue. Cursing, Swearing, Slandering, Scoffing, Filthy Speaking, Flattering, Censuring, Murmuring, Lying Boasting and Shewing* (London, 1663), sig. A3r.

13 John Dowland, trans. *Andreas Ornithoparcus His Micrologus, or Introduction: Containing the Art of Singing* (London, 1609; *STC* 18853), p. 6.

14 Robert Robinson, *The Art of Pronunciation* (London, 1617; *STC* 21122), p. 11.

15 See, among others, Margaret Ferguson, Maureen Quilligan, and Nancy Vickers, *Rewriting the Renaissance: The Discourses of Sexual Difference in Early Modern Europe* (Chicago: University of Chicago Press, 1986); Linda Boose, 'Scolding Brides and Bridling Scolds: Taming the Woman's Unruly Member,' *Shakespeare Quarterly* 42. 2 (1991): 179–213; Karen Newman, *Fashioning Femininity and English Renaissance Drama* (Chicago: University of Chicago Press, 1991); Catherine Belsey, *The Subject of Tragedy* (London and New York: Methuen, 1985); and Ann Rosalind Jones, *The Currency of Eros: Women's Love Lyric in Europe, 1540–1620* (Bloomington and Indianapolis: Indiana University Press, 1990).

16 Joseph Loewenstein, *Responsive Readings: Versions of Echo in Pastoral, Epic, and the Jonsonian Masque* (New Haven: Yale University Press, 1984), p. 54. Loewenstein offers a wealth of information about and richly developed readings of representations of Echo in the period. For more on literary representations of Echo, see John Hollander, *The Figure of Echo: A Mode of Allusion in Milton and After* (Los Angeles: UCLA Press, 1981).

17 There have been some attempts to historicize translations of the *Metamorphoses.* Some studies match particular Ovid translations with the early authors who draw on Ovid. See Robert H. Ray, 'Marvell's "To His Coy Mistress" and Sandys's Translation of Ovid's *Metamorphoses,' Review of English Studies* 44.175 (1993): 386–8; and Anthony Brian Taylor's numerous discussions of Shakespeare, Spenser and others' uses of Golding's translation ('Shakespeare and Golding: Viola's Interview with Olivia and Echo and Narcissus,' *English Language Notes* 15 [1977]: 103–6; 'Shakespeare's Use of Golding's Ovid as a Source for *Titus Andronicus,' Notes and Queries* 233 [1988]: 449–51; and 'Arthur Golding and the Elizabethan Progress of Actaeon's Dogs,' *Connotations* 1 [1991], 207–23). The purpose of these studies, primarily, is to shed light on non-Ovidian texts, not to explore the historical context of translations of Ovid. More thorough historical work has been done by those interested in contextualizing translators within a history of ideas. For instance, Pearcy's tightly theorized chapters on Sandys's translation deal with Sandys's use of Bacon and general relation to neoplatonic ideas. The essay that most closely models the kind of historical scholarship on the translated Ovid that I advocate is Raphael Lyne, 'Golding's Englished *Metamorphoses,' Translation and Literature* 5 (1996): 183–200. Lyne situates the translator Arthur Golding within his English Renaissance context, suggesting that Golding's 'language of heightened Englishness' may be evidence of his 'wish to promote his national culture' (p. 183). My approach differs from Lyne's and Pearcy's in that I focus on how early modern social conditions – specifically, early modern gender systems – might have influenced translations of Ovid.

18 Deborah Rubin, *Ovid's Metamorphoses Englished: George Sandys as Translator and Mythographer* (New York and London: Garland, 1985), p. 21.

19 Loewenstein, *Responsive Readings*, p. 48.

20 Arthur Golding, *The Fyrst Fouer Bookes of P. Ovidius Nasos worke, intitled Metamorphosis, translated oute of Latin into Englishe meter* (London, 1565), III, sig. B2r. Thomas Howell, *The Fable of Ovid treting of Narcissus* (London, 1560), sig. A2v. Emphasis added.

21 Golding maintains the sense of *forte* in his translation, beginning the line, 'By chance,' (III, sig. B2v); Thomas Howell, *The Fable of Ovid Treting of Narcissus* (1560), also introduces this moment with 'By chaunce' (sig. Aiiir). In Henry Reynolds's less literate translation (1632), Narcissus calls out to his friends because he hears a 'noise among the bushes greene / That unawares her [Echo's] foote did (tripping) make.' Echo's mishap, her unplanned misstep, thus serves as the catalyst for Narcissus's initiated discourse.

22 *The Compact Edition of the Oxford English Dictionary* (Oxford: Oxford University Press, 1971).

23 Many critics refer to Echo in these terms, but I am citing specifically SunHee Kim Gertz, 'Echoes and Reflections of Enigmatic Beauty in Ovid and Marie de France,' *Speculum* 73.2 (1998): 383.

24 *The Riverside Shakespeare*, 2nd ed. Boston & New York. (Houghton Mifflin Company, 1997).

25 I am referring here to Jonson's *Cynthia's Revels*, 1.2, where Mercury calls for Echo and she appears on stage, played by a visible actor. In Jonson's play, Echo does more than just repeat the ends of others' speeches – she speaks about forty independent lines.

26 Sandys completed his translation of the first five books of the *Metamorphoses* while settled in Virginia and published them in 1621 when he returned to England, making this the first printed work known to be written in the colonized New World. The first edition of this five-book translation has not been found, but a copy of the second edition is owned by the Folger Library (*STC* 18963.5). Sandys made very few changes to his translation as it moved from one edition to the next. For more publishing history and differences between editions, see Fredson Bowers and Richard Beale Davis, 'George Sandys: A Biographical Catalogue of Printed Editions in England to 1700' (New York: New York Public Library, 1950); and James G. McManaway, 'The First Five Bookes of *Ovids Metamorphosis*, 1621, Englished by Master George Sandys,' in *Papers of the Bibliographical Society of the University of Virginia* 1 (1848–9): 71–82.

27 Christopher Grose provides a helpful index of the names and places mentioned in Sandys's commentary section. See *Ovid's 'Metamorphoses': An Index to the 1632 Commentary of George Sandys* (Malibu: Undena Publications, 1981).

28 The influence of Baconian thought on Sandys's *Metamorphosis* is discussed at length by Pearcy. See also Grace Eva Hunter, 'The Influence of Frances Bacon on the Commentary of Ovid's *Metamorphoses* by George Sandys,' PhD diss. (State University of Iowa, 1949).

29 Francis Bacon, *Sylva Sylvarum, or a Natural Historie* (London, 1626), p. 249.

30 Echo's 'weake and shady' reflection further recalls her fictive nature by reference to Platonic ideas about the relation between art, nature, and truth.

31 I cite Sir Arthur Gorge's translation of Bacon's *De Sapientia Veterum, entitled The Wisdome of the Ancients* (London, 1619), p. 37.

32 Loewenstein, *Responsive Reading*, p. 24. Loewenstein's remarks on Bacon's view of Echo are worth quoting in full: 'Echo no longer appears as the uncanny discursiveness of the world; instead, Echo figures the conformity of discourse to the world. Echo no longer opposes human voice, no longer mimics our voice, for her voice has become ours.'

33 This version of the Pan-Echo relationship appears in Longus's narrative of *Daphnis and Chloë*, trans. George Thornley (London: Heinemann, 1916), Book III. 23.

34 Reynolds, *Mythomyastes*, p. 110.

35 On the centrality of sound to early modern modalities of perception and cognition, see Bruce R. Smith, *The Acoustic World of Early Modern England: Attending to the O-Factor* (Chicago and London: Chicago University Press, 1999).

36 Bacon, *Sylva Sylvarum*, no. 700.

37 Rubin, *Ovid's Metamorphoses*, pp. 156–8.

38 Elizabeth Harvey, *Ventriloquized Voices: Feminist Theory and English Renaissance Texts* (New York: Routledge, 1992), p. 120.

39 Ibid., pp. 122–3.

40 Ibid.

41 Deborah Greenhut, *Feminine Rhetorical Culture: Tudor Adaptations of Ovid's 'Heroides'* (New York: Peter Lang, 1988), p. 59.

42 Of course, neither Harvey nor Greenhut is specifically interested in the Echo figure of Ovid's *Metamorphoses*. By singling out their limited readings of echoic voice, I intend only to demonstrate that oversights of echoic vocal power can occur even amongst feminist critics who are familiar with Ovid and with his subversive representations of female speech.

43 Harvey, *Ventriloquized Voices*, p. 120.

44 Greenhut, *Feminine Rhetorical Culture*, pp. 11–12.

45 In addition to Harvey and Greenhut, see de Luce, 'O for a Thousand Tongues to Sing,' and Jones, *The Currency of Eros*. Amy Lawrence similarly posits Ovid's Echo as victim of 'a patriarchal system that wants to keep women silent.' In Lawrence's study of the female voice in cinema, Echo – her

'voice ... continually taken from her' – is a symbol of cinema's subordination of sound to image (*Echo and Narcissus: Women's Voices in Classical Hollywood Cinema* [Berkeley: University of California Press, 1991], p. 7).

46 Other critics who have discussed the significance of this conflation include Boose, 'Scolding Brides and Bridling Scolds'; Patricia Parker, 'On the Tongue: Cross Gendering, Effeminacy, and the Art of Words,' *Style* 23 (1989): 445–65; and Peter Stallybrass, 'Patriarchal Territories: The Body Enclosed,' in *Rewriting the Renaissance*, pp. 123–42.

47 Judith Butler, *Excitable Speech: A Politics of the Performative* (New York and London: Routledge, 1997), pp. 15–16.

48 Lynn Enterline discusses how the emergence of female subjectivity disrupts the stability of masculine identity. See especially her chapter 5, '"Hairy on the Inside": The Duchess of Malfi and the Body of Lycanthropy,' which discusses echoes and linguistic slipperiness, in *The Tears of Narcissus: Melancholy and Masculinity in Early Modern Writing* (Stanford: Stanford University Press, 1995), pp. 242–303.

49 Mary Ellen Lamb and Katharine Maus discuss Stoic silence as one such alternative model of female 'voicing.' Lamb and Maus point out ways that early modern women could work within the Stoic tradition of silence as a refusal to speak or express emotion, converting imposed constraints into heroic postures (Lamb, 'The Countess of Pembroke and the Art of Dying,' in *Women in the Middle Ages and the Renaissance: Literary and Historical Perspectives*, ed. Mary Beth Rose [Syracuse: Syracuse University Press, 1986]; Maus, *Inwardness and Theater in the English Renaissance* [Chicago: University of Chicago Press, 1995], chapter 3). Work on silence as an empowered stance importantly problematizes the overly simplistic conflation of speech and power that has been pervasive in feminist criticism. But, as Lamb herself points out, 'the cost exacted by these forms of heroism is high,' for Stoicism necessitates 'the suppression of the display of basic emotions ... without which no person can be whole' (p. 223). I would add that studies of silence exact a further cost, for they can perpetuate a misleading speech/silence binary: reexaminations of silence challenge one side of the speech/silence binary, but this leaves intact the other side, reinforcing a narrow signification of speech.

The Ovidian Hermaphrodite: Moralizations by Peend and Spenser

MICHAEL PINCOMBE

In the final stanzas of the three-book version of *The Faerie Queene* (1590), Edmund Spenser presents his readers with a visionary image of the reunion of the separated lovers Amoret and Scudamour. This reunion is a physical one, as is made clear by an intriguing comment of the author:

> Had ye them seene, ye would haue surely thought,
> That they had been that faire *Hermaphrodite,*
> Which that rich *Romane* of white marble wrought,
> And in his costly Bath causd to be site.[1]

It is very curious that Spenser should refer his readers to what appears to be a fairly obscure example of hermaphroditic statuary described in an epigram contained in the *Greek Anthology,* rather than to the *locus classicus* of the theme as depicted by Ovid in the tale of Hermaphroditus and Salmacis in the fourth book of his *Metamorphoses.*[2] But Spenser had his reasons. By calling up an image of luxury and titillation – for what other purpose can be served by the marble hermaphrodite in the decadent Roman's 'costly Bath'? – Spenser draws attention to the sinister side of the legend of Hermaphroditus as told by Ovid and passed on by earlier Elizabethan writers, in particular, by the adaptation of the tale by the little-known Thomas Peend in his *Pleasant Fable of Hermaphroditus and Salmacis* (1565).[3] Peend's poem helps us see what might be called the 'satirical' perspective on the 'hermaphroditic union' of Scudamour and Amoret in *The Faerie Queene.*

Here I take my lead from Jonathan Crewe's comments in his *Trials of Authorship* on what he calls 'a certain mimetic or identificatory desire' to produce large, synthesizing representations of counterontological innovation, displacement, gender-reversal, theatricality, positional mobility, power-shifting, dispersal, and cosmic remodelling.'[4] Crewe calls this a 'romantic' response to Renaissance literature; an interesting example of this kind of approach to the Ovidian myth of Hermaphroditus and Salmacis may be found in Jonathan Bate's interpretation of the fable in his study *Shakespeare and Ovid.* Bate speaks with some enthusiasm of the union between Hermaphroditus and Salmacis: 'This, we feel, is how sex should be.'[5] It is the 'ideal image of the union between a man and a woman' (p. 63). Or again: 'It might be described as the nearest thing available in a patriarchal culture to a myth of sexual equality' (p. 65). And perhaps most illuminatingly: 'the effect is a kind of polymorphous liberation' (p. 65).[6]

However, Crewe sets against this romantic tendency what he calls a 'satirical' countercheck: 'Not only resistance to radical change and dissolution (or merely to their hallucinatory representation), but a discounting of them, accompanied by a complex problematic of relative immobility, bondage, repetition, and pain, is as characteristic of the Renaissance as its quasi-revolutionary enterprises and representations' (p. 9). This is certainly the perspective on the Ovidian myth taken by Peend. Where Bate sees polymorphous liberation, Peend sees an allegory of enslavement. His Hermaphroditus is a young man 'Enthrald in slauyish woe.'[7] Here, then, is Crewe's 'complex problematic of relative immobility, bondage, repetition, and pain.'

I would argue that this satirical perspective is also present in Spenser's account of the reunion of Amoret and Scudamour. Or perhaps we should call it 'satyrical.' It is well known that Spenser probably had in mind a picture from an emblem-book such as Barthélemy Aneau's *Pictura poesis* (1552). Here we see an hermaphroditic figure curiously knotted into a tree (see opposite page).[8]

The motto seems to propose a sacramental reading of the hermaphrodite in terms of the spiritual and physical union of man and woman in holy wedlock. Perhaps it is the one taken by the figure to the left of the couple, who appears to be Moses. But there is another horned figure to the right – a satyr. The satyr, of course, was a symbol of the bestial aspect of human nature, particularly its primitive brutish lusts. Spenser, I suggest, wishes us to see Scudamour in terms of a morally ambivalent image of love and lust. The marble hermaphrodite is clearly not a 'primitive' piece of work, but highly sophisticated and 'civilized' (like *The Faerie Queene* itself). But the statue is still meant to appeal to sexual concupis-

Courtesy of the Special Collections of the Robinson Library of the University of Newcastle-upon-Tyne.

cence, and thus has links with the satyr, as a close examination of Peend's 'moralization' of the Ovidian tale may help to show. But first let us look at the original hermaphroditic figure in the *Metamorphoses.*

Ovid's Hermaphroditus as a *semimas*

The primary aetiological point of Ovid's fable is not to explain why we have hermaphrodites, but rather, as is stated quite explicitly at its outset: 'quare male fortibus undis Salmacis enervet tactosque remolliat artus' (IV. 285–6; 'Why Salmacis is ill thought of, how the evil strength / of its waters enfeebles and softens the limbs they touch').[9] Salmacis was a real spring in the ancient Carian city of Halicarnassus, but the origin of its well known and ill-famed powers was mysterious: 'causa latet, vis est notissima fontis' (IV. 287; 'The cause is obscure, but power of the spring is most famous'). It is Ovid's task to explain the hidden cause.

So it is that we learn of the son of Mercury and Venus, who, after fifteen years in the care of the naiads of Mount Ida, seeks adventure and makes his way southwards through the coastal regions of Asia Minor until he comes to a beautiful spring. Here he is encountered by an even more beautiful nymph, Salmacis. She propositions him; he spurns her; she retires – and hides behind a bush. And as he slips off his clothes and bathes in the pool, unseen as he thinks, she tears off her own garments and leaps in after him. There is a struggle, but she holds him fast in her embrace and prays to the gods that they may be inseparably united. The gods grant her wish, and the two bodies are miraculously merged into one.

This is the 'romantic' part of the fable; but Ovid then returns to his main purpose, which is to explain how these waters acquired their strange powers. It is because Hermaphroditus, mistakenly blaming his metamorphosis upon the waters rather than the gods, lays a curse on them, which is granted by his parents. From that moment on, any man whom the waters touch will be 'softened.' The emphasis on the softening effect of the waters is very marked. First Hermaphroditus sees that 'se liquidas, quo vir descenderat, undas / semimarem fecisse videt mollitaque in illis / membra' (IV.4.380–2; 'the transparent waters, to which he had gone down / a man had made him a half-male and that his limbs had been made soft'). And here is his curse: 'quisquis in hos fontes vir venerit, exeat inde / semivir et tactis subito mollescat in undis' (IV.385–6; 'whoever comes into this spring a man, let him come out from here / a half-man, softened immediately, he touches the waters'). So 'softening' involves a loss of virility. The most obvious physical effect would be a flaccid penis; and Marie Delcourt in her study *Hermaphrodite* (1956) says this of the pool of Salmacis: 'It was probably supposed to make impotent, more or less temporarily, any man who plunged into it.'[10] Ovid goes one mischievous step further. His Hermaphroditus is turned into a eunuch.

When Hermaphroditus sees that he has been turned into a *semimas*, he must see that he has been physically unmanned. The word *semimas* means 'castrated male.' When the new Hermaphroditus speaks, it is 'non voce virile' (IV.382; 'no longer with a man's voice'). He has suddenly acquired the high-pitched voice of a *castrato*. There are other tell-tale signs, too. The eunuch was also referred to as a *homo mollis*. Castration makes men corpulent, fleshy, and smooth-skinned. This is why Ovid insists on the word *mollis* and its cognates in this fable (they occur no less than six times). Hermaphroditus, then, is appalled at what has happened to him because he has been turned into a eunuch.

But how can we explain the fact that he is also a *semivir* and *biformis*? The word *semivir* is only used elsewhere in Ovid to refer to a being which is half-man and half-beast, such as the centaur.[11] But here he must be using it in a different way, presumably as an elegant variation on *semimas*. Still, how can the eunuch be 'two-formed'? This is a real problem. Here is what Ovid says of the transformation even as it takes place: 'nec duo sunt sed forma duplex, nec femina dici / nec puer ut possit, neutrumque et utrumque videntur' (IV.378–9; 'they were not two, but they had a dual form that could be said to be / neither woman nor boy, they seemed to be neither and both'). The *forma duplex* is what has given rise to the idea that the new Hermaphroditus is an hermaphrodite – and not unreasonably. But it could also be used to describe a eunuch, I think.

I would suggest that Hermaphroditus should now be seen as having paps which have become so soft and fleshy that they look like breasts. Here is the *femina*. And the *puer* is supplied by the eunuch's unmanned genitalia. Hermaphroditus may have lost his testicles, but castration did not usually involve the removal of the penis. However, this penis has lost its full phallic identity. It may be capable of erection, but not ejaculation; and this is why the new Hermaphroditus is not the sort of 'hermaphrodite' that Ovid would have known from the fertility cults. These hermaphroditic deities that he might have seen are not hermaphrodites in the modern anatomical sense. They do not have both male and female genitals. Usually they have breasts and also a phallus (or at least a beard). They have predominantly male bodies, who have both beards and breasts; and, on the other hand, they have predominantly female forms with strikingly erect phalluses.[12] But there are no images in which the genital area is occupied by phallus and pudendum – and it is difficult to see how this could be represented very clearly at all. But if we imagine a 'female' hermaphrodite with a permanently limp penis, then we may have a picture of Ovid's 'Hermaphroditus as Eunuch.'

Peend's Hermaphroditus as a *semivir*

By focusing with some insistence, then, on these textual clues, we may produce an appropriately satirical image of the 'hermaphrodite.' Ovid's

Hermaphroditus experiences no liberation in his polymorphousness, only its pain and humiliation. This is how we should regard Peend's Hermaphroditus, too. But Peend is not much interested in what new shape Hermaphroditus's body takes. He looks like 'man and woman both' and prays that other men may come out as 'halfe a man' when they swim in the pool (sig. A8v). No doubt he had some composite figure in mind such as we see in the emblem-books. But Peend is more interested in the moral aspect of the metamorphosis than the physical. And he uses the key word in the allegorical tradition relating to Ovid's fable of Hermaphroditus and Salmacis; '*effeminate.*'

We chaunge our nature cleane,
being made effemynat.
When we do yeeld to serue our lust,
we lose our former state.
It is the nature of that well,
that fylthy lothsome lake,
Of lust, the strengthe from lusty men
by hydden force to take ...(sig. B2v)

But what exactly does he mean?

We do not have space in this short essay to investigate in full the commentary tradition dealing with the detail of effeminacy. Suffice it to say that it was firmly embedded by the time that Raphael Regius compiled the various versions of his annotated edition of the *Metamorphoses* in the early sixteenth century. In the 1518 version, we read the following glosses on Ovid's *enervet* and *remolliat* (IV.286): '*Eneruet*: neruos ac vires eripiat; effeminet (*Eheruet*: snatches away his strength and vigour). *Remolliat*: molles ac effeminatos efficiat.' (*Remolliat*: renders him soft and effeminate)[13] Here is the loss of strength we find in Peend's moral, then. But Regius also includes a detail which suggests that 'effeminacy' need not imply impotence.[14]

Regius observes that people who drink the waters of the pool of Salmacis are 'vitio impudicitiae mollesceret' 'softened by the vice of lewdness.' Then he adds a very specific detail about the architecture of the building which housed the spring: 'aditus angustatus parietibus occasionem largitur iuuenibus petulantibus violando puerorum puellarumque.' The narrowed and walled entrance (to the building) gives ample opportunity for lascivious youths to violate boys and girls. From here it is but a short step to the idea that the hermaphrodite is a man who has intercourse with both sexes. And this, too, it seems could be described in terms of 'effeminacy,' as we can see from the comments on the fable made by George Sandys in his helpful volume *Ovid's Metamorphosis Englished, Mythologised, and Represented in Figures* (1632). These are very full, but the ones we are interested in are translated from one of the many versions of George Sabinus's annotated edition of the *Metamorphoses* (who in turn cites the Greek geographer Strabo):

> In *Caria* is the fountaine of *Salmacis,* I knowe not how infamous, for making the drinker effeminate: since luxury neither proceeds from the quality of the ayre nor water, but rather from riches and intemperance. *The* Carians *therefore addicted to sloath and filthy delights were called* Hermaphrodites; *not in that of both sexes, but for defiling themselves with either.*[15]

So 'effeminacy' is a word with complex associations in the context of the fable of Hermaphroditus. Ovid's *semimas* can have intercourse with neither sex, but the *hermaphroditus* of the commentary tradition seems to have sex with both.

However, the word 'effeminate' was by no means commonly used in this latter sense (if at all) in Elizabethan English. Rather, it was used to describe men who were unable to resist women, 'a lady's man.' Here is an amusing example of this kind of 'effeminacy' from the pen of Gabriel Harvey. He is writing a farewell letter to Spenser in 1579: 'Heus mi tu, bone proce, magne muliercularum amator, egregie Pamphile.'[16] Spenser is a 'good wooer,' a 'great lover of women' and an 'egregious Pamphilus' (Greek: 'All-Lover'). But Harvey goes on to warn him and the 'universa feministarum secta' that pursuing this 'yonkerly, and womanly humor' will come to no good. Spenser is a 'feminista,' then, because he is always chasing after women. This is what makes him 'womanly.' But it is also what qualifies him as a 'younker,' or 'young gallant.' On the other hand, 'effeminacy' also implied the supposed weakness of the female sex. A famous example is Samson's remark on his servitude to Dalilah in Milton's *Samson Agonistes* (1671): 'foul effeminacy held me yok't / Her Bond-slave.' This is the sort of effeminacy Peend has in mind: male sexual potency which yet lacks what Samson calls a 'grain of manhood well resolv'd.'[17]

Peend is not interested in *mollitia.* It is as if his eye simply never registered the word which Ovid uses so insistently. But he does see the pool as a place where men lose their strength. However, it is not so much physical strength that concerns Peend, as a man's moral strength to resist his own sensual nature. Young men are 'lusty' because they are physically vital ('younkers'). But they must also be wise enough to know what will happen if they allow their sensual nature too much rein. So it is tempting to see the image of the 'effeminated' Samson in phrases such as Peend's 'Enthrald in slauysh woe, he is / constrayned for to yeilde / To lust, and wyl' (sig. B2r). But Peend is really thinking in terms of bestiality. It is as if he had correctly interpreted Ovid's *semivir* as 'halfe a man' – and half a beast.

This is why Peend adds so much animal imagery to the poem. He amplifies Ovid's simile of the octopus and its prey by comparing Salmacis to a hawk, a hound, a pike, and Hermaphroditus to a partridge, a hare, and a 'lytle Roche' (sig. A7r). Hermaphroditus is also compared to a kid and a magpie. He is a 'dumb' beast, then, rather than a predator, and that is what makes him susceptible to the 'wily bait' put in his way by the world (Caria) and its vices (Salmacis). Unaware of his carnal nature, as Peend's moral explains at length, he is easily 'taken in the snare' (sig. B1v). The struggle with Salmacis is seen as grimly futile:

The more he striues, entangled once,
  the faster he is in.
Such is the nature of the bayte,
  and sleyght of that same gyn. (sig. B2r)

Sex is addictive, says Peend, and the more we indulge in it the more we become like beasts caught in a trap: 'Such is our beastly nature blynd, / so is our lust vnpure' (sig. B2r).

The bestial interpretation becomes clearer still when we consider an addition which Peend makes to Ovid when he comes to the physical appearance of the pool of Salmacis:

Much lyke vnto the well it was,
  wherto *Acteon* drew,
When that *Diana* and her Nymphes
  all naked in the same
He saw, by chaunce as he dyd seke
  hys lately coursed game. (sig. A4v)

In fact, Diana's pool is nothing like the spring of Salmacis. But it is nonetheless Actaeon who informs Peend's interpretation of Ovid's Hermaphroditus. Actaeon was a hunter who was turned into a hart and tracked down and killed by his own hounds. The fable was regularly moralized in terms of how a man 'puts off the mind of a man and degenerates into a beast.'[18] Shakespeare's Orsino in *Twelfth Night* (1623, performed 1602) is more explicit: 'That instant was I turn'd into a Hart, / And my desires, like fell and cruell hounds, / Ere since pursue me.'[19] In other words, where Ovid seems to have seen Hermaphroditus as a *semimas*, Peend sees him as a *semivir.* Ovid turns Hermaphroditus into a eunuch as a witty explanation of the impotence supposed to be brought on by the waters of the real pool of Salmacis in Caria. Peend sees the fable as an allegory of the lapse into 'our beastly nature' which awaits the sexually innocent 'younker.'

But this is not the end of the story. When Peend identifies the pool of Salmacis with a 'fylthy lothsome lake, / Of lust,' he means us to understand that it is a type of hell. To give in to bestial lust means risking eternal perdition:

So we do chaunge the happy hope
  of euerlastyng ioye,
Euen for the present pastyme, whych
  our selues doth moste anoye. (sig. B2v)

The phrase 'loathsome lake' was a cliché for the lakes of the classical underworld and for the Christian hell in the sense of a 'prison.'[20] For example, in his *Drum of Doomsday* (1576), George Gascoigne reminds his sinful readers of their likely destination: 'what a thinge it is to be for ever enclosed in the pryson of hell, in the myddest of unquencheable fyre, in a most fylthie stinckinge and lothesome lake.'[21] This hellish context is where the satirical credentials of Peend's poem make themselves felt most keenly.

The satirical image of the hermaphrodite has a long history. We can trace it back at least to Lucretius (99–55 B.C.). In his *De rerum natura,* he observes that lovers are driven by sexual desire to seek mutual incorporation, but that this, as Sandys has it, leads to 'vanity and vexation':

They greedily imbrace, ioyne mouthes, inspire
Their soules, and bite through ardor of desire:
In vaine; since nothing they can thence translate,
Nor wholy enter and incorporate.
For so sometimes they would; so striue to doe:
And cleaue so close as if no longer two.[22]

There is no 'polymorphous liberation' here. Lucretius thought that sexual desire was already too liberated and needed to be controlled by the exercise of reason. That is what gives these lines their satirical edge, and also the effects of bemused pity for these foolish worldlings.

But satire is also sometimes motivated more by repulsion than the desire to correct. Here, to take an example from the very other end of the time-scale, we might consider the punishment meted out to two sinners in the infernal city of Matapolis in Wyndham Lewis's novel *Malign Fiesta* (1954). Dr Hachilah thinks that Dante was too easy on Paolo and Francesca, who merely fly through the air 'still together' in the fifth canto of the *Inferno.* So he arranges a less 'sentimental' version of the punishment in a special cell devoted to those found guilty of fornication:[23]

> In the centre of the room were a man and woman strapped to one another. About four feet from the floor they were suspended from the ceiling, and arranged at an angle very near the horizontal, simulating flight.
>
> Dr. Hachilah went up to them, and slapping the woman upon the buttocks spoke in Italian.
>
> 'Ah, Francesca, how is love'?
>
> He asked Pullman to approach and pushing aside a garment revealed the fact that they were naked, and indecently glued to one another, the man exactly placed to facilitate sinful love.

'Sinful love.' It is a phrase that Peend might well have used. Love is not sinful for Lucretius, but vexatious. But Peend shares some of Lewis's disgust at 'beastly lust,' and is content to warn his readers that it will lead to the 'fylthy lothsome lake / Of lust' in the end.[24] And so, to a lesser extent, was Spenser.

Romantic and Satirical Perspectives on Amoret and Scudamour

There are several traces of Ovid's fable in Spenser's description of Amoret and Scudamour. Ovid uses the simile of a twig grafted on to a tree and gradually growing into it in order to describe the union between Hermaphroditus and Salmacis; Spenser says of his couple: 'No word they spake, nor earthly thing they felt, / But like two senceles stocks in long embracement dwelt' (3.12.45 [1590]; cf. Ovid, *Metamorphoses*, IV.375–6). The image is informative. There is no doubt that a passionate union between the two long-separated lovers has occurred; but the image of the stocks describes the moment *after* Amoret 'did in pleasure melt, / And in sweete rauishment pourd out her spright (3.12.45).' The two bodies may be still locked in genital union, but the spirits which usually inhabit them have left them in a long moment of ecstasy, so that these bodies are now no longer capable of sensuous – or sensual – experience but have become 'senseless.'

On the other hand, it is easy to understand the attractions of this image. Even the chaste Britomart is moved by it:

> So seemd those two, as growne together quite,
> That *Britomart* halfe enuying their blesse,
> Was much empassiond in her gentle sprite,
> And to her selfe oft wisht like happinesse? (3.12.46)

The image of the sexually united bodies of Amoret and Scudamour is an emblem of the disembodied union of their spirits (which is why it is Britomart's 'sprite' not her body that is moved). We cannot see the union of their spirits because spirits are invisible. But their bodies can give us an idea of this spiritual union. The emblem can be put to archly erotic purposes, of course. It is Donne's seductive argument in 'The Ecstasy': 'To our bodies turne we then, that so / Weake men on love reveal'd may looke.'[25] But that is not Spenser's purpose. To view their union in simply sexual terms is to miss what mattered most to Spenser. It risks reducing the image to the level of pornography – to the level of the Roman gazing at his marble hermaphrodite in his 'costly Bath.'

But this perspective is nonetheless present in the text. The Spenserian image of the embrace of Amoret and Scudamour is complicated by its apparent one-sidedness. It is only Amoret who experiences the spiritual release which should, we presume, accompany sexual orgasm. Scudamour's experience may be much more unregenerately carnal. In fact, he still retains much of the character of an earlier Spenserian type of Hermaphroditus: Red Cross Knight. In the first book of *The Faerie Queene* Queen, Red Cross abandons Una and takes up with Duessa; and so they come upon a lovely fountain. We learn that the nymph who dwelt in the pool was out of favour with Diana because one day whilst hunting she had stopped and sat down because she was tired. Diana cursed her pool: 'Thenceforth her waters waxed dull and slow, / And all that drunke thereof, did faint and feeble grow' (1.7.5) Red Cross is hot, too, and drinks of the well's water with predictable results: 'Eftsoones his manly force gan to faile.' But this does not prevent him (so it would seem) from having sex with Duessa:

> Yet goodly court he made still to his Dame,
> Pourd out in loosness on the grassy grownd,
> Both carelesse of his health, and of his fame – (1.7.7)

It is at this point that Orgoglio overpowers him and takes him away to his prison: 'as darke as hell, / That breathed euer forth a filthie banefull smell' (1.8.39). Here is the grim allegory of concupiscence and perdition which forms the ground of Peend's interpretation of the Ovidian fable. However, the sacramental allegory does redeem the situation to a certain extent. We note that Amoret 'pourd out her spright' in a similar effusion – but in lawful rather than unlawful love.

But it seems to me that Scudamour's part in this is merely instrumental. His attitude towards Amoret's body is still carnal:

> Lightly he clipt her twixt his armes twaine,
> And streightly did embrace her body bright,
> Her body, late the prison of sad paine,
> Now the sweet lodge of loue and deare delight.
> But she faire Lady ouercommen quight
> Of huge affection, did in pleasure melt,
> And in sweete rauishment pourd out her spright. (3.12.45 [1590])

The focus here is on Amoret. Only she has known the torments with which her body was afflicted whilst imprisoned in Busirane's castle. So it is that the pleasure which she feels when her own body is turned from a prison of pain to a lodge of love is so overwhelming. Just as her body has been set free from the prison of the castle by Britomart, so her soul is now set free from the prison of her body by Scudamour.

But Scudamour's relation to Amoret's 'sweet lodge of loue and deare delight' is different. It seems to me that Spenser applies another allegorical interpretation of the Ovidian fable in his case. Barthélemy Aneau declares quite roundly that the pool of Salmacis signifies the female pudendum: 'hic fons nihil est aliud, nisi cunnus ('This spring is nothing other than pudendum').'[26] Peend, I think, hints at this identification, too:

> By *Salmacis*, intende eche vyce
> that moueth one to ill.

And by the spring the pleasant sporte,
that doth content the wyll. (sig. B1v)

Strictu sensu, the spring signifies sexual intercourse; but the quibble on the word will is suggestive. If we read 'wyll' as 'penis,' then the word 'spring' seems to invite the reading 'pudendum.'

Peend's phrase may also throw light on the state in which Scudamour is found by Amoret upon her release from the castle: 'wilfull anguish and dead heauinesse' (3.12.43 [1590]). The dead heaviness reminds us of the enervated condition of Red Cross, both physical and moral. The enervation of the soul is, of course, despair; and Scudamour is 'Twixt dolour and despight halfe desperate.' But 'wilfull anguish' suggests sexual frustration. Scudamour wants to occupy Amoret's sweet lodge. She calls to him, and he comes back to life ('he reared light from ground'). Then he runs to her 'with hasty egernesse;' and here Spenser uses another simile which seems to echo Peend's bestial interpretation of the Ovidian fable:

Like as a Deare, that greedily embayes
In the cool soile, after long thirstinesse,
Which he in chace endured hath, now nigh breathlesse. (3.12.44)

Scudamour is likened to a thirsty deer escaping from its pursuers by diving into a pool during the chase. Perhaps it is too much to see an allusion to Actaeon here; but in other respects the image suggests that Spenser was thinking along the same lines as Peend. The word 'soil' is a term of venery, which means a pool of water in which an animal takes refuge. Does it echo Peend's 'fylthy lothsome lake' at one more metaphorical remove? The 'soil' is so called because it was originally used to denote a muddy pool in which a wild boar wallows.[27] Here is the very type of beastly sensuality. But it has affinities with the more 'civilized' image of the marble statue in the clear waters of the Roman's bath.

Conclusion

There is a scene in Blake's *Marriage of Heaven and Hell* (1793) in which the poet is warned of the 'hot burning dungeon' which awaits him if he perseveres in his infernal inquiry.[28] Then the poet metaphysically inverts the angel's view by taking him to the 'deep pit' to which access is gained through the Bible. The angel is appalled and says: 'Thy phantasy has imposed upon me & thou oughtest to be ashamed' (p. 93). The poet replies: 'We impose on one another, & it is but lost time to converse with you whose works are only Analytics.'

For hundreds of years it has been the angel's fantasy that has imposed upon our view of the sexual implications of Ovid's fable of Hermaphroditus and Salmacis. Now we tend to be 'of the devil's party.' When, for example, Bate talks of the 'celebration of sexuality' (p. 65) in the Ovidian myth, he imposes a modern 'romantic' fantasy on what the more angelic Spenser would have described as 'carnal concupiscence.' The sexual union of Amoret and Scudamour can be seen as an emblem of 'holy matrimony.' But we have learnt to distrust the institutions of holiness and wedlock. A 'lock' in this context seems to militate against the ideal of polymorphous liberation in the sexual arena. But Spenser asks us to consider the image of a man and a woman copulating as belonging to the evil pornographic context of the luxurious Roman villa. We recall the devils that Archimago sends to Red Cross to make him 'dreame of loues and lustfull play, / That nigh his manly heart did melt away, / Bathed in wanton blis and wicked ioy' (1.1.47).

Perhaps the devil's view imposes a little too strongly on the Ovidian hermaphrodite as it is represented in Elizabethan poetry. It seems doubtful whether either Spenser or Peend would have endorsed the notion of 'polymorphous liberation,' for example, in connection with the theme. However, works of criticism are not 'only Analytics,' as Blake's poet so scornfully puts it, but also works of faith and inspiration. It is obviously much more cheering to take the romantic view, but let us not lose sight of the more sombre satirical perspective.

NOTES

1 Edmund Spenser, *The Faerie Queene* (1590–1609), 3.12.46, in *The Poetical Works of Edmund Spenser*, ed. J.C. Smith and E. De Selincourt (London: Oxford University Press, 1912). All further references to this text are quoted parenthetically in the main text. Further references are to book, canto, and verse.

2 See James Nohrnberg, *The Analogy of 'The Faerie Queene'* (Princeton: Princeton University Press, 1976), p. 606. The tale of Hermaphroditus and Salmacis is in Ovid's *Metamorphoses*, book IV, ll. 286–414.

3 C.S. Lewis denounced Peend as a 'very, very bad' poet in his *English Literature in the Sixteenth Century* (Oxford: Clarendon Press, 1954), p. 250. A more sym-

pathetic account is given by James H. Runsdorf, 'Transforming Ovid in the 1560s: Thomas Peend's *Pleasant Fable,*' *American Notes and Queries* 5 (1992): 124–7. See also A.B. Taylor, 'Thomas Peend and Arthur Golding,' *Notes and Queries* 12 (1969): 19–20, and his 'A Note on Christopher Marlowe's 'Hero and Leander,' *Notes and Queries* 12 (1969): 20–1.

4 Jonathan Crewe, *Trials of Authorship: Anterior Forms and Poetic Reconstruction from Wyatt to Shakespeare* (Berkeley: University of California Press, 1990), p. 9.

5 Jonathan Bate, *Shakespeare and Ovid* (Oxford: Clarendon Press, 1993), p. 62. All further references to this text are quoted parenthetically in the main text.

6 Of course, much has been written on the hermaphrodite in Spenser. A representative selection might include the following: A.R. Cirillo, 'The Fair Hermaphrodite: Love-Union in the Poetry of Donne and Spenser,' *Studies in English Literature* 9 (1969): 81–95; Donald Cheney, 'Spenser's Hermaphrodite and the 1590 Faerie Queene,' *PMLA* 87 (1972): 192–200; and Lauren Silberman, 'The Hermaphrodite and the Metamorphosis of Spenserian Allegory,' *English Literary Renaissance* 17 (1987): 207–23.

7 Thomas Peend, *The Pleasant Fable of Hermaphroditus and Salmacis* (London: Thomas Colwell, 1565), sig. B2r. All references to signatures in this text are quoted parenthetically in the main text.

8 This figure is taken from p. 11 of the copy of Aneau's revised edition of *Picta poesis* (Lyon: Louis and Charles Pesnot, 1564), located in the Special Collections (Bai 1564 ANE) of the Robinson Library of the University of Newcastle.

9 The text of Ovid's fable is taken from the parallel edition by Donald Hill, ed. & trans., *Ovid: Metamorphoses I–IV* (Warminster: Aries & Phillips, 1985), IV.285–6. The translation deserves to be more widely used, as it is by far the most accurate I have encountered. All further references to this text are quoted parenthetically in the main text by book and line. Unless otherwise stated, all translations of Ovid are from this edition.

10 Marie Delcourt, *Hermaphrodite: Myths and Rites of the Bisexual Figure in Classical Antiquity* (1956; trans. Jennifer Nicholson; London: Studio Books, 1961), p. 54.

11 This point is taken from the second volume of Franz Bömer's commentary on *P. Ovidius Naso: Metamorphosen* (Heidelberg: Carl Winter Universitätsverlag, 1976), p. 131. My debt to Bömer will be apparent in the pages which follow.

12 See Delcourt, *Hermaphrodite,* p. 36.

13 Raphael Regius, ed. *Metamorphoses* (1518), ed. Stephen Orgel (New York & London: Garland, 1976), fol. 62v.

14 The Latin word *impotens* means not only 'impotent,' but also 'unrestrained.' Exorbitant lechery could be regarded as *impotens,* then, because the lecherer has no power over his passions.

15 George Sandys, *Ovid's Metamorphosis Englished, Mythologised, and Represented in Figures* (Oxford: John Lichfield, 1632), p. 161.
16 Gabriel Harvey (and Edmund Spenser), *Two Other Very Commendable Letters* (1580), in *The Poetical Works of Edmund Spenser*, ed. J.C. Smith and E. De Selincourt (London: Oxford University Press, 1912), p. 640.
17 John Milton, *Samson Agonistes* (1671; repr. Menston: Scolar Press, 1968), lines 409–11.
18 Sandys, *Ovid's Metamorphosis*, p. 100.
19 William Shakespeare, *Twelfth Night*, in *The Complete Works: Original-Spelling Edition*, ed. Stanley Wells and Gary Taylor (Oxford: Clarendon Press, 1986), 1.1.20–2.
20 See *OED*, *s.v. lake* 3. The phrase (or collocations with '*loathly*' or '*loathful*') is particularly common as a description of Avernus or Styx in mid-Tudor translations of the classics.
21 George Gascoigne, *The Drum of Doomsday* (1576), in *The Complete Works of George Gascoigne*, ed. John W. Cunliffe (Cambridge: Cambridge University Press, 1907–10), vol. 2, p. 391.
22 Sandys, *Ovid's Metamorphosis*, p. 160 (citing *De rerum natura*, 4.1110–13).
23 Wyndham Lewis, *Malign Fiesta* (1954; repr. London, Calder and Boyar, 1966), pp. 80–1.
24 I should also point out that Peend takes a much lighter view of the perils of sexual intercourse in the 'Pleasant Question' which follows and to some extent cancels his 'Moral.'
25 John Donne, 'The Ecstasy,' in *The Poems of John Donne*, ed. Herbert J.C. Grierson (Oxford: Clarendon Press, 1912), lines 69–70.
26 Cited by William Keach, *Elizabethan Erotic Narratives* (New Brunswick & Hassocks: Harvester, 1977), p. 263, n. 14. My translation.
27 See *OED*, s. v. *soil* §§1 & 2.
28 William Blake, *The Marriage of Heaven and Hell* (1793), in *William Blake's Writings*, ed. G.E. Bentley, Jr (Oxford: Clarendon Press, 1978), vol. 1. p. 91. There are intriguing connections between Blake's piece and Lewis's *Malign Fiesta*. In the devil's imposition on the angel's 'space,' strong monkeys prey upon weak monkeys, 'and with a grinning aspect, first coupled with them & then devourd them.' In the novel, Sammael (*alias* Satan) throws a woman sinner to the primitive satyr-like creatures who rape and devour her (simultaneously).

Ovid and the Dilemma of the Cuckold in English Renaissance Drama

BRUCE BOEHRER

At the climax of his fragmentary *Hero and Leander* (1593), Christopher Marlowe stages the initial sexual encounter between his poem's eponymous lovers, and he stages it as a kind of rape:

> Every kiss to [Hero] was as a charm,
> And to Leander as a fresh alarm.
> ...
> She trembling strove; this strife of hers (like that
> Which made the world) another world begat
> Of unknown joy. Treason was in her thought,
> And cunningly to yield herself she sought.
> Seeming not won, yet won was she at length,
> In such wars women use but half their strength.[1]

This assault comes as the crowning Ovidianism in a poem replete with Ovid; the base-text here, first rendered into English by Marlowe himself some years before the composition of *Hero and Leander*, is *Amores* 1.5. There Ovid describes an assignation with Corinna in much the same terms employed later by Marlowe, terms that construct the sexual encounter as a struggle in which the woman withholds her favours so as, paradoxically, to provoke a more ardent desire:

> I snatched her gown; being thin, the harm was small,
> Yet strived she to be covered therewithal,
> And striving thus as one that would be cast,
> Betrayed herself, and yielded at the last.[2]

Deripui tunicam – nec multum rara nocebat;
  pugnabat tunica sed tamen illa tegi.
quae cum ita pugnaret, tamquam quae vincere nollet,
  victa est non aegre proditione sua.[3]

The correspondence between these two passages – their mutual emphasis upon the idea of feminine self-betrayal and the commonplace of the *bellum amoris* – is only the most obvious aspect of a wide range of Ovidian attitudes toward feminine sexuality and physical constraint, attitudes that surface repeatedly in the literature of the English Renaissance. It is the purpose of this essay to examine these attitudes with particular reference to the Jacobean drama. As recent scholarship has shown, Renaissance poets like Marlowe derive from Ovid a sense of feminine identity as fundamentally split, as a discursive site onto which patriarchal desire projects its own contradictory impulses and behaviours, and clauses like 'victa est ... proditione sua' ('she has been conquered by her own treachery') illustrate the resulting fragmentation of feminine consciousness very clearly.[4] From this view, figures like Marlowe's Hero (and Ovid's Corinna), whose subsidiary social status renders them subject to sexual and economic exploitation, also provide evidence for the construction of a myth of femininity that justifies further exploitation of a similar variety. Hero and Corinna say no to masculine desire (so the story goes), but their eventual acquiescence proves that they never really meant it, and that – by extension – women in general may be defined by their inability to know what they want or say what they mean. Hence Marlowe's aphoristic summation: 'In such wars women use but half their strength.'

The present essay examines a parallel instance of sexual self-contradiction in Ovid and his Renaissance followers, an instance that once again involves the management of feminine sexuality but that is less concerned with constructing an abstract category of the feminine. I wish to focus here upon what I will call the dilemma of the cuckold in Ovidian verse, a dilemma that complements the situation of women in Ovid but that has elicited less scholarly attention, perhaps because it holds less immediate importance for feminist and neo-Marxist literary theories. Put simply, the dilemma of the cuckold is that by marrying, he has in a sense absorbed his wife's defects of character. Unable to correct or to uproot her feminine inconstancy, he becomes a site onto which – in a reversal of the discursive process whereby the category of femininity is itself initially constituted – *she* projects her own innate bad faith. In other words, if femininity itself is a discursive space created through the repression of social contradictions proper to various sorts of patriarchy, the cuckold in turn serves as an exemplary masculine figure for the return of what has been repressed. In what follows, I propose to document this return, first as it operates within Ovid, and then as it reappears in the early English drama, where it receives its most resonant treatment in Middleton's *Chaste Maid in Cheapside* and Jonson's *Volpone.*

1

Ovid's *Amores* celebrate the exploits of a cuckold-maker. Insofar as they have a unifying narrative (and they do not have much of one), Ovid's elegies tell the story of an adulterous seduction – the poet-narrator's conquest of Corinna – and the situational force of many specific poems in the series derives from their unashamed elaborations upon the theme of adultery. Thus, for instance, *Amores* 1.4 instructs Corinna on how to convey secret messages to her lover when at a supper-party in the company of her husband:

> When I (my light) do or say aught that please thee,
> Turn round thy gold ring, as it were to ease thee.
> Strike on the board like them that pray for evil,
> When thou dost wish thy husband at the devil. (1.4.25–8)

> cum tibi, quae faciam, mea lux, dicamve, placebunt,
> versetur digitis anulus usque tuis.
> tange manu mensam, tangunt quo more precantes,
> optabis merito cum mala multa viro.

Again, *Amores* 2.7 defends the narrator against Corinna's suspicions that he has slept with her handmaid. This poem, ironically exploiting the unfaithful wife's fears of her lover's infidelity, is then immediately followed by a secret note to the handmaid in question (*Amores* 2.8), a note in which the narrator wonders how Corinna could have got wind of their liaison. At moments like these, the *Amores* take an especial delight in the perfidies and subterfuges of adulterous love.

Given such a context, Corinna's cuckolded husband can hope for little sympathy and still less respect; he is, at best, a figure of contemptuous fun. *Amores* 1.4 thus opens with the cheerful asseveration, 'Thy husband to a banquet goes with me, / Pray God it may his latest supper be' ('Vir tuus est epulas nobis aditurus easdem – /ultima coena tuo sit, precor, illo viro!' [1.4.1–2]). In similarly derisive fashion, *Amores* 2.12 exults,

About my temples go, triumphant bays!
Conquered Corinna in my bosom lays,
She whom her husband, guard, and gate, as foes,
Lest art should win her, firmly did enclose. (2.12.1–4)

Ite triumphales circum mea tempora laurus!
vicimus: in nostro est, ecce, Corinna sinu,
quam vir, quam custos, quam ianua firma, tot hostes,
servabant, nequa posset ab arte capi!

Indeed, it is no surprise that within the self-glorifying narrative of an adulterous lover, the injured husband may appear both base and ridiculous, nor is it unexpected that the husband in question should be mocked for failing to preserve his wife's chastity. The really remarkable thing in Ovid is the utter inevitability of the cuckold's situation; no matter what he says or does in his efforts to manage his wife's sexuality, he is always in the wrong, and always will be.

Two elegies – *Amores* 2.19 and 3.4 – together provide a clear sense of the cuckold's dilemma in Ovidian amatory verse. On one hand, *Amores* 3.4 mocks as futile a jealous husband's efforts to place his wife in protective custody; on the other hand, *Amores* 2.19 upbraids another husband for not guarding his wife with sufficient vigilance. Between them, these two poems confront the Ovidian world's principal options for coping with a wayward wife, and neither course of action emerges as effective or as attractive. Indeed, the only good news that Ovid's verse offers to wronged husbands is implicit, for the logic rendering one option unsatisfactory is in potential conflict with the logic that opposes the second option. Thus, finally, we may see the Ovidian cuckold's eternal wrongness as a projection of contradictions within the central consciousness, masculine and adulterous, of the *Amores* themselves.

Amores 3.4 mounts an argument that will become axiomatic to early modern English writers: that no amount of masculine surveillance is sufficient to prevent a determined woman from committing adultery, and that any limited fidelity the surveillance may produce is in fact a sham. Ovid makes both of these points early in his poem, admonishing his reader that

'Tis vain thy damsel to commend
To keeper's trust: their wits should them defend.
Who, without fear, is chaste, is chaste in sooth:
Who, because means want, doeth not, she doth.
Though thou her body guard, her mind is stained:
Nor, lest she will, can any be restrained. (3.4.1–6)

Dure vir, inposito tenerae custode puellae
nil agis; ingenio est quaeque tuenda suo.
siqua metu dempto casta est, ea denique casta est;
quae, quia non liceat, non facit, illa facit!
ut iam servaris bene corpus, adultera mens est;
nec custodiri, ne velit, ulla potest.

Ultimately, this argument becomes so pervasive in early English writing that it can detach itself from the immediate question of wifely fidelity and function instead in a metaphorical capacity. Thus it can appear, for instance, as an element of Milton's plea for unlicensed printing in the *Areopagitica*: 'I cannot praise a fugitive and cloistered virtue, unexercised and unbreathed ... That virtue therefore which is but a youngling in the contemplation of evil ... is but a blank virtue, not a pure; her whiteness is but an excremental whiteness.'[5] For Milton, readers are like the wives in Ovid's *Amores* – only truly virtuous if exposed fully to temptation. To seek to preserve their virtue by physical constraint is futile and self-defeating.

Indeed, *Amores* 3.4 continues, not only is physical constraint useless as a guarantor of chastity; it can actually serve as a temptation to vice, for jealousy by nature renders its objects attractive to others:

What's kept, we covet more: the care makes theft;
Few love what others have unguarded left.
...
She is not chaste that's kept, but a dear whore;
Thy fear is than her body valued more.
Although thou chafe, stol'n pleasure is sweet play;
She pleaseth best, 'I fear' if any say. (3.4.25–32)

Quidquid servatur cupimus magis, ipsaque furem
cura vocat; pauci, quod sinit alter, amant.

non proba fit, quam vir servat, sed adultera cara;
  ipse timor pretium corpore maius habet.
indignere licet, iuvat inconcessa voluptas;
  sola placet, 'timeo!' dicere siqua potest.

This insight, in turn, provides the impetus for *Amores* 2.19, in which the poet-narrator tauntingly demands that a cuckolded husband increase the guard upon his wife so as thereby to enhance the speaker's own adulterous pleasure:

What flies I follow, what follows me, I shun.
But thou, of thy fair damsel too secure,
Begin to shut thy house at evening sure.
Search at the door who knocks oft in the dark,
In night's deep silence why the ban-dogs bark.
...
Let this care sometimes bite thee to the quick,
That to deceits it may me forward prick. (2.19.36–44)

  quod sequitur, fugio; quod fugit, ipse sequor.
At tu, formosae nimium secure puellae,
  incipe iam prima claudere nocte forem.
incipe, quis totiens furtim tua limina pulset,
  quaerere, quid latrent nocte silente canes,
...
mordeat ista tuas aliquando cura medullas,
  daque locum nostris materiamque dolis.

In effect, the *Amores* suggest, a cuckold's behaviour is inevitably wrong because it is inevitably inconsequential. Since nothing a husband can do will restrain a wife who is determined to stray, the cuckold functions as a peculiar case of reverse coverture – the legal condition 'of a woman during her married life, when she is ... under the authority and protection of her husband.'[6] Set inescapably at the mercy of his wife, the cuckolded husband may acquiesce to her infidelity with bad grace or with good, but acquiesce he must, and the best advice Ovid can offer a man in this dilemma is to submit good-naturedly:

Kindly thy mistress use, if thou be wise,
Look gently, and rough husbands' laws despise.

Honour what friends thy wife gives, she'll give many;
Least labour so shall win great grace of any;
So shalt thou go with youths to feast together,
And see at home much that thou ne'er brought'st thither. (3.4.43–8)

Si sapis, indulge dominae vultusque severos
exue, nec rigidi iura tuere viri,
et cole quos dederit – multos dabit – uxor amicos.
gratia sic minimo magna labore venit;
sic poteris iuvenum convivia semper inire
et, quae non dederis, multa videre domi.

In essence, the adulterous wife's inalienable control over her own reproductivity comprises the external limit of masculine authority within marriage, and the cuckold, subject to his wife's desire, exists somewhere on the far side of that limit. Hence his eternal inadequacy, and the withering scorn that accompanies it in the works of Ovid: in a sense the cuckold is not simply a failed husband, but an emblem of failed husbandship in general, or, worse yet, an intimation that husbandship can never really succeed on its own terms, as an institution created and upheld by masculine authority.

Given this broad iconic status, it is understandable that the very forms of the cuckold's inadequacy, as set forth in Ovid, should be contradictory and mutually discrediting. If, for instance, the husband of *Amores* 3.4 actually takes Ovid's advice and throws his household open to his wife's suitors, he will realize the condition to which Ovid himself has strenuously objected in *Amores* 2.19, the condition in which an absence of impediments to desire leads to the absence of desire itself. Indeed, Ovid's aphoristic 'Quod sequitur, fugio; quod fugit, ipse sequor' ('what follows, I fly; what flies, I follow in turn') would seem to offer the perfect course of action to a husband intent upon preserving his wife's fidelity; all he needs do is to offer her freely to all comers. But this gesture, the inveterate 'Take my wife – please!' of American stand-up comedy, is unthinkable in the Ovidian universe. Even when the speaker of *Amores* 2.19 threatens to abandon his girlfriend if her husband does not guard her more closely (2.19.47–8), the threat functions as a jocular expression of the unimaginable, for one of the main jobs of the *Amores* is to manufacture a notion of masculinity as boundless desire. This desire – so vast and unmitigated that it even exceeds the limits of the male body (cf., *Amores* 3.7)[7] – defines itself not against its own absence, but against the jealous, ever-desiring impotence that the figure of the cuckold represents. Thus the Ovidian cuckold has no choice but to be eternally, contradictorily wrong, for he exists as the projection of two separate anxieties that Ovid's protagonist-narrator cannot acknowledge as native to his own constitution: first, the anxiety that feminine reproductivity can never be placed under masculine control, and second, the fear that masculine desire, too, is beyond masculine governance. The cuckold neutralizes the former of these anxieties by functioning as an emblem for masculine sexual impotence – as the effeminized masculine figure against which a successful, sexually dominant man defines himself. Likewise, the cuckold responds to the latter anxiety by being eternally jealous, for the idea of a pervasive masculine sexual apathy, even in the case of a failed husband, is anathema to Ovid's verse.

2

In the early English drama, no play better approximates Ovid's contemptuous portrait of the willing cuckold than does Thomas Middleton's *Chaste Maid in Cheapside* (ca. 1612). Indeed, Middleton's character of Master Allwit could be a deliberate response to Ovid's advice that a husband 'honour what friends [his] wife gives.' Thus Allwit introduces himself with a lengthy soliloquy in which he descants upon the material benefits he has realized from his wife's lover:

> I walk out in a morning; come to breakfast,
> Find excellent cheer; a good fire in winter;
> Look in my coal-house about midsummer eve,
> That's full, five or six chaldron new laid up;
> Look in my backyard, I shall find a steeple
> Made up with Kentish faggots, which o'erlooks
> The water-house and the windmills:
> ...
> I see these things, but like a happy man
> I pay for none at all; yet fools think's mine;
> I have the name, and in his gold I shine.[8]

Allwit's situation fulfils the final promise of *Amores* 3.4, the promise that by indulging his wife a husband will discover 'quae non dederi[t], multa ... domi.' As for Allwit himself, he is apparently so taken with the personal comforts generated by his sexual acquiescence that he recognizes no disadvantage whatever to his situation. Quite the contrary, in fact: Allwit imagines himself enriched by his wife's adultery not only in terms of material well-being, but in terms of reputation as well. Thus he congratulates himself on 'pay[ing] for none at all' of his household comforts, and in the next breath he can refer scornfully to the 'fools' who believe him responsible for his own prosperity. For Allwit, in short, wittolry is a wonderful confidence-game, a supremely clever ploy through which the cuckold absorbs both the economic well-being and the honour, the 'gold' and the 'name,' of his wife's seducer.

In this latter respect, Allwit would again seem to be reacting to the wittol's situation as described by Ovid, for Ovid makes a point of observing that the acquiescent cuckold will enjoy a high level of social popularity; as the *Amores* put it, 'gratia sic minimo magna labore venit,' and hence the wittol will find himself a popular guest at dinner parties and similar festivities. But *A Chaste Maid in Cheapside* puts the wickedest possible twist upon the cuckold's popularity. Allwit may imagine that he 'shine[s]' in the 'gold' of his wife's lover, Sir Walter Whorehound, but he is an object of general contempt among the play's other characters. Thus his first appearance onstage – only a few lines before his long, self-congratulatory soliloquy upon the joys of a cuckold's life – is greeted by a serving-man's scornful exclamation, 'Honesty wash my eyes! I have spy'd a wittol' (1.2.1). Later, when the goldsmith Yellowhammer learns of the arrangement between Allwit and Whorehound, he exclaims in disgust, 'What an incomparable wittol's this! ... What a base slave!' (4.1.218–20). And the most memorable scene of Middleton's play is arguably a rewrite of the Ovidian promise that an acquiescent husband will find himself always dining among the young. In the case of Middleton's play, the dinner in question is a christening ceremony, hosted at the Allwit's home, in honour of Mistress Allwit's latest child; the child's natural father, Sir Walter Whorehound, stands as its godfather; and the gathering is not the graceful and witty 'convivi[um] iuvenum' imagined by Ovid, but rather an assembly of sharp-tongued, gluttonous gossips who do not scruple to abuse Allwit in his own presence:

4 GOSSIP. I promise you, a fine gentleman [i.e., Sir Walter] and a courteous.
2 GOSSIP. Methinks her husband shows like a clown to him.
3 GOSSIP. I would not care what clown my husband were too, So I had such fine children. (3.2.29–32)

If this is the cuckold's paradise promised by Ovid to the complaisant husband, one may be excused for declining the proferred delights. But the remarkable thing about Allwit is that he remains highly satisfied with his circumstances. C.S. Lewis once described the discourse of courtly love as 'Ovid misunderstood,'[9] but the phrase may in fact apply even more perfectly to Allwit's character, which is drawn so as to take the advice of *Amores* 3.4 literally, with no awareness of the irony and derision that inform it. And Allwit's general satisfaction, in turn, is made possible by one signal variance from the Ovidian model of cuckoldry – his absolute lack of sexual interest or appetite. This lack, signalled of course by the charactonym 'Allwit' (all mind, no libido) itself, is most manifest in contrast to Sir Walter Whorehound's anxious jealousy. On one hand, Sir Walter is so consumed with sexual possessiveness that he cannot abide the thought of Allwit approaching his own wife ('Yet, by your leave, I heard you were once off'ring/ To go to bed to her' [1.2.94–5]); on the other hand, Allwit exults in his own lack of jealousy – a quality that, like all of the other traditional burdens of a husband, he seems to have passed on wholesale to his wife's paramour:

> These torments stand I freed of; I am as clear
> From jealousy of a wife as from the charge:
> O, two miraculous blessings! 'Tis the knight
> Hath took that labour all out of my hands. (1.2.48–51)

In effect, Allwit has happily developed into a full-blown portrait of the Ovidian wittol because he, Allwit, has failed to grasp the extent to which wittolry effeminizes its subject. In his own self-aggrandizing fantasy life, Allwit imagines himself as co-opting the emblems of Sir Walter Whorehound's masculinity: 'I am like a man / Finding a table furnish'd to his hand' (1.2.11–12); 'I have the name, and in his gold I shine' (1.2.40); 'I live at ease, / He has both the cost and torment' (1.2.53–4). But the price Allwit pays for this fantasy (a price he cannot stand to admit to himself) is the abdication of his own manhood as figured through the exercise of domestic authority in general and sexual authority in particular. He stands bareheaded in Sir Walter's presence, a servant within his own home ('Now a stands bare ...; make the most of him, / He's but one pip above a serving man' [1.2.64–5]), not really even a household dependent, but rather the dependent of a dependent – his wife. Where he imagines that he has miraculously encompassed Sir Walter's income and reputation, surrounding circumstances suggest a contrary arrangement: one in which his own masculine status has been encompassed and obliterated by his wife's infidelity. Thus, if Allwit's lack of jealousy differentiates him from the pattern of the Ovidian cuckold, it ultimately reveals a model of unmanliness that Ovid's verse cannot bring itself to imagine: a model in which the cuckold himself is oblivious to just how completely his own identity depends upon his ability to control his wife's sexual behaviour.

3

If *A Chaste Maid in Cheapside* notably reworks the standard of acquiescent cuckoldry advocated by Ovid's *Amores* 3.4, Ben Jonson's *Volpone* (1606) offers a similarly remarkable embellishment upon the jealous cuckoldry encouraged in *Amores* 2.19. In the case of *Volpone*, moreover, the debt to Ovid is manifest and deliberate, perhaps most obviously so in Volpone's proposal that he and Celia should 'in changed shapes, act OVIDS tales'[10] while cuckolding Celia's husband, Corvino. But it is Corvino himself who embodies the mocking attitude towards husbandly jealousy projected by *Amores* 2.19. Taken together, Allwit and Corvino thus refigure the opposing horns of the Ovidian cuckold's dilemma; the former abdicates his manhood by surrendering his sexual identity, whereas the latter clings so tightly to his masculine prerogatives that those prerogatives themselves prove his undoing.

In part, at least, Corvino's problem arises from the fact that his masculine prerogatives are themselves fundamentally contradictory, and one of Jonson's great achievements in *Volpone* is arguably that he has recognized the nature and extent of this contradiction. On one level, the conflict is purely libidinal; as Katharine Maus has observed, 'The cuckold is entranced by the scene of his own betrayal,'[11] which constitutes both a titillating enactment of voyeuristic fantasy and a humiliating displacement from the sexual scene. Corvino is a classic case in point; on one hand, his character displays a positively febrile interest in the 'sports' his wife might enjoy behind his back, an interest that even leads him, in a court of law and before a tribunal of judges, to fabricate the details of a cuckoldry that never occurs:

> This woman (please your father-hoods) is a whore,
> Of most hot exercise ...
>
> I may say, these eyes
> Haue seene her glew'd vnto that peece of cedar,

That fine well-timber'd gallant: and ... here,
The letters may be read, thorough the horne,
That make the story perfect. (4.5.117–26)

On the other hand, however, Corvino's erotic fascination with his own cuckoldry is counterbalanced by rampant jealousy. Thus, after the famous scene in which Volpone impersonates a mountebank in order to get a glimpse of Celia from her bedroom window, and in which Celia encourages his attentions by dropping her handkerchief as a favour, Corvino promises to shackle his wife within a windowless room:

First, I will haue this bawdy light dam'd up;
...
Then, here's a locke, which I will hang vpon thee;
And, now I thinke on't, I will keep thee backe-wards;
Thy lodging shall be backe-wards; thy walkes back-wards;
Thy prospect – all be backe-wards; and no pleasure,
That thou shalt know, but backe-wards. (2.5.50–61)

It is no accident that Corvino's jealous fantasy of physical confinement should culminate in a thinly veiled threat of anal penetration; in Corvino's character, erotic excitement gives birth to jealous fear which in turn generates more erotic excitement.

This contradictory libidinal investment, in turn, is paralleled by broader contradictions in Corvino's exercise of husbandly and paternal authority. Celia is not only an erotic object for him; she is also a member of his family – a word *Volpone* employs in its Latin legal sense of 'household' or 'estate'[12] – and to this extent she is the most notable part of her husband's 'fortune' (1.5.81). Libidinal and economic investments merge, for Corvino, in the figure of his wife, who therefore becomes a test case for his ability to control his estate in general. When told that a certain physician has offered his daughter to Volpone in an attempt to revive the supposed invalid, Corvino himself frames the matter as a challenge to his own authority: 'Wherefore should not I / As well command my bloud, and my affections, / As this dull Doctor?' (2.6.70–2). Just as, on the erotic level, Corvino is both fascinated with and horrified by the prospect of his own cuckoldry, on the domestic level he seeks to control his wife both by keeping her entirely for himself and by putting her to public use. Thus, while pushing her into Volpone's bedroom, he can exhort her, 'If you bee / Loyall, and mine, be wonne, respect my venture' (3.7.36–7).

In a sense, Corvino's plight is the *reductio ad absurdum* of paternal absolutism. Pursuing an unattainable ideal of complete control over his estate, he is forced into a conundrum: can a husband prostitute his wife's chastity without making himself cuckold? This paradox – of the can-God-make-a-boulder-too-big-for-God-to-lift variety – generates growing anxiety in Corvino, who therefore casts about uneasily for reassurance: 'The thing, in't selfe, / I know, is nothing' (2.6.69–70); 'There is no shame in this, now, is there?' (4.5.127). Moreover, as a final irony, Corvino himself has been told that the ideal he is pursuing is unattainable: there is no such thing as *absolute* husbandly authority. He confesses as much to his own wife, in words that take *Amores* 3.4.6 ('Nec custodiri, ne velit, ulla potest') as their *locus classicus*:

> Doe not I know, if women haue a will,
> They'll doe 'gainst all the watches, o' the world?
> And that the fiercest spies, are tam'd with gold? (2.7.8–10)

Corvino, of course, is his own 'fiercest spie,' unmindful of the extent to which he himself has been 'tam'd with gold' through the offer of Volpone's inheritance. This lack of self-awareness, in turn, signals the extent to which the wisdom Corvino quotes remains unassimilated to his character; it is inert matter, irrelevant to the operations of his own jealousy and greed.

In other words, Corvino has never really learned the lesson that Ovid seeks to impress upon the addressee of *Amores* 3.4 – that in the end, a wife's reproductivity is beyond her husband's governance. Instead, Corvino remains steadfastly in the position that Ovid urges upon the husband of *Amores* 2.19. Bricking up windows and purchasing chastity belts, Corvino pursues a vision of husbandly security that simply does not exist, and in pursuing this vision he displays his own folly for the entertainment and enrichment of others. He too, like Allwit in *A Chaste Maid in Cheapside*, must watch his pretensions to independent manhood vanish, absorbed into a femininity that both encompasses and escapes it. To this extent, the figures of Corvino and Allwit recapitulate and enlarge disparate patterns of masculine anxiety explored by Ovid in the *Amores*.

4

Although Ovid's *Amores* dwell consistently upon the themes of love and adultery, they do not in fact have a single, continuous narrative line. *Amores* 2.19 and 3.4 offer a case in point; although they deal with the same general subject – how a husband should behave when his wife is being seduced – they give entirely different advice and therefore presuppose different audiences and situations. Indeed, some of their humour may derive from this discontinuity; as readers move from *Amores* 2.19 to 3.4, they may appreciate the cynical opportunism with which the poems' central consciousness modifies his language and strategies. In effect, the poet-narrator of the *Amores* tells different lies to different husbands. He encourages the husband of *Amores* 2.19 in the specious fantasy that wifely fidelity can be manufactured by physical constraint – that if one can only guard one's wife closely and jealously enough, one can transform her into the paragon of women and oneself into the happiest of men. To the husband of *Amores* 3.4, on the other hand, Ovid offers a different untruth: the notion that his wife's sexual behaviour is of no consequence whatever to his identity and reputation, except insofar as her infidelity may secure him the occasional dinner invitation.

These two lies in turn are both attractive because, despite their extreme dissimilarity of circumstance, they hold out the same promise. They both operate as fantasies of independence, in which an injured husband can recover his sense of self-sufficiency either through acts of discipline and surveillance or through parallel gestures of indifference and escape. In constructing the figures of Corvino and Allwit, Jonson and Middleton explore these two fantasies and suggest the extent to which they may be equally unattainable. Thus it is perhaps inevitable that Jonson and Middleton should both revise Ovid by taking the advice given in *Amores* 2.19 and 3.4, respectively, to its apparent extreme. For Jonson's Corvino, the fantasy of total husbandly control collapses into a self-discrediting conundrum, because any husbandly authority that is really total will sooner or later be called upon to transgress its own logic and limits. For Middleton's Allwit, likewise, the idea that a husband can hold himself aloof from his wife's infidelity is equally untenable, given the social grounding of marriage and masculinity.

To this extent Jonson's Corvino and Middleton's Allwit are virtually unique dramatic characters; they unambiguously embody the most extreme possible formulations of cuckoldry-anxiety to be encountered on the early English stage. Yet in another respect, these characters remain impressively typical, for they illustrate, in its purest and most diametrically opposed forms, the most pervasive and paradigmatic sexual concern of their day. This essay scarcely needs to register the ubiquity of the cuckold's horns in early modern cultural expression; students of the

Renaissance encounter them everywhere, in visual art and literary representation, historical event and legal records. On the stage alone, one can scarcely encounter a play of the period that does not contain some form of nervous response to the cuckold's dilemma. As a parallel to Jonson's Corvino, for instance, we may consider the situation of Francis Ford in Shakespeare's *Merry Wives of Windsor* (1597). Ford is so haunted by the possibility of wifely infidelity that spousal surveillance becomes an *idée fixe* for him. Thus, between disguised reconnaissance missions, he ridicules the trusting nature of other husbands, most particularly his neighbour George Page: 'Page is an ass, a secure ass; he will trust his wife, he will not be jealous. I will rather trust a Fleming with my butter, Parson Hugh the Welshman with my cheese, an Irishman with my aqua-vitae bottle, or a thief to walk my ambling gelding, than a wife with herself.'[13]

For one recent scholar, Ford's ridiculous suspicion illustrates his 'miserliness' rather than any particular 'erotic energy,'[14] and to this extent it becomes worthy of comparison to Corvino's similarly acquisitive jealousy. Likewise, the complacent openness of Middleton's Allwit meets its like in the credulous Camillo of Webster's *White Devil* (1611). Fearful, like Ford, of cuckoldry ('You know not where my nightcap wrings me'),[15] Camillo nonetheless unwittingly contributes to his wife's adultery by allowing himself to be locked into his own bedroom while she is given full freedom of movement. The reason? As Camillo's brother-in-law, the pander Flamineo, explains, spousal surveillance is the surest way to encourage infidelity:

> Women are more willingly and more gloriously chaste, when they are least restrained of their liberty ... These politic enclosures for paltry mutton makes more rebellion in the flesh than all the provocative electuaries doctors have uttered since last Jubilee. (1.2.90–6)

Thus Camillo discovers, like Ovid's dupes before him, that there is no completely reliable way to manage feminine sexuality, nor any surety for wifely chastity.

But perhaps the most curious and resonant restatement of such themes occurs not in the early modern English drama, but rather in the dramatic arena of the early modern English courtroom. I refer to that most protracted and ugly of Jacobean sex scandals – the 1613 wedding of Frances Howard, formerly Countess of Essex, to Robert Carr, Viscount Rochester, with all that the wedding entailed. There is no space here for a detailed discussion of the event;[16] in brief, however, the union between Howard and Carr was impeded by the notorious fact of Howard's prior wedding (in 1609) to Robert Devereux, third Earl of Essex. This match, originally prompted by political considerations, seems to have repelled Howard from the moment of its inception, and her response to it was twofold: first, she stubbornly refused to have conjugal relations with her husband, and second, she pursued a variety of extramarital flirtations, culminating in the public spectacle of an adulterous affair with Carr. Faced with such wifely misbehaviour, Essex responded with the full range of tactics recommended by Ovid. To begin with, he sought to prevent sexual mischief by placing his wife under guard, even going to such lengths as to sequester her in his country estate at Chartley; these efforts failing, he then resorted to the opposite extreme of allowing her to reside independently, in a separate household. Predictably, neither of these expedients contained the growing scandal, and thus, in the end, Essex had no choice but to sue for marital annulment on the grounds of non-consummation. Nor was this a satisfactory solution to his problem; on the contrary, it had the unfortunate effect of turning Essex into a public laughing-stock, reputedly both impotent and cuckold, a walking embodiment of the Ovidian husband's eternal and contradictory wrongness. In literary cases such as those of Webster, Shakespeare, Jonson, and Middleton, and in historical situations like that of Essex, we may glimpse the pervasive influence of sexual attitudes and concerns elaborated compellingly in the *Amores.*

If Ovid is so central to early modern constructions of sexuality, in turn, that is arguably because his work articulates a sexual unease that exceeds the poet's own attempts to contain it. Thus Ovid's treatment of cuckoldry consistently assumes that husbands are conflicted and dependent, and the *Amores* use this insight as the basis for offering tongue-in-cheek advice on how to deal with wifely infidelity. Yet Jonson and Middleton, on the other hand, construct dramatic characters who take Ovid's advice in deadly earnest and carry it to extremes not imagined in Ovid's own verse. In the process, these characters act out an anxiety that the central consciousness of the *Amores* exists to deny: the anxiety that masculinity itself might be an unattainable fantasy, an ideal of self-containment and self-control whose indices – wifely chastity and masculine libido – are always beyond one's management. In short, Jonson and Middleton suggest that the cuckold's dilemma is not at all unique: it is, in its broadest and simplest terms, the dilemma of being a man.

NOTES

1 *Hero and Leander*, sestiad 2, ll. 283–96, in *Christopher Marlowe: The Complete Poems and Translations*, ed. Stephen Orgel (New York: Penguin, 1979).

2 Ovid's *Elegies*, 1.5.13–16, in *Christopher Marlowe: The Complete Poems and Translations*, ed. Stephen Orgel (New York: Penguin, 1979). Further references to the *Amores* in English will be to this translation, and identified by book, poem, and lines.

3 *Amores*, 1.5.13–16, in *Ovid: Heroides and Amores*, trans. Grant Showerman, The Loeb Classical Library (Cambridge, MA: Harvard University Press, and London: William Heinemann, 1977). Further references to the Latin text of Ovid will be to this edition.

4 I acknowledge the help of Geraldine Thomas with this translation. For two well-known applications of this argument to the early English drama, see Jonathan Dollimore, *Radical Tragedy: Religion, Ideology and Power in the Drama of Shakespeare and His Contemporaries* (Chicago: University of Chicago Press, 1984), esp. pp. 40–50; and Catherine Belsey, *The Subject of Tragedy: Identity and Difference in Renaissance Drama* (London: Methuen, 1985), esp. pp. 149–91. As Belsey summarizes, 'The justification of the absolutist definition of marriage is the frailty of women' (p. 168).

5 John Milton, *Areopagitica*, in *John Milton: Complete Poems and Major Prose*, ed. Merritt Hughes (Indianapolis: Odyssey, 1957), p. 728.

6 *OED*, s.v. Coverture 9. For a recent application of the legal theory of coverture to the drama of the English Renaissance, see Frances Dolan, *Whores of Babylon: Catholicism, Gender, and Seventeenth-Century Print Culture* (Ithaca: Cornell University Press, 1999), pp. 61–75.

7 For a discussion of *Amores* 3.7 as an expression of masculine literary and erotic anxieties, see Bruce Boehrer, 'Behn's "Disappointment" and Nashe's "Choise of Valentines": Pornographic Poetry and the Influence of Anxiety,' *Essays in Literature* 16.2 (1989): 172–87.

8 Thomas Middleton, *A Chaste Maid in Cheapside*, ed. R.B. Parker (London: Methuen, 1969), 1.2.22–40. Further references are to this edition.

9 C.S. Lewis, *The Allegory of Love: A Study in Medieval Tradition* (Oxford: Clarendon Press, 1936), p. 7.

10 Ben Jonson, *Volpone*, 3.7.221, in *Ben Jonson*, ed. C.H. Herford and Percy and Evelyn Simpson, 11 vols. (Oxford: Clarendon, 1925–52), vol. 5. Further references are to this edition.

11 Katharine Maus, 'Horns of Dilemma: Jealousy, Gender, and Spectatorship in English Renaissance Drama,' *ELH* 54.3 (1987): 566.

12 *Oxford Latin Dictionary* s.v. 'Familia' 1 and 6. As Friedrich Engels noted (*The Origin of the Family, Private Property, and the State,* in *The Marx-Engels Reader,* ed. Robert C. Tucker [New York: Norton, 1978], p. 737), 'Famulus means a household slave and familia signifies the totality of slaves belonging to one individual. Even in the time of Gaius, the familia, id est patrimonium (that is, the inheritance) was bequeathed by will.' For examples of this usage in *Volpone,* see 1.3.34–5; 1.5.46–9; 5.4.14.

13 William Shakespeare, *The Merry Wives of Windsor,* 2.2.300–5, in *The Riverside Shakespeare,* ed. G. Blakemore Evans et al. (Boston: Houghton Mifflin, 1997).

14 Grace Tiffany, *Erotic Beasts and Social Monsters: Shakespeare, Jonson, and Comic Androgyny* (Newark: University of Delaware Press, 1995), p. 148.

15 John Webster, *The White Devil,* ed. John Russell Brown (London: Methuen, 1960), 1.2.87. Further references are to this edition.

16 For readable accounts of the Essex annulment and Carr's courtship and marriage of Howard, see Anne Somerset, *Unnatural Murder: Poison at the Court of James I* (London: Weidenfeld and Nicolson, 1997), esp. pp. 98–141; Edward Le Comte, *The Notorious Lady Essex* (New York: Dial, 1969), pp. 33–135; and Vernon Snow, *Essex the Rebel: The Life of Robert Devereux, Third Earl of Essex* (Lincoln: University of Nebraska Press, 1970), pp. 9–70.

PART III

Textualization

Lyrical Wax in Ovid, Marlowe, and Donne

RAPHAEL LYNE

In his book *Writing Matter* Jonathan Goldberg advocates working towards a 'cultural graphology,' which aims to evaluate how available technology and materials affect the writing and thought of a period.[1] A similar approach has been adopted very suggestively in Jocelyn Penny Small's work on memory and literacy in the classical world, which shows how tools and writing surfaces defined the tasks required and achieved. One of the important tools she discusses is the wax tablet, citing examples of writers comparing the act of memorization to making impressions on wax.[2] From a literary perspective the wax tablet is of interest because it is frequently depicted, in Latin love poetry, as the vector for the lovers' messages. The materials of writing are not necessarily the mundane starting points from which poetry ascends, and in Ovid especially the wax can assume considerable importance as its properties reflect the emotional dynamics of the poem (and vice versa). This essay will look at what happens to this literary feature of a 'cultural graphology' when a text is imitated or translated. What happens, in the Ovidian poems of Marlowe and Donne, when the wax arrives in a culture of ink and paper? In Ovid's poetry the physical nature of wax leads to an implicit connection with bodies and their warmth and pliability; the texture of the surface is a starting point for evoking a physically intimate poetry, the immediacy of which is reflected in the marks on the wax. This corporeal connection also finds counterparts in English imitations.

Wax features in Ovid's epic *Metamorphoses* at two important junctures which provide a link between writing and the body. One is during Pythagoras's speech (XV.165–72), where the preservation of the soul's constancy, despite its change of shape, is likened to the moulding of wax. The philosopher's oration offers a picture of a world of constant change, one which relates in complex ways to the metamorphoses which happen throughout Ovid's poem. If wax represents an analogy of metamorphoses, it may also represent an analogy of the *Metamorphoses*, and a metaphor for the shaping of the poem in all its variety. Ovid also seems to use wax to evoke the act of poetic creation in the story of Pygmalion, where the transformation of his statue is likened to the moulding of wax. Pygmalion is a sculptor and the tactile image is therefore all the more appropriate:

> temptatum mollescit ebur positoque rigore
> subsidit digitis ceditque, ut Hymettia sole
> cera remollescit tractataque pollice multas
> flectitur in facies ipsoque fit utilis usu. (X.283–6)[3]

> [The ivory grew soft to his touch and, its hardness vanishing, gave and yielded beneath his fingers, as Hymettian wax grows soft under the sun and, moulded by the thumb, is easily shaped to many forms and becomes usable through use itself.]

This simile transcends the scene of wonderful transformation with the idyllic vision of a bee-covered mountainside, but it continues in a way which leaves a problematic residue: the statue is likened to wax which becomes 'utilis usu.' This captures the subtext to this story that Pygmalion's idealized bride is a conveniently passive vehicle for his desire – something designed to be used, not loved. Also, there is the connection of flesh, supple and soft, with wax, and again the connection of creation with wax. The personae of love elegy and the creative action of Pygmalion have been connected by A.R. Sharrock, who sees the statue as a refraction of the love object of Latin love poetry. In the comic aspects of Pygmalion's devotion (for instance, in lavishing gifts on the statue) and in the self-obsession of the hero's love for his creation, there may be a reflection on the circular interests of poetry like the *Amores*.[4]

In Ovid's love poetry wax, the usual writing surface, is connected to the act of creation, the physical nature of the body, and the urgent sexual desire of the poet. It is most prominent in *Amores* 1.11 and 1.12, paired poems about the giving and receipt of a set of 'tabellae' (wax writing tablets). They start on familiar territory (as in *Amores* 1.6 and 2.3), with Ovid demanding a servant's help:

accipe et ad dominam peraratas mane tabellas
  perfer et obstantes sedula pelle moras! ...
si quaeret quid agam, spe noctis vivere dices;
  cetera fert blanda cera notata manu. (1.11.7–8, 13–14)[5]

[Receive and take early to your mistress these tablets I have inscribed, and care that nothing hinder or delay! ... Should she ask how I fare, you will say my hope of her favour lets me live; as for the rest, it is charactered in the wax by my fond hand.]

She is to carry the reply to Corinna's imagined question as to Ovid's welfare, and the wax tablets which will themselves carry a vague message: 'cetera,' 'other things.' These 'cetera' are imprinted on the wax of the tablet with a 'blanda manu.' The adjective 'blandus' can simply mean 'fond,' but it also has a sense of 'fondling,' 'caressing.' The wax will show the stroked words, softened by a passionate heat. The properties of wax as a surface for writing draw the poet towards the idea of intimate expression. In the advice for users of 'tabellae' in Ovid's *Ars Amatoria*, as well as describing the dangers involved, Ovid says wax is 'conscia mentis,' a reliable index of the lover's mind, and must try the way on his behalf, acting like a lover ('imitataque amantem').[6] The physicality of writing love poetry on wax is also seen in the distinctive word 'peraratas' ('ploughed' or 'furrowed').[7] *Amores* 1.11 continues with Ovid urging Nape to make Corinna answer. He impresses upon her the urgency of the situation and of the messages contained (ll. 15–18), and requests a reply:

nec mora, perlectis rescribat multa, iubeto;
  odi, cum late splendida cera vacat.
conprimat ordinibus versus, oculosque moretur
  margine in extremo littera rasa meos. (1.11.19–22)

[And do not wait, but bid her write much in answer when she has read; I hate when a fine, fair page [literally, wax] is widely blank. See she pack the lines together, and long detain my eyes with letters traced on the outermost marge.]

The word 'versus' offers the idea that the elegiac poet may be sending a verse message (as he often does, as in 2.1 and 3.1), although it does not necessarily make this the case, since there are hints that his message is of a more direct and pragmatic kind.[8] Having made a pseudo-emotional impression on the wax with his warm, caressing hand, Ovid has ironically high hopes for the immediacy of its effect. His belief that as long a reply as possible would be better does not last: at the end of *Amores* 1.11 all he wants is one imperative word: 'veni' ('come!'). The brief command is the antithesis of poetic eloquence, an ironic counterpart to the overall mood of the *Amores*, in which the power of poetry is so evident. In this Ovid extends an irony present in Propertius 3.23, in which another poet loses his 'tabellae.'[9]

Ovid continues the story of his 'tabellae' in *Amores* 1.12 with their return, and his request for an assignation is refused. The poem rails against the wax tablets themselves, seeing something pernicious in every part of them, contrasting the everyday nature of the wax tablets with the importance of their message (ll. 21–6).[10] The wax comes from poor quality bees visiting poisonous flowers and it is tinted with blood, while the wood comes from a tree crowded with dubious omens (ll. 7–20). In line 21 he calls the writings on the tablets 'amores,' which could be the loves of his life, or the Loves that are the *Amores* – a question on which critics differ. Duncan Kennedy says the word 'renders the act of making love and the act of writing about it open to being seen as manifestations of a single sphere of activity.'[11] This is in opposition to Gordon Williams, who sees simply 'love-messages' scratched in the wax.[12] There is no prompt from Ovid for a reader to resolve an ambiguity in this way – it is a paradox which is central and intriguing. *Amores* 1.12 ends with a reference to the construction of the 'tabellae' from two hinged wooden leaves ('duplices'), and in this is seen the origin of their duplicitous nature (ll. 27–30). After all, for a poet apparently so keen on his posterity, wax itself is a curious place on which to picture himself writing, given its capacity to hold dangerous earlier messages and to lose the poet's own so quickly.[13] Ovid's *Amores* depict a world of words, and Ovid takes an interest in the material on which they appear – in his own 'cultural graphology.' The wood of the tablet proves fertile, but it is the wax which elicits a repertoire of ideas which prove challenging to imitators in a different culture.

When Christopher Marlowe translated Ovid's *Amores* 1.11 and 1.12, he transformed the wax tabellae into leaves of paper. At times Marlowe preserves features of the tabellae which seem out of place once the presence of paper and pen is established; at others he resolves potential dissonances. The 'tabellas' of 1.11.7 are rendered as 'lines': 'Receive these lines, them to my Mistrisse carry.' The English word need not necessarily denote lines of verse, but that meaning is present.[14] The movement between writing cultures is more complete in line 14, where the 'cera notata manu' changes:

> If, what I do, she askes, say hope for night
> The rest my hand doth in my letters write. (1.11.13–14)[15]

The 'hand' is preserved, but now it writes as if on paper rather than wax. The adjective 'blanda,' which provided a tactile edge to Ovid's depiction of the wax tablets, is not translated by Marlowe. Something is lost with the disappearance of waxiness as the paper and pen take over. Marlowe tends to use 'lines' to translate 'tabellae' when it concerns a message between lovers. He does this at 2.5.5 and 2.19.41, and at 3.13.31 he wonders 'why see I lines [for 'tabellas'] so oft receiv'd and given.'[16] As 1.11 continues Marlowe moves closer than Ovid towards placing these 'lines' in a poem, and the importance of the new medium grows:

> Straight being read, will her to write much backe,
> I hate fair Paper should writte matter lacke.
> Let her make verses, and some blotted letter,
> On the last edge to stay mine eyes the better. (1.11.19–22)

The 'verses' of line 21 match 'versus' in Ovid, but they contain a more concrete sense of poems being written. In Latin 'versus' has the same range of possible meanings as the English 'line,' while English 'verses' are more directly literary. The commentaries of Dominicus and Micyllus state that poetry is not necessarily implied by this line in the *Amores*, and that Ovid wishes to depict the packed lines of epistolary script.[17] Marlowe, though, seems to recognize the poetic origin of the imagined interaction between Ovid and Corinna, and preserves it. The most concrete change is that 'splendida cera' becomes 'fair Paper.' The whiteness of the page, contrasted with the blackness of the ink, is a symbol of purity which clashes with the preference the poet has for a surface blackened with words. Marlowe does not simply ask for a well-filled page in return, as Ovid does (filled 'margine in extremo'). He asks for her to write up to the edge and then put in a 'blotted letter.' The overflow of ink acts as a metaphor for the hoped-for overflow of passion.[18]

While writing on wax is effectively replaced, Marlowe does not effect a complete transposition between cultures. Other aspects of the Latin medium are handled differently. 1.11 continues as follows:

> What neede she tyre her hand to hold the quill,
> Let this word, come, alone the tables fill.
> Then with triumphant laurell will I grace them
> And in the midst of Venus temple place them.
> Subscribing that to her I consecrate
> My faithfull tables being vile maple late. (1.11.23–8)

An Ovidian 'graphium' becomes a 'quill,' but the end of 1.11 sees a movement back towards the Latin object, even including the fact that the tabellae are made of maple wood.[19] This detail interrupts the replacement of wax tablets with ink and paper, but the incongruity is partly resolved by the connection provided through the 'tables.' In English this word retains its etymological connection to the Latin 'tabellae,' and can denote a two-sided tablet for writing, much like Ovid's. Also, though, it can mean a notebook of less specifically Latin style. The *Oxford English Dictionary* derives the relevant meaning of 'table' from the Latin 'tabula,' although its predominantly plural appearances show that 'tabellae' are another origin. The entry in Cooper's Thesaurus for 'tabellae' is 'A table to write in: a littell table,' and this is qualified by reference to the *Amores* and *Ars.*[20] In the commentary of Dominicus which appeared in some editions there is a lengthy explanation printed alongside 1.11.7 which traces their use back to times long before Homer, and cites Ovid and Propertius for Roman descriptions. Marlowe's imaginatively inconsistent response reflects the fact that 'tables' (like Hamlet's) and 'tabellae' are objects at home in both past and present. Throughout the *Elegies* translation Marlowe combines moments of English colour with exact preservation of Latin details, as in his preservation of the joke about losing a foot of the pentameter line in 1.1.5–8, even in couplets with lines of equal length. Lee Pearcy has noticed that Marlowe sometimes tends towards an exaggerated Latinity, as when he occasionally employs a convoluted Latin-sounding word order not derived from the Latin original.[21] Roma Gill praises a maverick technique's 'schoolboy howlers ... Marlowe sticks closest to his text when he is least interested in its subject.'[22] She echoes here the received wisdom that such a close translation (matching line for line) probably dates from the poet's student days.[23]

When the tabellae return at the beginning of 1.12 it seems that the moment of 'maple' Latinity has been temporarily forgotten. Marlowe translates 'tabellae' as 'booke' (l. 1) although he is faithful to all the other details of the lover's advice to the servant. The passing of messages seems to remind him of a more English-style passing of poems, but he does not follow this through by altering the physical characteristics of the tabellae when Ovid mentions them in detail. The presence of wood, and cleverly altered wax, returns as 1.12 continues:

Hence luck-lesse tables, funerall wood be flying
And thou the waxe stuft full with notes denying.
Which I thinke gather'd from cold hemlocks flower
Wherein bad hony Corsicke Bees did power.
Yet as if mixt with red leade thou wert ruddy,
That colour rightly did appeare so bloudy. (1.12.7–12)

Now 'tabellae' are 'tables' again and they are made of 'funerall wood.' For once, the wax is mentioned, but line 8 seems to separate it from the writing itself. For the wax to be 'stuft full with notes denying' opens the possibility that it is a seal.[24] This makes more sense of the exaggerated redness of Marlowe's 'ruddy' and 'bloudy' wax, which is not faintly blushing like Ovid's. The seal motif reappears in 2.15, in which Ovid imagines being Corinna's ring, and describes himself sealing 'tabellae': Marlowe substitutes sealed papers (ll. 15–16). *Amores* 1.12 continues with Ovid hurling abuse at his tabellae and finding every part of them full of ominous history. Marlowe's version again preserves Latin detail – 'evill wood' (l. 13) – which is inconsistent with his introduction of paper and ink. The final complaints show Marlowe's translation at its best, embellishing Ovid:

To these my love I foolishly committed
And them with sweete words to my Mistrisse fitted.
More fitly had they wrangling bondes contained
From barbarous lips of some Atturney strained,
Among day bookes and billes they had laine better
In which the Merchant wayles his banquerout debter,
Your name approves you made for such like things
The number two no good divining bringes.
Angry, I pray that rotten age you wrackes,
And sluttish white-mould overgrowe the waxe. (1.12.21–30)

Marlowe is not tempted by the 'amores' of line 21, and chooses a generalized 'love' rather than poetic 'Loves.' More expansive is the line, 'In which the Merchant wayles his banquerout debter,' which is freer than most of the *Elegies* translation and introduces a new character to the sordid story of the tabellae. The poem ends ambiguously with an incongruous reference to the two leaves of the tabellae, and it is still not easy to define what the 'waxe' is. When Ovid's tabellae are given concrete physical characteristics in Latin these are mostly kept by Marlowe. At some points, though, the attraction of his own ink-based culture makes him depict the messages sent by Ovid on leaves of paper. The messages are also made more clearly into poems by Marlowe, as the idea that Ovid could send anything other than poems to Corinna is apparently inconceivable. Throughout his *Elegies* – the first verse translation of the *Amores* in any vernacular – he creates a version which combines vibrant excursions into contemporary scenery with rigorous adhesion to some local details of Latin culture.

Donne's amatory poems take Marlowe's transformations a stage further and in his poems it is the corporeal associations of the wax, rather than a cultural graphology, which come to the fore. Ovid is by no means their only source but discernibly Ovidian features are evident, and Donne often creates something very original from his source material.[25] One possible reaction to classical elegy and to Ovid is the fact that verbal communication between lovers is far less productive in Donne's poems than secret signs and nonverbal codes. Indeed, the appearance of the poet's writings (whether letters or poems) is always after the love has ended – in 'Valedictions,' for example. Behind Donne in his predilection for secretive communication lie numerous episodes in Latin elegy. In Ovid's *Amores* 1.4 and 2.5 the poet describes the cunning nods and signs which lovers can share at the dinner table, but Ovid never relinquishes the power of language to persuade and to shape the world, and it is this which Donne undermines. That Donne differs from Ovid in his moments of more desperate passion has been noted with regard to his debt to Propertius, and his difference in attitude to secret signs should be noted with regard to Tibullus.[26] Behind 'Elegie VII; Nature's lay Ideot,' for example, lies Tibullus's 1.6, although Helen Gardner and J.B. Leishman understate its place.[27] It describes a feeling of resentment as the woman deceives the poet with his own tricks (ll. 9–20). Ovid's *Amores* 1.4 describes a scene of teaching, but Tibullus gives Donne his precedent in showing the lessons rebound on the teacher.

Many of Donne's *Elegies* show lovers employing deceitful signs rather than words, like the 'becks, winks, looks' and 'dialogues with our feet' of 'Elegie XII: His parting from her' (ll. 51–2).[28] When, for example, 'sonnets' appear, in 'The Canonization' (l. 32), and 'Elegie X: The Dreame' (l. 19) they are not part of a vital, thriving love: they are a dream, or a memory of the past. The victory of codes over words is complete in the Tibullan 'Nature's lay Ideot':

> I had not taught thee then, the Alphabet
> Of flowers, how they devisefully being set
> And bound up, might with speechlesse secrecie
> Deliver arrands mutely, and mutually. (ll. 9–12)[29]

The phonetic closeness of 'speechlesse' and 'secrecie' displays a natural contiguity. That between 'mutely' and mutually,' though, is more notable since it enacts the affinity that these apparently contradictory terms enjoy in Donne's new linguistic order. The gentleness of these flowers and their aura of innocence stand in effective contrast to their secretive purpose. Thomas Docherty usefully introduces the themes of Frank Kermode's *The Genesis of Secrecy* while describing this form of communication.[30] Docherty sees a concealed meaning in the 'Alphabet of flowers' (which seems not to describe more usual means of attributing symbolic meaning to particular flowers), one which is only revealed to those already in the know. All they can do is remind the recipient of a union already established.

Donne's narrator recalls a past of malleable innocence which was only briefly improved by his teachings. When things leave his control he turns to wax as a potent image. In doing so, however, he does not effect anything like Marlowe's partial Englishing in 'Elegy VII: Nature's Lay Ideot':

> Thy graces and good words my creatures bee,
> I planted knowledge and lifes tree in thee,
> Which Oh, shall strangers taste? Must I alas
> Frame and enamell Plate, and drinke in glasse?
> Chafe waxe for others seales? breake a colts force
> And leave him then, beeing made a ready horse? (ll. 25–30)

The narrator shows great bitterness at his wasted labour, making his lover more usable (the rubbing of wax, the breaking of a colt) and more attractive ('framing' and 'enamelling' plate). The wax image incorporates the common place of wax in English writing – as a seal – and Donne may be evoking an embrace here. There is also the word 'Chafe,' which gives a rather Ovidian sense of the lover moulding a woman into a congenial shape. Indeed, it is quite possible that Donne is reponding specifically to Ovid's Pygmalion story in *Metamorphoses* X: like Ovid's his wax evokes artistic creation. There is another example of a possible echo of Pygmalion in a waxy context in 'A Valediction: of my name, in the window.' This poem is typical of Donne's love poetry in its doomed quest for a verbal language of real substance.[31] The poet describes his wish to make a lasting mark, and to find a more enduring presence, textual and physical, for the poet and for his name. The suggestive writing surface adds its properties to the scene – glass is breakable, in need of the narrator's questionable 'firmnesse' (l. 2). Its transparency allows a metaphorical breakdown of the barriers between things ('Here you see mee, and I am you,' l. 12). When the prospect of infidelity looms, the 'firmnesse' and substance threaten to become fluid:

> And when thy melted maid,
> Corrupted by thy Lover's gold, and page,
> His letter at thy pillow'hath laid,
> Disputed it, and tam'd thy rage,
> And thou begin'st to thaw towards him, for this,
> May my name step in, and hide his. (ll. 49–54)

Gold and a letter have caused the woman to become a 'melted maid,' wherein her change is all the more nightmarish because her liquification thwarts the male presence. (Patrides glosses 'page' as 'a male servant' but the presence of a 'letter' in the next line blurs the carrier and the paper itself.) The 'thaw' means that the melting may refer to ice, but the Petrarchan combination of icy constancy and heated passion has as an accompaniment the idea that it may be a maid of wax which is melting, with the story of Pygmalion and its erotic undertones hovering in the background. The melting takes the lover's warming and shaping a stage further, as the problematic substance refuses to be controlled – it is quite possible that, when Pythagoras describes the soul holding its essence like wax, Ovid allows a certain irony to gather because when wax melts its substance is compromised. In Donne's poem the name in the window is supposed to interfere with the woman's reply to her suitor's letters:

And if this treason goe
To an overt act, and that thou write againe;
In superscribing, this name flow
Into thy fancy, from the pane.
So, in forgetting thou remembrest right,
And unaware to mee shalt write. (ll. 55–60)

The point of the written name formerly was its fixed, diamantine permanence. Now it is asked to 'flow,' like a word carried on water or melting wax, into the letter. Donne evokes the literature of wax tablets in the reference to 'superscribing': in the *Ars Amatoria*, in particular, Ovid describes exactly this and the problems it can cause (2.395–6).[32] Donne shares an interest in the experience of the surface of writing with classical elegists, with Ovid to the fore. The final stanza reflects the decline of his poem's paradoxical wish for firmness and the ability to flow: 'But glasse, and lines must bee, / No meanes our firme substantiall love to keepe' (ll. 61–2). Vitally, there is a lack of substance in the name written in the glass, and 'lines' in general (where, as in the Latin 'versus,' the word implies poetry but without certainty). This poem's grasp at the idea of lasting substance is denigrated as the product of a 'dying,' 'idle' mind: a dreamy 'murmure' (ll. 64–6).

This is the most sustained exploitation of refractions of wax imagery in Donne's poems, but there are other significant instances. In 'Elegie VI: Oh, let me not serve so' the image of a wax heart recalls a time when the poet's lover was compliant and constant:

When my Soule was in her owne body sheath'd,
Nor yet by oathes betroth'd, nor kisses breath'd
Into my Purgatory, faithlesse thee,
Thy heart seem'd waxe, and steele thy constancie. (ll. 11–14)[33]

The contrast of wax and steel is worryingly reversible. Even this way round anything made of 'steele' is hardly congenial and a heart made of wax can be melted and moulded by anyone. In 'Sapho to Philaenis' Donne finds another way to use the idea of wax. Here it becomes a figure for memory, representing the remains of the lover in Sapho's heart. Donne allows it to come into contact with the clichéd fires of passion:

Onely thine image, in my heart, doth sit,
But that is waxe, and fires environ it.

My fires have driven, thine have drawne it hence;
And I am rob'd of Picture, Heart, and Sense. (ll. 9–12)[34]

Donne depicts wax melting away to nothing, caught in the crossfire of paradoxically complementary passions, one assailing the wax from the outside, one from the inside. Again the sense that wax is a version of flesh is suggestive, as the body becomes less and less substantial as time passes. As a final example, the word 'wax' can denote the substance but it can also serve as a synonym for 'grow.' Only in 'Elegy XII: His parting from her' does this seem to be an occasion for wordplay, where the word is accompanied by references to temperature:

The Pole shall move to teach me ere I start;
And when I change my Love, I'll change my heart,
Nay, if I wax but cold in my desire,
Think, heaven hath motion lost, and the world, fire. (ll. 35–8)

Love seems like a melted state in which a heart of wax has been melted by the fire of love. So the line, 'if I wax but cold,' captures two meanings, and the 'fire' of the next line is both necessary to heat the poet but also to melt his metaphorical waxen state. These last two examples show the waxen state anxiously poised, and this may be what makes the image so fertile in Donne's hands. It captures the fragile state of human bodies: it is noteworthy that John Carey's biography of Donne has consecutive chapters on 'Bodies' and 'Change.'[35] It also captures the combination of moments of power and moments of futile fleetingness which makes his love poetry so vital.

NOTES

1 Jonathan Goldberg, *Writing Matter: From the Hands of the English Renaissance* (Stanford: Stanford University Press, 1990), pp. 2–4, citing Jacques Derrida, *Of Grammatology*, trans. Gayatri Chakravorty Spivak (Baltimore: Johns Hopkins University Press, 1976).

2 Jocelyn Penny Small, *Wax Tablets of the Mind: Cognitive Studies of Memory and Literacy in Classical Antiquity* (London: Routledge, 1997), p. 150.

3 Quoted from the Loeb *Metamorphoses*, trans. and ed. Frank Justus Miller, 3rd ed., rev. G.P. Goold, 2 vols. (Cambridge, MA: Harvard University Press, 1984). References are to book and line number.

4 See A.R. Sharrock, 'Womanufacture,' *Journal of Roman Studies* 81 (1991): 36–49.

5 From the Loeb *Heroides and Amores*, trans. Grant Showerman, 2nd ed., rev. G.P. Goold (Cambridge, MA: Harvard University Press, 1977).

6 See the Loeb *The Art of Love and Other Poems*, trans. J.H. Mozley, 2nd ed., rev. G.P. Goold (Cambridge, MA: Harvard University Press, 1979), 1.437–40.

7 I.M. LeM. Du Quesnay, 'The *Amores*,' in *Ovid*, ed. J.W. Binns (London: Routledge, 1973), p. 17, points out the inventiveness of the image.

8 John Barsby, *Ovid's Amores Book One* (Oxford: Clarendon Press, 1973), p. 133, says that 'versus does not here imply poetry,' although it is difficult to see why he is sure. The ambiguity contained in the word 'versus' is also exploited in the tale of Byblis and Caunus in *Metamorphoses* IX.565.

9 Propertius, *Elegies*, ed. and trans. G.P. Goold (Cambridge, MA: Harvard University Press, 1990). References are to book and poem numbers.

10 Small, *Wax Tablets of the Mind*, p. 150, says they were 'preferred temporary repositories for almost every kind of written transaction.' See also Catullus, poem 50, in *Catullus, Tibullus, and Pervigilium Veneris*, trans. F.W. Cornish, J.P. Postgate, and J.W. Mackail, 2nd ed., rev. G.P. Goold (Cambridge, MA: Harvard University Press, 1988), where two poets have a friendly writing competition on wax, and Ovid, *Tristia* 5.12.33–6, in *Tristia and Ex Ponto*, trans. A.L. Wheeler, 2nd ed., rev. G.P. Goold (Cambridge, MA: Harvard University Press, 1988), where Ovid composes his poems on a tablet.

11 Duncan Kennedy, *The Arts of Love: Five Studies in the Discourse of Roman Love Elegy* (Cambridge: Cambridge University Press, 1993), p. 82. See also Robert J. Baker, 'Duplices Tabellae: Propertius 3.23 and Ovid, *Amores* 1.12,' *Classical Philology* 68 (1973): 109–13.

12 Gordon Williams, *Tradition and Originality in Roman Poetry* (Oxford: Oxford University Press, 1968), p. 490.

13 On the erasability of 'tabellae,' see Bernhard Bischoff, *Paläographie des römischen Altertums und des abendländischen Mittelalters* (Berlin: Schmidt, 1979), pp. 28–30. Also Small, *Wax Tablets of the Mind*, pp. 145–8, and Robert Maichal, 'Les Tablettes à écrire dans le Monde Romain,' in *Les Tablettes à écrire de l'Antiquité à l'époque Moderne*, ed. Élisabeth Lalou, *Bibliologia*, vol. 12 (Turnhout: Brepols, 1992), pp. 165–85.

14 The *Oxford English Dictionary* suggests that the poetic sense of 'Line' (23e) dates from the second half of the sixteenth century. Its older meaning – a short message (23c) – is also important here.

15 From *The Complete Works of Christopher Marlowe, vol. 1: Translations*, ed. Roma Gill (Oxford: Clarendon Press, 1987), p. 29.

16 Poem 3.13 in Marlowe is 3.14 in the Loeb and other modern editions of the

Amores. Marlowe's text may have been a London Plantin-type like *Publii Ovidii Nasonis Heroidum Epistolae Amores Libri III* (London: J. Harrison, 1594). This text was chosen as the one used by Marlowe by Eric Jacobsen, *Translation: A Traditional Craft: An Introductory Sketch with a Study of Marlowe's Elegies* (Copenhagen: Gyldendalske, 1958), p. 163, after an extensive survey, despite this particular example being printed after Marlowe's death. Texts differ only slightly and Marlowe was enough of a scholar to have used several editions and possibly even to have made his own emendations. Roma Gill, *The Complete Works of Christopher Marlowe*, suggests a 1575 edition, *P. Ovidii Nasonis Heroidum Epistolae, Amorum Libri III* (Antwerp: C. Plantin, 1575), but says (p. 6) that her choice was made 'more or less at random.' There is no problem with the Basel Hervagius texts like that suggested by Millar Maclure, ed., *The Poems* (Manchester University Press, 1968), p. xxxiii, on *P. Ovidii Nasonis Amatoria* (Basel: Hervagius, 1568).

17 Commentaries cited from *P. Ovidii Nasonis Poetae Sulmonensis Opera Quae Vocantur Amatoria* (Basel: Hervagius, 1549), p. 266.

18 Contemporary sonnet writers frequently also see the outflow of their passion in the pen's effusion. See in particular Sidney's *Astrophel and Stella* (where the blackness of Stella's eyes tests the poet's ink), in *The Poems of Sir Philip Sidney*, ed. William A. Ringler (Oxford: Oxford University Press, 1962), esp. 6.9–14; 19.5–8; 34.12–14; 70.9–14; 93.1–4; 102.12–14; and Song 8.41–4.

19 See Richard H. Rouse, and Mary A. Rouse, 'The Vocabulary of Wax Tablets,' in *Vocabulaire du Livre et de l'Ecriture au Moyen Age*, ed. Olga Weijers (Turnhout: Brepols, 1989), pp. 220–30.

20 Thomas Cooper, *Thesaurus Linguae Romanae et Britannicae* (London: H. Wyke, 1565).

21 See Lee Pearcy, *The Mediated Muse: English Translations of Ovid, 1560–1700* (Hamden: Archon, 1984), p. 5.

22 Roma Gill, 'Snakes Leape By Verse,' in *Christopher Marlowe*, ed. Brian Morris (London: Benn, 1968), p. 137.

23 Clifford Leech, *Christopher Marlowe: Poet for the Stage*, ed. Anne Lancashire (New York: AMS Press, 1986), p. 26, says that although dating to Cambridge 'cannot be proved ... it does look like that.' U.M. Ellis-Fermor, *Christopher Marlowe* (Hamden: Archon, 1967), pp. 10–14, sites it firmly in the Cambridge years.

24 Margreta de Grazia, 'Imprints: Shakespeare, Gutenberg and Descartes,' in *Alternative Shakespeares, vol. 2*, ed. Terence Hawkes (London and New York: Routledge, 1996), pp. 63–94, explores some imaginative nuances of seals and their relationship to the imprinting of identity.

25 N.J.C. Andreasen, *John Donne: Conservative Revolutionary* (Princeton: Prince-

ton University Press, 1967), pp. 53–77, sets out three 'strands' in Donne's love poetry – Ovidian, Petrarchan, and Platonic – but three seems the minimum number.

26 See Stella Revard, 'Donne and Propertius: Love and Death in London and Rome,' in *The Eagle and the Dove: Reassessing John Donne*, ed. Claude J. Summers and Ted-Larry Pebworth (Columbia: University of Missouri Press, 1986), pp. 69–79. See also A.J. Peacock, 'Donne's *Elegies* and Roman Love Elegy,' *Hermathena* 119 (1975): 20–9; and Roma Gill, 'Musa Iocosa Mea: Thoughts on the *Elegies*,' in *John Donne: Essays in Celebration*, ed. A.J. Smith (London: Methuen, 1972), pp. 47–72.

27 See J.B. Leishman, *The Monarch of Wit: An Analytical and Comparative Study of the Poetry of John Donne*, 6th ed. (London: Hutchinson, 1962), p. 62, and the notes in Helen Gardner, ed., *The Elegies and Songs and Sonnets* (Oxford: Oxford University Press, 1965). See also Peter De Sa Wiggins, 'The Love Quadrangle: Tibullus 1.6 and Donne's "Lay Ideot,"' *Papers on Language and Literature* 16 (1980): 142–50; and M.L. Stapleton, '"Why Should They Not Alike In All Parts Touch?": Donne and the Elegiac Tradition,' *John Donne Journal* 15 (1996): 1–22.

28 References to, and quotations from Donne's poems are from *The Complete English Poems of John Donne*, ed. C.A. Patrides (London: Dent, 1985). 'Elegie XII' is excluded from the canon by Helen Gardner, although its manuscript tradition is not very bad. She judges its quality too uneven (see pp. xl–xliii, 225–6).

29 On the 'praeceptor amoris' tradition in which this poem is placed, see A. Labranche, 'Blanda Elegeia: The Background to Donne's *Elegies*,' *Modern Language Review* 61 (1966): 357–68, and Alan Armstrong, 'The Apprenticeship of John Donne: Ovid and the *Elegies*,' *ELH* 44 (1977): 419–42.

30 See Thomas Docherty, *John Donne, Undone* (London: Methuen, 1986), p. 195, citing Frank Kermode, *The Genesis of Secrecy: On the Interpretation of Narrative* (Cambridge, MA: Harvard University Press, 1973), p. 3.

31 See John Bernard, 'Orthodoxia Epidemica: Donne's Poetics and "A Valediction: Of my Name in the Window,"' *South Atlantic Quarterly* 71 (1972): 377–89.

32 Both Gardner and Patrides gloss 'superscribing' as 'addressing,' citing *OED* sense 2. Again, though, the idea of 'overwriting' can complement the act of 'addressing.'

33 On this poem see Achsah Guibbory, '"Oh, Let Me Not Serve So": The Politics of Love in Donne's Elegies,' *ELH* 57 (1990): 811–33.

34 'Sapho to Philaenis' is another poem excluded from Helen Gardner's canon but this is questioned usefully by Janel Mueller, '"Troping Utopia": Donne's

Brief for Lesbianism,' in *Sexuality and Gender in Renaissance Europe*, ed. James Grantham Turner (Cambridge: Cambridge University Press, 1993), pp. 183–4; see also Stella Revard, 'The Sapphic Voice in Donne's "Sapho to Philaenis,"' in *Renaissance Discourses of Desire*, ed. Claude J. Summers and Ted-Larry Pebworth (Columbia: University of Missouri Press, 1993), pp. 63–76.

35 John Carey, *John Donne: Life, Mind, and Art*, 2nd ed. (London: Faber and Faber, 1990), pp. 117–83, particularly p. 162 on the word 'melt.'

Engendering Metamorphoses: Milton and the Ovidian Corpus

ELIZABETH SAUER

He who would not be frustrate of his hope to write well hereafter in laudable things, ought him selfe to bee a true Poem, that is, a composition, and patterne of the best and honourablest things.

John Milton, *Apology for Smectymnuus*

The language of metamorphosis and dismemberment haunts Milton's writings, despite the 'highly individualized "portrait of the artist" that Milton himself constructed so authoritatively' by transmitting his life and voice through print.[1] The unifying imperatives developed by Miltonists have advanced this view of the writer; as Mary Nyquist and Margaret W. Ferguson observe in *Re-membering Milton,* Milton 'continues to enjoy the status of the most monumentally unified author in the canon.'[2] An analysis of episodes from Milton's literary life and works, especially *Paradise Lost,* enables an investigation of his ongoing exchanges with Ovid, by whom he is first enchanted. Milton's scenes of Ovidian metamorphosis, I argue, transform the coherent 'idea of a literary career,' identified with this Christian *vates* (the Virgilian prophet-poet or poet-priest). By unsettling the poet's powerful self-presentation, this paper also challenges the arch-spectre of Milton criticism that upholds the integrity of his poetic identity and *oeuvre.*

The first half of my argument considers Milton's response to the 'smooth elegiac poet' who initially seduces him. The sites of conscious self-fashioning in Milton are scenes of reading which put the autonomous literary life in jeopardy. A discussion of the early years and works provides in turn a context for studying the influence of the *Metamorphoses* on *Paradise Lost.* In anatomizing and reanimating the Ovidian (literary) corpus, Milton focuses on the *Metamorphoses* which, along with the works of Homer and Euripides, delighted him most.[3] Curiously, the Ovidian presence does not fade in Milton's mature poems but rather produces a dynamic relationship between the two poets, which Thomas De Quincey would describe as a 'wedding of male and female counterparts.'[4] While the Milton-Ovid marriage soon ends, the intensity of their affair endures.

Initially, Ovid performs important work for Milton, who borrows from the classical poet in reinventing his own gendered persona. Later, however, Milton engages his Ovidian, feminine side in order to renounce it and cultivate his masculinity. Milton's experimentation with his gendered identity gives way to anxieties about another form of mutability and mutation: dismemberment – both of the poet's body and his body of works. The dismembered Orphic poet,[5] who is the figure of Ovid in Milton's work,[6] is an image as well of Milton and his ill-fated writings, which in the Restoration period, as he laments, are 'fall'n on evil days ... and evil tongues.'[7]

Paradise Lost, in particular, is rich in evidence of Milton's fascination and continuing struggle with metamorphosis. The scenes of transformation in the text, especially in the creation account, tend to invert those in Ovid by exhibiting 'movements from non-life to life, from the static to the mobile, from lower to higher forms.'[8] Still many other metamorphoses throughout *Paradise Lost* are construed as destructive and involve moral and physical degeneration. Such is the case with the self-conscious or self-referential passages in the epic. In this paper, I depart from Michael Lieb's provocative discussion of Milton's metamorphosis, bisexuality, and dismemberment (*sparagmos*) by demonstrating that Milton, in an effort to preserve the image of the Christian *vates* who maintains his moral and sexual purity, projects his anxieties about personal and textual mutability onto sites of (satanic) contagion and onto the female body, which is depicted as 'double-form'd' (*PL* 2.741), monstrous, and essentially Ovidian.

Anatomizing the Literary Corpus

I

Developments in print culture in the seventeenth century transformed the notion of authorship. The printed book became identified with the corpus carrying the life and spirit of the author, who in turn developed a pattern of a literary career, often in imitation of classical writers. In the case of Spenser, Jonson, and Milton, as well as Daniel, Drayton, and Chapman, we find 'a complete cultural artefact – "a Renaissance idea of a literary career,"'[9] which marked a Virgilian progression from pastoral to epic. Richard Helgerson's *Self-Crowned Laureates* characterizes the literary careers of Spenser, Jonson, and Milton as Virgilian in terms of their common mandate to make literature serve the nation. The careers of Lyly, Sidney, and Donne, by contrast, were modelled on Ovid (or Petrarch) insofar as they wrote poetry in their youth and then served the state in some other capacity in their later years.[10] Despite his departure from the works and life pattern established by Ovid, Milton continues his engagement with Ovidian *cursus* and the Ovidian corpus even in his mature poems.

Milton's readings of Ovid are recorded from the earliest stages of his literary career. His first documented creative moment, which is described in 'Elegy I to Charles Diodati,' is an Ovidian one in that he not only imitates Ovid's style but also shares with Ovid – to whom he refers in lines 21–2 – a common experience of exile. Banished by Augustus to the city of Tomis in A.D. 8, Ovid devotes books 3–5 of his elegiac *Tristia* to bemoaning his fate. Ovid's banishment in his old age needs, however, to be distinguished from Milton's rustication in his youth when he was sent home to London after a conflict with his Cambridge tutor. 'Elegy I,' which is a study in defiance, intellectual sophistication, and playfulness, shows Milton adapting to the situation much better than Ovid had. Milton dedicates himself to a life of leisure in the company of the Muses and his books, which absorb him wholly and even transport him (ll. 25–6). His passion is also enflamed, however, by the maidens he spies in the pastoral setting he describes thereafter. This scene is coloured and eroticized by an Ovidian lens, specifically a reading of the *Metamorphoses*. The poet is struck dumb by the divine – and mythological – female forms, which he pursues until chastity and reason come to his aid in the form of moly; his austere mood is then restored:

Ast ego, dum pueri sinit indulgentia caeci,
Moenia quam subito linquere fausta paro;
Et vitare procul malefidae infamia Circes
Atria, divini Molyos usus ope. (ll. 85–8)

[But for my part – while the blind boy's indulgence permit it – I am preparing the speediest possible departure from this city of delights –

> preparing with the help of divine moly, to secure the safety of distance from the infamous halls of the deceiver, Circe]. (p. 10)

In reading the Elegies in their likely order of composition, a similar history of the poet's development from sensual indulgence to his repudiation of the passionate in favour of the moral and spiritual is discernible. However, at the same time that the Elegies reveal an obvious indebtedness to Ovid's *Tristia,* they also expose Milton's attraction to the *Amores,* as is apparent in Elegies I, III, and notably IV.[11] 'Elegy V' is a study in paganism, eroticism, and the renewal of creative energy. However, in the following elegy, Ovid again becomes for Milton a battleground of the erotic and moral or divine. The first 35 lines of this poem, 'Elegy VI,' portray Milton as 'a young Ovid'; but then we witness the birth of the Puritan who pursues an ascetic way of life. Like 'Elegy I,' 'Elegy VI' is dedicated to Diodati, who offered Milton a model of chastity. The figures Milton includes in the latter part of the Elegy are known for having curbed their appetites: Tiresias as ascete and priest; Orpheus in his old age; Ulysses who successfully resists the charms of Circe and the Sirens; and Ovid, an inspired poet who in the *Fasti*[12] sings of divine things (ll. 67–8).

'Elegy VII,' which presents the traditional Ovidian theme of the poet conquered by Cupid, was printed with a retraction in 1630. 'Haec ego mente olim laeva studiosque supino / Nequitiae posui vana trophaea meae' (ll. 1–2) ('These are the monuments to my wantonness that with a perverse spirit and a trifling purpose I once erected'): Milton rejects the empty tokens, the products of youthful folly. 'Cincta rigent multo pectora nostra gelu' (l. 8) ('Thenceforward my breast has been rigid under a thick case of ice'): having extinguished the flames of desire, the chastened poet now keeps Cupid and Venus (and Ovid) at bay through an encasement of ice, which stiffens his breast. Since his youth, the development of Milton's poetic identity was predicated upon sexual renunciation, Milton implies. While the passage from the sensual to the moral becomes a convention of early modern literary narratives, the journey Milton plots is unparalleled – and by no means linear. *L'Allegro* and *Il Penseroso,* likely composed shortly after the Elegies, do not chart a direct movement from mirth to melancholy. Rather than dismissing the premises of *L'Allegro, Il Penseroso* serves as a companion poem to the other by anatomizing a complementary psychic state, that of pensiveness. David P. Harding's conclusion, perhaps informed by a literal interpretation of the 'Elegy VII' retraction, that by 1630 Milton's apprenticeship to Ovid as the poet of love was officially over (p. 57), is valid; but one should not assume that the poets' association ended as a result. In fact, their relationship became symbiotic: Milton engages Ovid in fashioning his own identity, while Ovid, who had invested the future generations of his readers – and printers – with the power to grant him immortality, is reanimated by virtue of his indelible name; 'nomenque erit indelebile nostrum' ('[his] name will be indelible among us').[13]

II

The relationship that Milton developed with Ovid thereafter must be contextualized in terms of the printing history and received tradition of the *Metamorphoses* in the Renaissance. The three primary, often interconnected, ways of reading the *Metamorphoses* which emerged were the allegorical, rhetorical, and epical. The Christianized allegorical and rhetorical reading of Ovid encouraged by Arthur Golding's translation – four books in 1565 and fifteen books in 1567 – was especially influential; the translation in fact acquired national importance. Later George Sandys's sanitized, allegorical version of the *Metamorphoses*, entitled *Ovid's Metamorphosis, Englished, Mythologized and Represented in Figures*, appeared, first as five books in 1621, then as a complete text in 1626, and finally with commentary in 1632. 1632 was also the year of Prynne's *Histriomastix*, which fueled the Puritan opposition to the stage and to mythology. While allegory went out of style by the mid century, Sandys's edition was reprinted almost every decade in the 1600s.[14]

The actual edition of the *Metamorphoses* that Milton possessed was probably sold, along with many of his other books, by his daughters, who had served as his readers and amanuenses. Milton's scepticism of glosses and commentaries on the *Metamorphoses* meant that he likely owned a Latin copy of the text. Despite his preference for the original, however, he inevitably contributed to the metamorphosis of the text and to its reading history.

Milton's continuing need to control his self-presentation helps to explain his engagement with and fears about metamorphosis, which he often characterizes in terms of changes in sexuality and gender. Six years before the composition of *The Ludlow Mask*, Milton comments in 'Prolusions VI' on the epithet 'Lady' ascribed to him:

> Have I slain some serpent and incurred the fate of Tiresias? Has some Thessalian witch poured magic ointment over me? Or have I been violated by some god, like Caeneus of old, and won my manhood as the

> price of my dishonour, that I should be thus suddenly changed from woman into man? Some of late called me 'the Lady.' But why do I seem to [my contemporaries at Cambridge] too little of a man ... But I wish they could leave playing the ass as readily as I the woman.
>
> (*Prose*, vol. 1, pp. 283–4)[15]

The Ovidian legends of Tiresias, the Thessalian witch, and Caenis are related insofar as they include scenes of involuntary, unmerited, and violent sexual metamorphosis.[16] Milton likewise views arbitrary change as dangerous and disabling in all respects, and in the tradition of medieval and Renaissance commentaries on Ovid, attributes a psychological and moral significance to physical transformations.

In 'Prolusions VI,' Milton exerts a masculine effort to retain a sense of integrity by rejecting the nickname 'Lady.' While in the same passage he embraces rather than denies the ascription of effeminacy[17] – just as he will recuperate his association with Tiresias in 'Elegy VI' – he does so in order to support his self-presentation and self-preservation as a whole, chaste man. Anxieties about the failure to control the process of self-fashioning are projected onto his accusers, the 'jolly fellows.'

The contrast between the poet who does not lose his form and his companions and adversaries who do reminds us of another scene of (averted) metamorphosis – that of Odysseus and his companions in their encounter with Circe. The following allegorical interpretation of this account is taken from George Sandys's commentary, printed with his translation of the *Metamorphoses*:

> Yet *Ulysses* could not lose his shape with the rest, who being fortifyed by an immortall power, was not subject to mutation. For the divine & caelestiall soule, subsisting through the bounty of the Creator, can by no assault of nature be violated nor can that bee converted into a beast which so highly participates of reason.[18]

Sandys goes on to explain that moly, a present from Mercury, protected Ulysses from Circe's spells (p. 654). Like Sandys, Milton identifies moly with the activation of reason and practice of morality and chastity, which render the bewitching power of Circean metamorphosis ineffective. Moly or *Haemony*, mentioned in 'Elegy I,' is said by the Attendant Spirit in *The Ludlow Mask* to be 'yet more med'cinal ... than that *Moly* / That *Hermes* once to wise *Ulysses* gave' (ll. 636–7) to protect its users from enchantment. The power of moly, a form of integrity or Christian grace for Milton, is represented by steadfastness in the Lady, which enables her to resist Comus – the offspring of Circe and Bacchus (l. 522).

Following the composition of *The Ludlow Masque* in 1634, Milton, in a 1637 letter to Diodati, confesses to an obsessive search for an image of supreme beauty: 'Not so diligently is Ceres, according to the Fables, said to have sought her daughter Proserpina, as I see for this idea of the beautiful, as if for some glorious image, throughout all the shapes and forms of things' (*Prose*, vol. 1, p. 326). As he announces in the *Apology for Smectymnuus*, the pursuit leads him to abandon Ovidian eroticism to follow instead 'the two famous renowners of *Beatrice* and *Laura* [Dante and Petrarch], who never write but honour of them to whom they devote their verse.' Published anonymously, *Apology for Smectymnuus* develops a portrait of the artist that is (re-)made in the image of his own composition – in the image of 'a true Poem, who is, a composition, and patterne of the best and honourablest things' (*Prose*, vol. 1, p. 890).

Metamorphoses of the Body

I

Milton's attraction to the *Metamorphoses* can be attributed to the comprehensiveness of its subject matter; the nonlinear narrative structure; its multiple narratives and voices, which are nevertheless managed by a dominating narrator; its creation accounts; and its interest in the universal theme of mythic and psychological changes rather than in empire and war, which fascinated classical epic poets. *Metamorphoses* celebrates the human spirit; it is a counter-classical defence of individuality in the face of 'ferocious and arbitrary attempts to control human nature,' and Milton associates individuality with both poetic achievement and free will.[19]

The timelessness of the *Metamorphoses* would also have impressed Milton, as would the notoriety that it bestowed upon its author. In the *Amores*, Ovid had announced triumphantly that poetic immortality liberated him from the oppression of kings: 'carmina morte carent. / cedant carminibus reges regumque triumphi' ('[The] song is untouched by death. Before the song let monarchs and monarchs' triumphs yield'). At the end of the *Metamorphoses*, Ovid likewise rejoices in the fame he achieves through verse: 'quaque patet domitis Romana potentia terris, / ore legar populi, perque omnia saecula fama, / siquid habent veri vatum praesagia, vivam' ('Wherever Rome's power extends over the conquered world, I shall have mention on men's lips, and, if the prophecies of bards have any truth, through all the ages shall I live in fame').[20] Poetry confers new life on the writer, which enables him to transcend the changeability associated with material or corporeal forms. Furthermore, Ovid's habit of inscribing his name in his texts – part of the 'heavily graphic emphasis in Ovid's fantasies about his own social, authorial identity'[21] – reinforces his concern about self-presentation and enduring fame.

As a testament to the greatness of Milton's achievement, *Paradise Lost* also celebrates the poet as much as his subject matter. Poet and poem are perceived as being immune to corruption – whether of kings or 'an age too late, or cold / Climate, or Years' (*PL* 9.44–5), or even editorial changes, which Jonathan Richardson would describe as a 'Kind of Licentiousness.'[22] After citing the famous passage from the *Areopagitica* about the '*Pretious Life-Blood of a* Master-Spirit' that is contained within every good book, Richardson declares:

> Whatsoever Suggestion or Assertion, in Jest or in Earnest, concerning Some Unknown, Pragmatical, or Rascally Editor has been flung out ... [it] shall not hurt the Book, That, and its Author are safe. So – *Go thy Ways, the Flour and Quintessence of all Editors.* the [*sic*] Edition of 1674 is the Finish'd, the Genuine, the Uncorrupted Work of *John Milton.* (310)

Richardson's assurance that 'the Book ... and its Author are safe' remains virtually unchallenged by Miltonists through the centuries. But a different story unfolds when we locate the epic in a counternarrative of Milton's affair with Ovid.

The cultivation of the poet's image is compromised by various kinds of mutability, which become most apparent, perhaps ironically, in the masterwork of the 'Uncorrupted' 1674 edition. The numerous scenes of metamorphosis in *Paradise Lost*, moreover, all reinforce the Renaissance notion that physical, psychological, moral, and even linguistic transformation go hand in hand. In examining several of these scenes, I take exception to DuRocher's observation in *Milton and Ovid* that reliance on a Christian muse enables Milton 'paradoxically, to pour Ovid's fables of mythological change in *Paradise Lost* abundantly, without anxiety that they might destroy his comprehensive Christian epic' (p. 74).

The epic journey begins with a descent into the underworld by the poet-narrator, who follows the course taken by Virgil in the *Aeneid*, Orpheus/Ovid in the *Metamorphoses*, and of course Satan in *Paradise Lost*. The first words uttered by the fallen angel speak of change, specifically the alteration Satan discerns in Beelzebub: 'If thou beest hee; But O how fall'n! how chang'd / From him, who in the happy Realms of Light / Cloth'd with transcendent brightness didst outshine / Myriads though bright' (*PL* 1.84–7). Here Milton recalls Aeneas's encounter with Hector's ghost, who represents both the defeated warrior and the prophet who foretells Aeneas's triumph.[23] Satan is interested in his companion's countenance and words first because they reflect back his own fallen condition. Though fallen, Satan possesses a form which had 'yet not lost / All her Original brightness' (*PL* 1. 591–2) and insists on his unaltered psychological and mental state. At the same time, Satan becomes the author of his own counter-epic, who rewrites the past and produces a history of metamorphoses in which he performs the lead role.

Satan's epic narrative features scenes of physical, psychological, and sexual change. An encounter with Sin awakens Satan's recollection of his attraction to Sin and of his crimes of pride and lust. In this episode, Sin becomes the agent who forces Satan to confront his duplicitous self. Having immediately recognized her father (*PL* 2.727), Sin is surprised by Satan's failure to know her as she once was: 'Hast thou forgot me then, and do I seem / Now in thine eye so foul, once deem'd so fair / In Heav'n? ... Likest to thee in shape and count'nance bright' (*PL* 2.747–9, 756). Now, half woman, half serpent, Sin, who is made in the image of Satan and Ovid's Scylla, attempts to convince her progenitor and lover of their relatedness and relationship: 'Thou art my Father, thou my Author, thou / My being gav'st me; whom should I obey / But thee, whom follow?' (*PL* 2.864–6).

Sin's history of her creation, which she recounts to Satan, is a demonic recasting of the Ovidian myth of Narcissus: 'full oft / Thyself in me thy perfect image viewing / Becam'st enamor'd' (*PL* 2.763–5). The Ovidian myth is prefaced by an account of Cephisus's rape of Liriope who gives birth to Narcissus. It includes an exchange in which Liriope asks Tiresias whether her son Narcissus will live to a ripe age. The response is 'si se non noverit' ('If he ne'er know himself'; 3.348). In Milton's allegorization of the Ovidian account, the encounter with the once desirous image of himself ends for Satan, as for Narcissus, in the confrontation with Death. The story of Satan's former attraction to Sin forces him to acknowledge the 'dire change / Befall'n' (*PL* 2.820–1) them both.

The sites of physical metamorphosis in *Paradise Lost* are linked with the erotic, the demonic, and the feminine. The more grotesque scenes of metamorphosis are projected onto the female body, which becomes the locus for mutability as well as the register of the patriarchal attitudes to women conveyed by early modern culture. Satan's sinful state is portrayed as intellectual when Sin, the doubly formed creature of his own depraved mind, emerges fully formed from his head. Sin's own corruption, in contrast, is physically manifest in her monstrous shape and the monsters she bears. The account of her horrific metamorphosis allegorizes, and, according to the example offered by George Sandys, moralizes the Ovidian myth of Scylla, who undergoes a monstrous transformation by the jealous Circe in book XIV of the *Metamorphoses.*[24]

Two separate scenes involving prelapsarian Eve also invite Ovidian readings. In fact, Ovid is most often invoked in *Paradise Lost* when Eve is on site. The myth of Narcissus is transferred to book 4 by way of Eve, whose narcissistic encounter with her own reflection anticipates the fall. Though the temptation to read the scene as Ovidian must be resisted in this prelapsarian setting, Ovid nevertheless haunts the episode, which recalls book III of the *Metamorphoses* (ll. 402–510).

Similarly, in his description of Eden prior to the episode of Eve's self-encounter, Milton invokes and at the same time again steers us away from Ovid; Eden is dissociated from 'that fair field / Of *Enna,* where *Proserpin* gath'ring flow'rs / Herself a fairer Flow'r by gloomy *Dis* / Was gather'd' (*PL* 4.268–71; *Metamorphoses* V.385–92). Later, when Satan spies Eve separate from Adam in book 9, the Ovidian reference reappears and is applied to her: 'Each Flow'r of slender stalk ... she upstays / Gently with Myrtle band, mindless the while, / Herself, though fairest unsupported Flow'r, / From her best prop so far, and storm so nigh' (*PL* 9.428–33). The rape in the garden that is anticipated and which brings to mind the reference to Proserpina – who is mentioned in passing in book 4 of *Paradise Lost* – provides evidence of Ovid's presence in paradise. Eve herself is identified with the garden that Satan violates and transforms through his corrosive gaze and then by his multiple (anti)incarnations. Satan is described in terms of a series of mythological figures who underwent transformations, including Harmonia ('*Hermione*'), Cadmus, Aesculapius ('the God / In *Epidaurus*'), Jupiter Ammon ('*Ammonian Jove*') (*PL* 9.506–8). Thus when Eve is compared to Circe immediately thereafter (*PL* 9.522), Satan 'uncall'd before her stood' (*PL* 523), having already voluntarily transformed himself into a bestial form. However, Eve becomes spell-bound by his words, thus making Satan the true Circean figure in the poem.

The original fall triggers various transformations, all with moral and psychological implications. Adam and Eve's internal corruption is conveyed by their lust and 'guilty shame' about their nakedness, which they attempt to conceal with the leaves of the 'Figtree ... to *Indians* known / In *Malabar* or *Decan*' (*PL* 9.1101–3). Their altered, partially clad postlapsarian state, which is contrasted to their 'first naked Glory' (*PL* 9.1115), also connects them to 'Th' *American* so girt / With feather'd Cincture, naked else and wild' (*PL* 9.1116–17). Milton thus imports the images of defilement from both the feminized East and the New World in order to compound the shame of the barbaric transgressors.

II

In the *Areopagitica*, Milton explains to his readers that Ovid's banishment in his old age for 'the wanton Poems of his youth' was 'but a meer covert of State over some secret cause'; and besides, Milton continues, 'the Books were neither banisht nor call'd in. From hence we shall meet with little else but tyranny in the Roman empire, that we may not marvell, if not so often bad, as good Books were silenc't' (*Prose*, vol. 2, 499–500). Ovid's punishment is now visited on Milton in his late years. And the two are linked through the figure of Orpheus who, as I previously mentioned, in some ways represents 'the figure of Ovid in [Milton's] work' (DuRocher, *Milton and Ovid*, p. 65).

Reference to the legend of Orpheus reminds us that the most barbarous form of metamorphosis has yet to be examined – dismemberment. Fears of dismemberment are concentrated at the heart of the epic and apply to the Orphic poet who falls prey to the 'wilde Rout' of Maenads/ Bacchantes (*PL* 7.34). In *Metamorphoses* XI.1–55, Orpheus is torn apart by Maenads, frenzied female followers of Dionysius. While the legend of Orpheus was conventionally used to represent the civilizing power of poetry (Orpheus's ability to impose order on nature), it was also used to illustrate the acrimonious relationship between the poet and an uncivil society.

In *Paradise Lost*, the poet will reject the Muse, Calliope, who could not prevent the dismemberment of her son, Orpheus (*PL* 7.37–8; also see *Lycidas*, ll. 58–9). The failure of Orpheus's mother to save him leads, John Shawcross argues, to Milton's 'rejection of Calliope as his muse in *Paradise Lost*, and his hope and faith in himself.'[25] Faith in himself depends, however, on sustaining an active dialogue with a Christian muse.

Ovid intervenes in that exchange and in fact, as we have seen, continually disrupts the poet's song. But Ovid and Milton share a concern about the fate of the poet in a hostile society. The myth of Orpheus provides them with a language to describe, in different ways, the dangers associated with the poet's role. Milton's anxiety about his sexual identity is replaced in his later poems by his fears about his dismemberment as an Orphic poet and about his texts, which are 'fall'n on evil days ... and evil tongues' (*PL* 7.25–6). The demonic dissonance that his poetry attempts to evade threatens the song and the singer:

> But drive far off the barbarous dissonance
> Of *Bacchus* and his Revellers, the Race
> Of that wild Rout that tore the *Thracian* Bard
> In *Rhodope*, where Woods and Rocks and Ears
> To rapture, till the savage clamor drown'd
> Both Harp and Voice. (*PL* 7.32–7)

John Hales's article in the inaugural issue of *Modern Philology* explicates the Orpheus passage in relation to the opening of the eleventh book of Ovid's *Metamorphoses*, which describes the Maenads drowning out the notes of the lute before slaying the Thracian bard:

> ... ad vatis fata recurrunt
> tendentemque manus atque illo tempore primum
> inrita dicentem, nec quicquam voce moventem,
> sacrilegae perimunt, ... (XI. 38–41)

> [They run back to make an end of the bard; and him stretching out his hands toward them, and on that occasion for the first time speaking vainly and moving nothing with his voice, sacrilegiously they slay.][26]

Sandys explains that the *Thracian Bacchides* attacked the Prophet Orpheus for avoiding the female sex 'as a hinderance to the study of philosophy, & administration of civill affairs: he esteeming the propagation of wisdome & virtuous endeavours, more noble and immortall then that of posterity' (p. 519). For Milton's desexualized Orphic/Ovidian poet, who desires intercourse only with a Christian muse (*PL* 1.19–23), 'barbarous dissonance' is a product both of the fallen satanic discourse that pervades and threatens the epic and of the historical political conditions to which it is answerable: 'Could the character of Charles the Second, with its rabble rout of riotous courtiers, or the cavalier spirit and party just after the Restoration, be marked stronger and plainer than in the beginning of the seventh book?' asks one eighteenth-century commentator on *Paradise Lost.*[27] The royalist revelry – which 'fatally stupifi'd and bewitch'd' the masses in Circean fashion (*Prose*, vol. 3, p. 347) – poses the same danger as the 'language of [the Tory scribblers'] infernal pamphlets' (*Prose*, vol. 7, p. 452), which maligned Milton. Sandys had interpreted the scene of Orpheus's dismemberment in the *Metamorphoses* in terms of the scattering of the 'reliques of learning' (XI.519), thus anticipating Milton's description of the (female) body of Truth, which is hewn into a thousand pieces (*Areopagitica*, *Prose*, vol. 2, p. 549) and the dismemberment of the poet who asserts eternal providence. The recollection of Orpheus's fate leads the poet-revolutionary in the Restoration years to distance himself from the classical tradition, and in turn to transform the royalist pamphleteers, whose 'savage clamour' (*PL* 7.36) would drown both song and singer, into Meanads. Ovidian language and scenes of metamorphoses that pervade Milton's poems and prose works are projected onto the unruly, demonic, and the feminine, which constructs 'the other.'

Milton's conflicted changing personal and poetic affiliation with Ovid, from whom he had long beforehand publicly divorced himself, haunts the poem. The scenes of self-presentation which frequently involve an encounter with the Ovidian/feminized other unsettle 'that naïve wholeness of one's notions about the self that lies at the heart of the lyric, epic, and tragic image of man.'[28] The Ovidian possibility, it seems, always resurfaces and surprises the poet just as Sin surprises her Author in whose image she is made.

Epilogue

His harmonicall, and ingeniose soule dwelt in a beautifull & well proportioned body – In toto nusquam corpore menda fuit. Ovid

(Aubrey, *Minutes*, p. 4)[29]

I conclude this narrative of Milton's metamorphoses and lifelong relationship with Ovid with another scene of reading. *The Life of Mr. John Milton*, assumed to be authored by Edward Phillips (Milton's nephew), describes gender relations and the domestic politics in the Milton household.[30] Elaborating on an anecdote provided in Phillips's *Life*, Thomas Birch describes an episode 'communicated to [him] by Mr. John Ward' about Mrs Deborah Clarke's relationship and that of her sisters to their father as 'uncomprehending conduits of the *classical* languages' they recited to him. Before her death, Deborah explained 'that she and her Sisters us'd to read to their Father in eight Languages;

which by practice they were capable of doing with great readiness and accuracy, tho' they understood what they read in no other language but English.' The writings that appealed to her father most, she remembers, were Isaiah, Homer, and Ovid's *Metamorphoses*.[31] Ironically, the words of Ovid had all along been ventriloquized by a woman and chanelled to Milton through the conduit of a *female* body, one which resembled Milton's own, according to John Ward, and one which carried the '*Pretious Life-Blood*' of the master.[32]

NOTES

I gratefully acknowledge the assistance of M. Morgan Holmes and Goran Stanivukovic in the preparation of this essay. Funding for my research was generously provided by the Social Sciences and Humanities Research Council of Canada.

1 Leah S. Marcus, *Unediting the Renaissance: Shakespeare, Marlowe, Milton* (New York: Routledge, 1996), p. 221.

2 Margaret W. Ferguson, *Re-membering Milton: Essays on the Texts and Traditions* (New York: Methuen, 1987), p. xii. On Milton's authorial self-presentation and its discontents, see also John Rumrich; in a period in which 'intense impatience with the status quo [has] pervaded American culture especially in the academy, ' Milton scholarship has seldom shown any discontent with itself (Rumrich, 'Uninventing Milton,' *Modern Philology* 87.3 [1990]: 249; Rumrich *Milton Unbound: Controversy and Reinterpretation* ([Cambridge: Cambridge University Press, 1996], p. 2).

3 Samuel Johnson, *Lives of the English Poets*, ed. George Birkbeck Hill, 3 vols. (New York: Octagon Books, 1967), vol. 1, p. 154.

4 Thomas De Quincey, *Collected Writings of Thomas De Quincey*, ed. David Mason, 14 volumes (Edinburgh: Adam and Charles Black, 1889–90). I refer to the reprint of this work (New York: AMS Press, 1968), vol. 11, p. 449.

5 On Milton and Orpheus, also see Michael Lieb *Milton and the Culture of Violence* (Ithaca: Cornell University Press, 1994), chapter 3; and Rachel Falconer, *Orpheus Dis(re)membered: Milton and the Myth of the Poet-Hero* (Sheffield: Sheffield Academic Press, 1996).

6 See Richard J. DuRocher, *Milton and Ovid* (Ithaca: Cornell University Press, 1985), p. 65.

7 *Paradise Lost*, in *John Milton: Complete Poems and Major Prose*, ed. Merritt Hughes (New York: Odyssey Press, 1957), book VII, lines 25–6. All citations of Milton's poems, including translations, are from this edition. References

are to book and line numbers. Citations of Milton's prose are from *Complete Prose of John Milton*, ed. Don Wolfe, et al., 8 volumes, (New Haven: Yale University Press, 1953–82). References are to volume and page number.

8 Joseph H. Summers, *The Muses Method*, p. 139, quoted in Catherine Gimelli Martin, *The Ruins of Allegory: Paradise Lost and the Metamorphosis of Epic Convention* (Durham: Duke University Press, 1998), p. 244.

9 Patrick Cheney, *Marlowe's Counterfeit Profession: Ovid, Spenser, Counter-Nationhood* (Toronto: University of Toronto Press, 1997), p. 6.

10 Richard Helgerson, *Self-Crowned Laureates: Spenser, Jonson, Milton, and the Literary System* (Berkeley: University of California Press, 1983).

11 On Milton's indebtedness to Ovid's *Amores* and *Tristia* in 'Elegy IV,' see David P. Harding, *Milton and the Renaissance Ovid* (Chicago: University of Illinois Press, 1946).

12 Ovid, *Fasti*, trans. Sir James Frazer, 2nd ed. (Cambridge, MA: Harvard University Press, 1989), book 6, 5–8.

13 Ovid, *Metamorphoses*, trans. Frank Justus Miller, The Loeb Classical Library (Cambridge, MA: Harvard University Press, 1984), XV.876. References are to book and line numbers. On Ovid's indelible name, see Lynn Enterline *The Rhetoric of the Body from Ovid to Shakespeare* (Cambridge: Cambridge University Press, 2000), pp. 52–3.

14 On Renaissance editions of *Metamorphoses*, see Harding, *Milton and the Renaissance Ovid*, pp. 21–4.

15 See John Aubrey, *Minutes, Early Lives of Milton*, ed. Helen Darbishire (London: Constable, 1932), p. 3. On the nature of the poetic process that allows 'a model of reading that does not exclude "female"' and on the poet's female sensibilities, see James Grantham Turner: *One Flesh: Paradisal Marriage and Sexual Relations in the Age of Milton* (Oxford: Clarendon Press, 1987), pp. 186–7; and Falconer, chapter 7. On Milton's identification with the feminine, see John T. Shawcross, *John Milton: The Self and the World* (Lexington, KY: University Press of Kentucky, 1993), pp. 185–92. The translator of the Prolusions in the Yale edition of Milton's *Complete Prose* is Phyllis B. Tillyard.

16 Tiresias undergoes a sex change for his violence to a pair of mating serpents in *Metamorphoses* 3.324–31. On the Thessalian witch, see Ovid *Amores*, trans. Sir James Frazer, 2nd ed. (Cambridge: Cambridge University Press, 1989), a book 7.27. References are to book and line numbers. The Thessalian girl, Caenis, demands a change of sex to a male from Neptune as amends for his violence to her in *Metamorphoses* 12.189–209.

17 Katharine Eisaman Maus, 'A Womb of His Own: Male Renaissance Poets in the Female Body,' in *Inwardness and the Theater in the English Renaissance* (Chicago: University of Chicago Press, 1995), p. 199. On the connection between

the Lady in *Comus* and Milton's nickname at Cambridge, see pp. 198–200.

18 George Sandys, 'Upon the Fourteenth Booke,' in *Ovid's Metamorphosis, Englished, Mythologized and Represented in Figures*, ed. Karl K. Hulley and Stanley T. Vandersall (Lincoln: University of Nebraska Press, 1970), p. 654. Ovid mentions that Mercury (Hermes) gave Ulysses advice in addition to moly, but the nature of the advice is unknown; see Leonara Brodwin, 'Milton and the Renaissance Circe,' *Milton Studies* 6 (1974): 26. Moly is the plant given to Odysseus by Hermes as a protection against Circe's spells (*Odyssey* 10.281–306).

19 W.R. Johnson, 'The Problem of the Counter-classical Sensibility and Its Critics,' *California Studies in Classical Antiquity* 3 (1970): 147.

20 Ovid, *Ovid with an English Translation: Heroides and Amores*, ed. and trans. by Grant Showerman (Cambridge, MA: Harvard University Press, 1914, repr. 1958), 15.32–3. References are to book and line numbers.

21 Enterline, *The Rhetoric of the Body*, p. 53. Enterline recalls one of the more impressionable scenes of inscription in Ovid's works: *Ars Amatoria* ends with the narrator fantasizing about his readers writing 'Naso' on the bodies of their erotic victims.

22 Jonathan Richardson, *The Early Lives of Milton*, ed. Helen Darbishire (London: Constable, 1932), p. 308.

23 Virgil, *The Aeneid*, trans. John Dryden, ed. Robert Fitzgerald (New York: Macmillan, 1965), 2.358–9; 2.381–2.

24 Milton allegorizes Ovid; for recent studies of Milton's indebtedness to the Ovidian tradition, see Judith E. Browning, who examines Sin's narrative in relation to the myth of Circe ('Sin, Eve, and Circe: *Paradise Lost* and the Ovidian Circe Tradition,' *Milton Studies* 26 [1990]: 135–57).

25 John Showcross, *John Milton*, pp. 188–9.

26 John W. Hales, 'Milton and Ovid,' *Modern Philology* 1 (1903–4): 144; see Lieb, *Milton and the Culture of Violence* (pp. 70–80), for a biographical, historical interpretation of the passage. Although the Latin text is quoted from the Loeb edition, the English translation is Hales's.

27 Francis Blackburne, comp., *Memoirs of Thomas Hollis, Esq.*, vol. 2 (London: J. Nichols, 1780), p. 623.

28 M.M. Bakhtin, *Problems of Dostoevsky's Poetics*, ed. & trans. Caryl Emerson (Minneapolis, MN: University of Minnesota Press, 1984), p. 120.

29 Nowhere in his whole body was there a blemish.

30 Richardson, *The Early Lives of Milton*, ed. Darbishire.

31 Deborah was made in the image of Milton, according to Ward (Thomas Birch, 'An Historical and Critical Account of the Life and Writings of Mr. John Milton,' in *A Complete Collection of the Historical, Political, and Miscella-*

neous Works of John Milton, vol. 1 [London, 1738], pp. lxi–lxii). Also see Samuel Johnson, *Lives of the English Poets*, vol. 1, p. 154; and Kevin Pask, *The Emergence of the English Author: Scripting the Life of the Poet in Early Modern England* (Cambridge: Cambridge University Press, 1996), p. 158.

32 Birch, 'An Historical and Critical Account,' vol. 1, p. lxii. Stephen B. Dobranski offers a provocative interpretation of this phrase as semen and as 'the viscous mixture of oil and resin used to make printer's ink,' which was applied with a pair of ink balls (*Milton, Authorship, and the Book Trade* [Cambridge: Cambridge University Press, 1999], p. 120).

The Girl He Left Behind: Ovidian *imitatio* and the Body of Echo in Spenser's 'Epithalamion'

JUDITH DEITCH

Criticism on the subject of Ovid in the Renaissance has traditionally focused on translation, reworking of *epyllia*, and imitation of Ovidian style, tone, and wit.[1] Criticism interested in the figure of Echo has, while usually taking brief note of the version of the myth in *Metamorphoses*, Book III, focused attention immediately on the abstractions of echo and echoing – as intertextuality, resonance, imitation, or belatedness – leaving the girl behind. The Echo of Ovid's myth is adduced only to transcend her in favour of literary allusivity (Hollander), deconstructive repetition (Goldberg), or in a recuperative effort of current feminism (Greenberg, Mudge) or Freudian psychoanalytic Narcissism (Spivak).[2] This paper will attempt to bring the strands of literary *imitatio* and concern with the politics of the female body together. I will argue that when Spenser invokes Echo in each stanzaic refrain of the *Epithalamion* ('The woods shall to me answer and my Eccho ring')[3] he is purposefully revealing himself as an imitator of Ovid. But since in Ovid's myth Echo only passively re-sounds other voices, she embodies classical imitation at its most facile and fragmented, as an icon of failed poetic descendance. The invocation of Echo in close proximity to a female body in Spenser's poem, however, cancels any figuration of the poet as epigone by transferring the ineffectual image onto the available woman. The image of Echo thus accrues to the bride, who is inscribed as passive reflector, while the male poet retains his role as active originator. Bodying forth the girl as the place for creating poetry casts the potentially effeminized lover and Renaissance author back into the masculine role of dominance and control. This allows Spenser to construct his own secure authorial identity in relation to the *auctoritas* of ancient exemplars.

Echo's body transposed into the body of the bride complements male poetic creation by absorbing any notion of *imitatio* as female re-iteration.

In order to see how this kind of Ovidian *imitatio* works we must first of all restore the material body of Echo – in many different ways 'the girl left behind' – to Spenser's poem. Two problems seem to impede such a move. First, Echo, the initially talkative, vocal nymph of *Metamorphoses*, Book III, whom Ovid so skilfully pairs with the ocularly obsessed Narcissus, is ultimately conspicuous by her absence – that is, her lack of a body: she is the girl whose voice is left behind after the slow dissolution of her flesh and bones. How can we restore a body which is hollow space? Second, adducing the pathetic story of Echo's unrequited love and Juno's curse of eternal re-sounding injects a note of doom, failure, and frustration into what is otherwise a celebratory wedding song – a gift from Spenser to his second wife, Elizabeth Boyle. Perhaps Echo ought to be left behind so as not to ruffle the placid surface of the vatic ceremony and bring anxieties into the poem. I hope to demonstrate, however, that just as her body is materialized in order to then make a space for the poet's song, so the threat of Echo as doomed repetition is evoked in order to be revoked, rejected, and transcended.

The problem with most modern academic discussions of Echo is that they pass too quickly over the Ovidian myth: when scholars and critics use Echo to talk about intertextuality or allusiveness, belatedness or 'anxiety of influence,' resonance or deconstructive repetition, they too leave the girl behind. The present analysis also requires the abstraction of Echo, as a kind of failed poetic imitation, but the nymph's body and Ovid's treatment of it must be restored to the discussion prior to such a move. In other words, both the body and Ovid are key to understanding Spenser's position as classical imitator.

Ovid's *Metamorphoses* is a book about bodies in flux: the very first line of the 'carmen perpetua' declares that it will tell about bodies changed to other forms. In Book III, when Ovid introduces the nymph Echo already in love with Narcissus, he emphasizes her corporeal existence: 'Corpus adhuc Echo, non vox erat' (III.359). Arthur Golding's 1567 translation gives: 'This Echo was a body then and not an onely voyce' (III.447);[4] and George Sandys's 1632 translation makes it more concise: 'Eccho was then a body, not a Voyce' (p. 89).[5] Ovid sets up the contrast between body and voice not only to stress the separation of the two, which will allow Echo's peculiar continued existence as a voice alone (this is an etiological tale); but also to show how, at the moment of metamorphosis, the loss of body creates the space for the transition from girl to abstract resonance, and thence to the permanent space for echoing.

Therefore Ovid again emphasizes Echo's body at her death, after the final rejection by Narcissus:

extenuant vigiles corpus miserabile curae
adducitque cutem macies et in aëra sucus
corporis omnis abit; vox tantum atque ossa supersunt:
vox manet, ossa ferunt lapidis traxisse figuram.
inde latet silvis nulloque in monte videtur.
omnibus auditur: sonus est, qui vivit in illa. (III.396–401)

Her wretched body pines with sleeplesse care:
Her skinne contracts: her blood converts to ayre.
Nothing was left her now but voyce and bones:
The voyce remaynes; the other turne to stones.
Conceal'd in Woods, in Mountaines neuer found,
Yet heard by all; and all is but a Sound. (trans. Sandys, p. 90)

The last line in the Latin original is an Ovidian semantic tour-de-force which seems to say that Echo retains a living absent body even after her dissolution: 'sonus est, qui vivit in illa' (III.401), literally, 'there is sound which lives in her' or 'the sound is that which lives in her.' The sound is living in the place where her body used to be – as well as the places her body used to be, that is, the places she frequented as rejected, elegiac lover. Ovid uses the word 'corpus' twice in these lines to underscore the process of distilling voice out of body; he also uses the transformation word 'figura' which denotes the shape or form her bones leave as a phantom silhouette in stone. Thus Echo's metamorphosis is not a complete dissolution, but an erasure which leaves an outline, as it were, of where the body was – a shell circumscribing a space within which sound can reverberate.

Echo's petrified bones conjure up man-made architectural structures where echoes sound, complementing the natural places like woods and caves. Sandys already made this logical connection in his gloss on the third book of the *Metamorphoses*: 'Eccho is here said to conceale her selfe in woods and mountaines: but chiefly in winding vallies, rocky caues, and ruinous buildings' (p. 104). What specific images would the term 'ruinous buildings' suggest to a Renaissance poet? Besides the dissolved monasteries of the English countryside, the obvious 'ruins of time' would be the buildings that were the glory of classical Rome. The notion of echoes sounded in these monuments strongly suggests the irretrievability of the past – indeed, it was only modern archaeology that could make these stones 'speak.' To be in the position of Echo, according to the nymph's absented body, therefore, is merely to sound hollowly, with no possibility of reproducing meaning, or even transmitting it. As *imitatio* it is a position of ineptitude if not failure, and wholly passive; not a desirable place of descendence for a masculine poet.

Turning to Spenser's *Epithalamion*, it is notable that amongst the vocal plenitude of the poem the bride is peculiar for her muteness. Practically everything else thinkable in the world of the poem – from the gods of classical myth to roisterous Elizabethan urchins – is called upon to sound, and each is assured by the bard in the final line of stanzas 1 through 16 that 'the woods shall answer and your echo ring.' Only the bride – chaste, silent, and obedient – will not initiate any echoing response; her passive speechlessness is total. This seems logical: since it is the beloved's praises which are being rung it would not be fitting for her to add her own voice. However, it does set her apart among the vocalic positions of the poem – everything else sounds, except the woods which re-sound, and the bride who is mute. Since muteness is a condition of echoing – one cannot choose to echo; it is an involuntary act (something which Ovid stresses) – the two positions (echoing and muteness) are closely correlative and disjunctive from the initiating of sound.

More importantly for associating the bride with Echo is the description of her female body as an architectural space:

> Her snowie necke lyke to a marble towre,
> And all her body like a pallace fayre,
> Ascending uppe with many a stately stayre,
> To honors seat and chastities sweet bowre. (ll. 177–80)

Of course this is part of a set-piece blazon in stanza 10 deriving in general from the biblical Song of Songs. But the notion of contained space in the specific words 'tower' and 'palace,' as well as the staircase ascending to the throne and chamber ('seat' and 'bower'), present prime locations for echoing. The bride's body is thus spatialized like the dissolved body of Echo in Ovid's myth – the living marble neck, a cylindrical tower, replicates the nymph's petrified remains; the stairwell and chamber the ruinous places she haunts.

Besides the authority and tradition of the Hebrew Bible, the body as building, according to Sheila Delany, appears in two of the most privileged medieval discourses: medical discourse and 'Pauline and Augustinian injunctions to think of the body as temple or altar.'[6] In her discussion of fifteenth-century hagiographer Osbern Bokenham, Delany notes that '[f]or Augustine, in fact, the architectural image – specifically for the female body – goes all the way back to Genesis.' This is because the Vulgate says that the Lord God 'built up the rib' of Adam to make Eve (*aedificavit*), which Augustine glosses '"as if there was a question of a house rather than a human body" (Gen. 9.13).'[7] Thus the body – and especially the female body – as building is not an innovation on Spenser's part. It was part of an available patristic tradition; but his conflation of the spatialized biblical female body and the Ovidian vocalic echoing nymph is a new and powerful syncretic statement which helps him to define by dissociation his own position as male poet.

It is true that there are other standing structures besides the images of the bride's body in Spenser's poem: the temple gates and altar where the wedding ceremony takes place in stanzas 12 and 13; the walls at the return home sprinkled with wine to make them drunk in stanza 14; and the heavens as temple of the gods in stanza 23. But the first two hardly conjure up spatialized structures in the same way the image of the bride-cum-palace does, and no other person is represented as architectural space; indeed, only the temple of heaven forms an acceptable parallel to the architectural body of the bride.

In the last full stanza of the poem the heavenly temple of the gods is called upon to 'pour out' blessings 'plenteously' and 'rain' down 'happy influence,' images of the overflowing masculine potency of the deity as father sky. The result of this elemental fertility imagery is to 'raise a large posterity' to bless the earth, combining the Stoic theme of immortality through progeny with Judaic election. The complementary motion of mounting up to the 'haughty palaces' of the heavenly hereafter – landing places for the 'blessed saints' – spatializes that otherworld in terms which directly recall the description of the bride. There is also an invocation of the feminine aspect of God in this contained space, especially in the throne and tabernacle which signify the ark of the divine presence (the *Shekhina* of the kabbalah).[8]

The parallel between the bride-as-palace and heaven-as-palace also correlates in terms of another important spatialization of the beloved's body – as a container for the production of offspring. The bridegroom-poet had just told of 'the chaste womb inform[ed] with timely seed' in stanza 21, appropriating and revaluing the effete emptiness of Echo's female form by injecting it with re-productivity (again the girl is left behind). It is, notably, 'the' womb, not 'her' womb, absenting the human woman too and claiming the procreative moment for a relationship between the poet-husband and the divine in the form of the goddess Cynthia. Thus materializing the absent body of Echo reveals how the embodiment of the major female figure of the poem partakes of an erased corporeality, both as passive hollow structure waiting to resound and as container for the masculine poet's procreativity.

The Echo of the *Epithalamion* is Ovidian Echo. There is, however, an alternative tradition which gave to Echo a greater, more positive status. Joseph Loewenstein, while cognizant of the debilities of the Ovidian myth, presents a much more complicated model of Echo as *imitatio.* Loewenstein includes both earlier and later mythographies of the vocal nymph: her prophetic ability to give good advice (often evident in the genre of echo-poems); her association with Orpheus; and her association with Pan (who is often read as Nature or Christ).[9] The concord between Echo and Pan was interpreted, Loewenstein asserts, as an animate voice of nature which could subdue the daemonic to the human.[10] Loewenstein also discloses that Echo had a reputation which linked her to the muses. As he states, in the *Genealogia Deorum,* Boccaccio called her 'Parnasi nympha potissime' (the most powerful nymph of Parnassus); and in a collection of Renaissance echo-lyrics published in Venice in 1648, the Dutch editor, Johann van der Does, extended her prestige when he inscribed her on the title page of his second edition as 'Echo, quae novem regens musis, ceu decimam comitem addidit' ('Echo who rules with the muses, as if adding a tenth member to their cohort).[11] Loewenstein deduces from this information that '[i]n the Renaissance, an era of explicitly imitative poetic production, Echo had come to seem a muse of modernity,' where modernity is the 'preservation and modernization of antique modes and manners.'[12] Or as Elizabeth Harvey puts it in her book *Ventriloquized Voices,* there is often a 'self-conscious construction of Renaissance culture as the inheritor, voice, and disinterrer of the classical past.'[13] Following Bacon's representation of Echo as an ideal philosophical discourse, Loewenstein sees her place in Ben Jonson's mythography as an 'idealized figure for imitative poetry, a tradition of modern making that revalues its models with free and knowing respect.'[14]

Loewenstein has valuably identified a tradition of Echo as a positive form of *imitatio,* but he seems to want to meld the two divergent strands – the Ovidian nymph's inept re-sounding and the Muse's voice as disinterrer of the classical past – into one. He tries to integrate all the variousness into one model of 'cultural memory'[15] – a model predominantly positive in its ability to modernize the past, as for Jonson, but also construing the 'modernity' of the Renaissance as anticipating the melancholic anxieties of twentieth-century modernity, especially in his article on Orpheus and the *Epithalamion*.

In my view, it would be preferable to preserve the distinction between two alternative traditions for Echo: the one linking her to the muses, the resounding (*resonare*) of pastoral, and 'the preservation of antique modes'; the other – Ovidian – tradition linking her to effete and epigonic reiteration. As so many other scholars do, Loewenstein moves too quickly from girl to abstraction, from the nymph's body to the conceptual aspects of language, and he often includes in his analysis instances in which Echo is not specifically present at all, or only present by association, not in name or direct allusion. This method of abstraction is particularly detrimental to his discussions of Ovid's treatment of Echo, the most well-known and influential version of the myth in the period. To my mind there is real analytic use in describing and maintaining two distinct traditions, one Ovidian and one non-Ovidian.

Just as Echo has a double tradition, so Ovid himself was subject to two different evaluative assessments in the Renaissance. Jonathan Bate, in his book *Shakespeare and Ovid*, quotes Shakespeare's contemporary Francis Meres who praised Shakespeare as 'infused with the sweet and witty soul of Ovid';[16] Ovid thus serves as a positive model for imitation. *Imitatio* here, Bate is at pains to assert, is an affiliation 'broadly paradigmatic,'[17] rather than apelike reproduction of the original. In Shakespeare's sonnets we have an imitation of Ovid's elegance and facility, allowing room for difference as well as similarity.[18] Thus Shakespeare's Ovidian *imitatio* is, as Puttenham puts it, an imitation of antiquity which dignifies English poetry by offering a paradigm or example which authorizes as a precedent.[19] But there is also a negative valuing of Ovid as a model for imitation. This is well known in the dismissal of Ovid for licentiousness and moral laxity which lurks behind a preliminary section in George Sandys's translation of the *Metamorphoses* called 'Ovid Defended' (it is interesting to note that Ovid still needed defending in 1632).

The two negative traditions – of author and myth – are brought together for chastisement by the minor Elizabethan poet and translator Joshua Sylvester. Sylvester had greater reason to feel anxious and threatened by Ovidian Echo as a model for poetic identity than Spenser did. Sylvester 'lamented that he was in a manner enforced to be a Translator rather than a "native Poet"' due to poverty.[20] A translator is of course more open to the charge of simplistic echoing than a 'native poet,' and thus may have more care to distance himself from any model which suggests apelike and empty replication. Sylvester is best known for his successful translation of Du Bartas's *Divine Weekes and Workes,* first printed in 1598, and in eight successive issues and editions between then and 1632.[21] In the 'Translator's Invocation' to this work, Sylvester emphasizes his belatedness by calling on his 'tardy Muse,' and protests his lack of skill in his 'Art-less pen' (p. 99). Nonetheless, he would like to dignify English poetry by ridding the country of Ovidian imitators:

O! furnish me with an un-vulgar stile
That I by this may wain our wanton ILE
From Ovid's heires, and their un-hallowed spell
Here charming senses, chaining soules in Hell. (p. 99)

Indeed, Ovid is to be replaced by 'My dear sweet Daniel,' and 'our new NASO,' Drayton, a good candidate for replacing Ovidius Naso because he nativized the *Heroides* in the *Heroick Epistles.*

In his translation of the first day of the second week of creation, discussing Eden before the fall, Sylvester speaks of the birds' and angels' song praising the great Maker. But his description of Echo is jarringly out of sync with the tone of celebration here:

Th'Air's daughter Eccho, haunting woods among,
A blab that will not (cannot) keep her tongue,
Who never asks, but onely answers all,
Who lets not any her in vain to call;
She bore her part; and full of curious skill,
They ceasing, sung; they singing, ceaséd still:
There Musicke raign'd, and ever on the plain,
A sweet sound rais'd the dead-live voyce again. (p. 127)[22]

The notion of Echo as the daughter of Air and Language fits into the negative Ovidian tradition and derives from an epigram of Ausonius, which also calls her the mother of blind judgment, 'a voice without a mind. / I only with others language sport: / And but the last of dying speech retort' (trans. Sandys, p. 104). Sylvester's 'dead-live voyce' succinctly summarizes the absent body/present sound of the girl left behind, the dissolved and erased Echo, the voice without a mind. In calling Echo a 'blab,' not only a tell-tale but a kind of vocalic slut who responds to any call, Sylvester intensifies the defamation that the English translator Golding had already heaped upon her:

A babling Nymph that Echo hight, who hearing others talke,
By no meanes can restraine hir tongue but that it needes must walke,
Nor of hir selfe hath powre to ginne to speake to any wight ...
Yet of hir speach she had that time no more than now the choyce,
That is to say, of many wordes the latter to repeate. (III.443–9)

Translators can make choices, however, and it is instructive to compare this with Sandys's translation, which is much closer to the Latin and less disparaging of the girl than either Sylvester's or Golding's treatment:

The vocall Nymph, this louely Boy did spy
(She could not proffer speech, nor not reply) ...
Eccho was then a body, not a Voyce:
Yet then, as now, of words she wanted choyce;
But only could reiterate the close
Of euery speech. This *Iuno* did impose. (p. 89)

The 'curious skill' of Sylvester's description of Echo, paired with Sylvester's own modest invocation of his 'Art-less pen,' seems to rebuke the skilled art*ful*ness of Echo's author Ovid, as well as his blabbing nymph. In fact, the description of Echo in Book III of *Metamorphoses*, before she receives her curse, already emphasizes her licentious speaking – excessive, skilled, and put to immoral purpose: for often, while Jove dallied with her fellow-nymphs, she had detained Juno through her skill in speaking at length ('illa deam longo prudens sermone tenebat,' III.364; Golding translates as 'tatling talk,' Sandys 'long discourses'). This makes Echo the same kind of tale-spinner as the ill-fated daughters of Minyas who appear in the next book of the *Metamorphoses*; and, more importantly, it parallels her to the supreme weaver of tales, Ovid himself. Ovid's link to these feminine weavers of *texta*, however, must be seen as a complicated strategy on the part of the male poet. Ovid frequently speaks from the position of the female voice in his works, most notably in the *Heroides*. But as Elizabeth Harvey cautions, 'Ovid can write from the perspective of the woman precisely because he is not himself a woman ... [Although] Ovid uses the metaphor of woman as a lever for dismantling certain patriarchal values ... he simultaneously partakes of the very privilege he seeks to expose.'[23]

Yet Ovid's role as male poet in relation to, and defined against, female bodies and voices goes even further. Building on the work of A.M. Keith, it is important to note that Ovid frequently casts his poetic works in the form of female bodies: the *corpus poematis* is also the *corpus puellae.* Ovid scholars have long noted the initial programmatic poem of each book of the *Amores* as participating in the ancient debate about aesthetics. For example, in the first poem in Book III of that work a personified Elegia appears walking with a slight limp ('pes illi longior alter erat,' III.1.8), 'so that her walk mimics the rhythmic alternation of hexameter and pentameter lines in the elegiac couplet.'[24] Keith notes the conflation of the elegiac style with the elegiac mistress, and more generally, the conflation of the physical incarnation of poetic form with the *puellae* in other poems of the collection. This gives a deeper grounding to the Ovidian practice of what she punningly calls his *corpus eroticum.* The poems identified, she argues, promote the interpretation of the beloved as a literary construction – for example, when Corinna's body 'displays a perfection realizable only in a work of art such as a marble statue, an ivory carving, or a finely-crafted book of poetry.'[25] Therefore, in several cases Corinna is 'simultaneously girl friend and literary project.'[26]

One of the poems, *Amores* 2.4, presents a catalogue of *puellae*: the poet-lover admits that he can love them all – tall, short, dark, fair:

tu, quia tam longa es, veteres heroidas aequas
et potes in toto multa iacere toro.
haec habilis brevitate sua est. corrumpor utraque;
conveniunt voto longa brevisque meo.
non est culta – subit, quid cultae accedere possit;
ornata est – dotes exhibet ipsa suas.
candida me capiet, capiet me flava puella,
est etiam in fusco grata colore Venus.
seu pendent nivea pulli cervice capilli,
Leda fuit nigra conspicienda coma;
seu flavent, placuit croceis Aurora capillis. (II.4.33–43)[27]

[You, because you are so tall, are not second to the ancient daughters of heroes, and can lie the whole couch's length. Another I find apt because she is short. I am undone by both; tall and short are after the wish of my heart. She is not well dressed – I dream what dress would add; she is well arrayed – she herself shows off her dower of charms. A fair white skin will make prey of me, I am prey to the golden-haired, and even love of dusky hue will please.

> Do dark locks hang on a neck of snow – Leda was fair to look upon for her black locks; are they of golden hue – Aurora pleased with saffron locks.]
>
> (trans. Showerman)

Keith notes that 'the beauty and manners of many of the *puellae* catalogued in the poem intersect with the poetic program of the elegist ... In particular, Ovid exploits a variety of adjectives in order to bring together *puellae* of differing physical proportions in such a way as to evoke the metrical norms of elegiac verse.'[28]

At least one Renaissance reader of Ovid had noted the same Ovidian practice of conflating or superimposing girls' bodies and a male author's poetic works; that reader was Erasmus. In the *Ciceronianus*, his contribution to the discussion of *imitatio* and specifically Ciceronianism in the Renaissance, Erasmus argues for emulation as opposed to imitation of classical models. He rejects the 'verbal correctness' of those who would conform to Cicero's Latin in all things. Towards the end of the dialogue, the reader is exhorted to follow Ovid's example in his eclectic taste in *puellae* (referring to *Amores* 2.4) and take from any writer that which is good:

> quin potius quod Naso ludens narrat sibi accidisse in puellarum amoribus, id nos serio praestemus in autorum lectione. Ille proceram commendabat puellam, quod heroina videretur, breuis placebat ob commoditatem, primam aetatem flos ipse commendabat, grandiorem rerum vsus, in illiterata delectabat simplicitas, in erudita ingenium, in candida coloris gratiam amabat, in fusca nescio quid latentis gratiae sibi fingebat. Eodem candore si nos ex singulis scriptoribus excerpemus quod habent probandum, nullum fastidiemus, sed ex omnibus aliquid delibabimus, quod nostram condiat orationem.[29]

> [Rather let us, in reading our authors, display in all seriousness the attitude of mind which Ovid jestingly tells us he found himself displaying in his various affairs with girls. He found a tall girl attractive because of her heroic stature, a short one attractive because she was easy to handle; youthful bloom commended a young one, experience one who was a bit older, the naivety of an uneducated girl was delightful, in an educated one the attraction was wit, in a fairskinned girl he adored the loveliness of her colouring, in a dusky one he imagined I know not what lurking charm. If we show the same generosity of spirit and extract from each writer

whatever deserves commendation, we shall disdain none of them, but channel off something from each to give a flavour to our own speech.][30]

Whereas Keith draws out the references to elegiac poetics embodied in the girls of the poem – for example, in the juxtaposition of tall and short we have the characteristic alternation of hexameter and pentameter lines of verse[31] – Erasmus is specifically interested in Ovidian *puellae* in a context of *imitatio* as different rhetorical styles: the elevated high style of the tall girl, the brevitas of the short one; the epideictic praise of youth or maturity; the humble simplicitas of the uneducated girl, the learned wit of the educated one; the rhetorical colours of the fair girl, the concealed artistry of the dark one. It is likely that Erasmus gave currency to this renewed Ovidian practice, as the *Ciceronianus* was well known in the period, and is quoted, for example, in the preface to Sandys's translation entitled 'Ovid Defended'; and Spenser's friend Gabriel Harvey composed his own *Ciceronianus.* Thus Erasmus served as a justifier of the author of the *Amores* and the *Metamorphoses,* and more specifically as the originator of the construction of the textualized female body as an explicitly Ovidian way of emulating classical authors.

Spenser also employs a parallel embodiment of woman and form. In the envoys to Spenser's *Shepheardes Calendar* we can read the aspect and gesture of the bride of the *Epithalamion* as referring back to this earlier work. Both Spenser's 'little book' and his spouse of the 'Epithalamion' embody modesty – the calendar following Chaucer and Langland with a 'lowly gate,' while the bride ever keeps her eyes 'upon the lowly ground affixed' (l. 161). More importantly, however, Spenser's Ovidian *imitatio* is characterized, I would argue, by outdoing his classical precedent. If Bate sees Shakespeare's imitation of Ovid as asserting Ovid's immortality and his own in mutual, respecting share, I see Spenser's imitation as surpassing the model. In Spenser's self-construction as *vates,* supremely in control, and in his choice of Echo, a manifestly Ovidian female character, as the rejected or transcended embodiment of his poetic production, he proves himself not just equal to but capable of overgoing the master. For the poet-husband of the 'Epithalamion' not only initiates but can also terminate re-sounding at will, as the refrain of the second half of the poem makes clear, 'The woods no more shal answere, nor your echo ring (l. 314).'[32] Unlike Loewenstein, I detect no Orphic anxiety in the use of Echo as poetic imitation; instead of an 'anxiety of influence,' we have a case of 'the more predecessors, the better' –

a more accurate description of Ovid's own attitude to his poetic precursors.[33] In the assured transposition of the body of Echo into a feminized space for sounding, in the syncretic projection of this spatialized body onto his humble spouse – a move of supreme masculine power and brilliance[33] – Spenser out 'Ovids' Ovid: once the girl is left behind the voice remaining is his alone.

NOTES

1 This paper was first presented to The English Renaissance Group at the University of Toronto in April 1998; my sincere thanks to organizer Glenn Loney for giving me that opportunity. Barkan's work seems to continue the tradition established by Boas, Wilkinson, and Martindale's volume, while some incisive rethinking is effected by Bate and Stapleton. See Leonard Barkan, *The Gods Made Flesh: Metamorphosis and the Pursuit of Paganism* (New Haven: Yale University Press, 1986); Frederick S. Boas, *Ovid and the Elizabethans* (London: The English Association, [1947?]; L.P. Wilkinson, *Ovid Recalled* (Cambridge: Cambridge University Press, 1955); Charles Martindale, ed., *Ovid Renewed* (Cambridge: Cambridge University Press, 1988), especially Laurence Lerner, 'Ovid and the Elizabethans,' pp. 121–35; Jonathan Bate, *Shakespeare and Ovid* (Oxford: Clarendon Press, 1993); M.L. Stapleton, *Harmful Eloquence: Ovid's* Amores *from Antiquity to Shakespeare* (Ann Arbor: University of Michigan Press, 1996).

2 John Hollander, *The Figure of Echo: A Mode of Allusion in Milton and After* (Berkeley: University of California Press, 1981); Jonathan Goldberg, *Voice Terminal Echo: Postmodernism and English Renaissance Texts* (New York: Methuen, 1986); Caren Greenberg, 'Reading Reading: Echo's Abduction of Language,' in *Women and Language in Literature and Society*, ed. S. McConnell-Giret, Ruth Barker, and Newlly Furman (New York: Praeger, 1980); Bradford K. Mudge, 'Echo's Words, Echo's Body: Apostasy, Narcissism, and the Practice of History,' *Tulsa Studies in Women's Literature* 10 (1991): 197–214; and Gayatri Chakravorty Spivak, 'Echo,' *New Literary History* 24 (1993): 17–43.

3 All references to the poem are from *Amoretti and Epithalamion*, ed. Alexander Dunlop, in *The Yale Edition of the Shorter Poems of Edmund Spenser*, ed. William Oram et al. (New Haven: Yale University Press, 1989), pp. 584–679.

4 *Ovid's Metamorphoses: The Arthur Golding Translation 1567*, ed. John Frederick Nims (New York: Macmillan, 1965).

5 George Sandys, *Ovid's Metamorphosis Englished Mythologized and Represented in Figures* (Oxford, 1632; repr. New York: Garland, 1976).

6 Sheila Delany, *Impolitic Bodies: Poetry, Saints, and Society in Fifteenth-Century England: The Work of Osbern Bokenham* (Oxford: Oxford University Press, 1998), p. 75. She cites as examples John 2:19–21; 1 Cor. 6:19; and Saint Augustine, *De Doctrina Christiana* 3.14.22.

7 Delany, *Impolitic Bodies*, pp. 75–6, notes, in addition, that Plato's *Timaeus* 'employs architectural imagery in recounting the creation of humankind: chamber, apartment, wall, citadel ...' (sec. 70A).

8 For a very interesting discussion of the feminine aspects of God in kabbalistic thought, including the imagery of the *Shekhina* as bride, bridal chamber, and throne, and reflection of or containment within the male, see Elliot R. Wolfson, *Through a Speculum That Shines: Vision and Imagination in Medieval Jewish Mysticism* (Princeton: Princeton University Press, 1994). Although beyond the scope of the present essay, it would be relevant to apply Wolfson's findings to Spenser's text.

9 See Joseph Loewenstein, *Responsive Readings: Versions of Echo in Pastoral, Epic, and the Jonsonian Masque* (New Haven: Yale University Press, 1984); and 'Echo's Ring: Orpheus and Spenser's Career,' *English Literary Renaissance* 16 (1986): 287–302.

10 Loewenstein, *Responsive Readings*, p. 11.

11 A place usually reserved for Sappho. See Loewenstein, *Responsive Readings*, p. 5.

12 Loewenstein, *Responsive Readings*, p. 5.

13 Elizabeth D. Harvey, *Ventriloquized Voices: Feminist Theory and English Renaissance Texts* (London: Routledge, 1992), p. 10.

14 Loewenstein, *Responsive Readings*, p. 5.

15 Ibid.

16 Bate, *Shakespeare and Ovid* (Oxford: Oxford University Press, 1994), p. 84.

17 Ibid., p. 85.

18 Ibid., p. 87.

19 Ibid., p. 84.

20 Alexander B. Grosart, 'Memorial Introduction' to *The Complete Works of Joshua Sylvester*, ed. A.B. Grosart, vol. 1, Chertsey Worthies Library (Edinburgh: Edinburgh University Press, 1880), p. xxv.

21 According to Susan Snyder, the English vogue of du Bartas was endorsed by such Spenserian associates as Sidney and Gabriel Harvey, and 'Spenser seems to have shared the general esteem for du Bartas.' It is worth noting that his works gained longer popularity in Renaissance England than in France through the translations of Sylvester. See Snyder, 'du Bartas,' in *The Spenser Encyclopedia*, A.C. Hamilton, general editor (Toronto: University of Toronto Press, 1990), p. 80.

22 The line immediately preceding this section on Echo mentions Orpheus ('And Nightingales sung like divine Arion, / Like Tracian Orpheus, Linus, and Amphion'). It is clear that Sylvester is making a clear distinction between Orpheus and Echo; he is either directly rejecting the positive tradition which merged them together, or just as emphatically underlining of the negative, Ovidian one.

23 Harvey, *Ventriloquized Voices*, pp. 39–40.

24 A.M. Keith, '*Corpus Eroticum*: Elegiac Poetics and Elegiac *Puellae* in Ovid's *Amores*,' *Classical World* 88 (1994): 27.

25 Keith, '*Corpus Eroticum*,' p. 31.

26 Ibid., p. 32.

27 Ovid, *Heroides and Amores, with an English translation by Grant Showerman*, 2nd ed., revised by G.P. Goold, Loeb Classical Library (London: Heinemann, 1986), p. 392.

28 Keith, '*Corpus Eroticum*' p. 33. I would like to acknowledge here the formative influence of Keith on my own reading of Ovid.

29 Erasmus, 'Dialogus Ciceronianus,' in *Opera Omnia*, ed. Pierre Mesnard, vol. 1, pt 2 (Amsterdam: North-Holland, 1971), pp. 708–9.

30 Erasmus, *Ciceronianus*, in *Literary and Education Writings 6*, ed. and trans. A.H.T. Levi, *Collected Works of Erasmus*, vol. 28 (Toronto: University of Toronto Press, 1986), pp. 446–7.

31 Keith, '*Corpus Eroticum*' p. 34.

32 As those familiar with the poem know, the refrain for stanzas 17 through 23, like that of 1 through 16, is not standardized, but includes slight verbal variations in each instance.

33 See Stephen Hinds, 'Medea in Ovid: Scenes from the Life of an Intertextual Heroine,' *Materiali e discussioni per l'analisi dei testi classici* 30 (1993): 9–47. I am indebted to Hinds's oral version of this paper, given at the University of Toronto in March 1991, for the stunning insight into Ovid's use of his predecessors.

34 Spenser seems to have learned well from his poetic master; as Lerner notes, for an Elizabethan contemporary ('Ovid and the Elizabethans,' p. 126) 'What Donne takes from Ovid may be above all his masculinity: masculine cynicism, masculine power, masculine brilliance.'

'If that which is lost be not found': Monumental Bodies, Spectacular Bodies in *The Winter's Tale*

LORI HUMPHREY NEWCOMB

It is hard to imagine *The Winter's Tale* as a lost play when it is so prominently placed as the last of the comedies in Shakespeare's First Folio. Yet the oracle's famous warning that order will not be restored 'if that which is lost be not found' briefly applied to at least one crucial copy of the play, which was misplaced while the Folio was in press. An August 1623 record (itself now lost) in the Revels office licensed 'the king's players' to perform 'an olde playe called *Winters Tale*, formerly allowed of by Sir George Bucke, and likewyse by mee on Mr. Hemmings his worde that there was nothing prophane added or reformed, thogh the allowed booke was missinge.'[1] Textual scholars have speculated about the nature of this 'allowed booke,' seeking to link it to the text transmitted in the pages of the Folio. Was that allowed book a 'fair copy,' that most sought-after of Shakespearean texts? The vanishing of that perhaps authoritative copy has tantalized textual scholars. So, too, has the more temporary misplacement of the play from the Folio itself, where it was printed significantly later than the other comedies. The delay is signaled by breaks in the textual body of the Folio – an unprecedented blank verso page following *Twelfth Night*, a tail-ornament that was dented by wear between its appearances in the two comedies.[2]

To early textual scholars, it seemed more than coincidental that *The Winter's Tale* went missing from two different venues on or about August 1623. Could the use of the 'allowed text' in the printing house have rendered it unavailable for performance licensing? Or conversely, could the 1623 performance of *The Winter's Tale* have temporarily derailed its publication? Alfred W. Pollard mused in 1907: 'If only one manuscript of the play was available, and that was wanted for use in the theatre when the end of the comedies was reached, there may have been a delay in printing this one play ... But we cannot be sure that we have anything more than a coincidence.'[3] Later scholars have dismissed the link that Pollard tried to forge: W.W. Greg estimated that the play was printed no later than winter 1623, albeit as 'an afterthought' among the comedies (p. 439); J.H.P. Pafford, dubious that there had been 'only one manuscript' available, concluded that the Revels record 'has no bearing at all on the apparent delay in printing *The Winter's Tale*' (pp. xvi–xvii). There is no reason to identify the two misplacements, or to seek in the convergence proof of any one text's authority. Still, Pollard's 'coincidence' begs to be read as a fable of competition between the printing of the play and its performance. In this fable, if the play joins the Folio to become a monument, it becomes impervious to performance; if the play is brought to the stage, its constant reenactment makes the fixity of the monumental impossible.

That tendency to see page and stage as competitors has been reversed in much contemporary Shakespeare criticism, which, by arguing for the indeterminacy of early modern textual and stage practices, has assimilated the free play of the text to the playfulness of theatre. But to the extent that the early modern meanings of page and stage are founded in broader conceptions of the body, I believe that the two are neither mutually exclusive nor fully assimilable. I see tension between page and stage throughout the Folio *Winter's Tale*, a play-text uniquely poised between impulses that I call monumentalizing and spectacular, impulses that evince very different conceptions of the body. On one hand, the play is marked by a strong tendency to monumentalize: to shape and fix texts, to demand singular control of the art object, to memorialize the body in an exact duplicate, to contain women in immobility.[4] On the other hand, it also dares to be spectacular – to leave texts behind, to embrace collaboration and proliferation, to celebrate the changefulness of the human body, even the female body.[5] In *The Winter's Tale*, the monumental, by recording the absence of the female body, maintains the presence of the purified male body, the 'issue.' The spectacular, by accepting the evanescence of all bodies, maintains metamorphosis as the only human constant. Monuments depend on what is lost; spectacle celebrates what is found.

These impulses are fundamental to the performance of early modern English gender and sexual difference: their 'ritualized repetition' works to 'produce and stabilize not only the effects of gender but the materiality of sex' in the forms characteristic of that culture.[6] It is widely held that sexual difference in early modern patriarchal culture turns on a

Bakhtinian opposition between closure and openness.[7] By revising this opposition, which can figure openness as patriarchy's other, to the pairing of monumental and spectacular impulses, I emphasize that both impulses are constitutive of patriarchal constructions of sex. The monumental fantasy of 'masculine' closure is legible in comportment, building, writing, printing; the spectacular fantasy of 'feminine' openness provokes (and problematizes) movement, sexual acts, visual arts, and of course theatre. Patriarchy taps *both* impulses in sustaining its norms. Crucially, however, the two cannot be reconciled, for each questions the very grounds on which the other understands the body. The monumental insists that identity is recorded only by eradicating fluid forms; the spectacular insists that the body must be presented and can never finally be represented. Their tension is what threatens early modern norms of sex and gender. Although the spectacular impulse imagines a body that escapes texts, I see the impulse itself as being enacted textually, as it is in *The Winter's Tale.* Judith Butler's work has linked gender norms to playtexts *metaphorically*: gendered bodies act their parts 'within the confines of already existing directives ... just as a script may be enacted in various ways, and just as the play requires both text and interpretation.'[8] I would argue that a printed script, straining with material traces of both textuality and embodied interpretation, is not just similar to, but instrumental in, the shaping of the 'materiality of sex' in its historically specific form.

Both monumental and spectacular impulses are strongly present in the Folio *Winter's Tale.* In broad terms, its plot can be said to condemn monumentalizing and embrace spectacle, while its transcription works to re-monumentalize the text, to empty out the play's performing bodies and curb its metamorphic qualities. Hermione's change from monument-to-a-woman-lost to woman-not-a-monument strikingly embodies the play's alternation between monumentalized textual body and spectacular theatrical body. The final act, apparently about a substitute for an absent body, opens into living bodies and their proliferation through time. The fable of the revived statue draws on Ovid's Pygmalion narrative to condemn monumentalization in favour of dramatic, dynamic metamorphosis. But at the same time, the monumentalizing environment of the Folio tends to curb the gender instabilities introduced by this spectacular, Ovidian resolution.

Although we can name some of the men who helped to shape the play's intersecting impulses – Ovid, Robert Greene, William Shakespeare, John Hemings, and Henry Condell, the other King's Men, Ben Jonson, Ralph Crane, William and Isaac Jaggard, compositors A, B, and so on – the accumulated effect cannot be attributed to particular individuals. Nor, in the end, can parties or states be securely labelled. For throughout this play's First Folio embodiment, the monumentalizing text and the embodied performance are problematically imbricated in one another. Just when the text most asserts its monumentality, it too is losing and finding bodies, or tripping over their fluid genderings; conversely, even in the final scene, as the spectacle of the performing body triumphs, monumentalizing claims are mouthed by actors. The printed text acts up, the theatrical text weighs down. The monuments of loss in this play, and the spectacles of finding, intersect and cross in a complex performance of the gendering of bodies.

What text was lost in August of 1623, or whether it was found, remains for an oracle to discover. We can imagine, though, that if that lost 'allowed booke' encountered the play's First Folio embodiment, it might ask, as Hermione asked of Perdita: 'Tell me (mine owne) / Where haft thou bin preferu'd, where liu'd? How found.'[9] Hermione greets Perdita, herself the fairest of copies, as her 'yffue' (5.3.3340). Unlike Perdita, the First Folio is an 'yffue' whose textual journeys and parentage cannot be named. Finding one text does not yield a lineage of those that are lost. Finding is spectacular, even in the monument that is the Folio.

'Counterfetted corse': The Monumental Body and the Metamorphic Tradition

Ovid never says whether Pygmalion, after his statue metamorphosed into a living wife, regretted the loss of his masterpiece – but surely that loss is implied. Indeed, once Venus gives life to his artwork, Pygmalion as artist disappears from the narrative, superseded by his wife's awakening to 'hir lover and the light at once,' and a concluding account of the couple as progenitors.[10] The man gives up not just his artificial woman, but his art form, in order to acquire a real woman and a line of heirs. If the story of Pygmalion, like so many of the depetrifications and petrifications on which Ovid builds his *Metamorphoses*, weighs art against nature, it may strike an especially hard bargain, one that implies that the artist-made body must be sacrificed to gain a natural body and descendants. Most readings of the tale see this exchange as a gain: the lost artwork is a mere copy, while the found human body is an original. Artists could argue that the cost is too high, for the perfected artistic reproduction, the copy so fair that it disappears back into its original, will never be replaced, while natural reproduction will continue for generations, regardless of human imperfections. Pygmalion apparently refuses the opposite course – to rest satisfied with the statue, to suppress the desire for a living replacement, with its promise of erotic pleasure and of progeny. This tale of rivalry between artistic/representational and living/natural making is also always a tale about gender; it reverses the male patriarchal fantasy that an ideologically impeccable 'counterfetted corse' (X: 272) may replace the more problematic but pleasurable living partner. And beneath that monumental fantasy lies a different knowledge – that the two ways of knowing woman, like the two ways of making bodies, challenge the very grounds of one another.

Can we be certain, though, that the Pygmalion story endorses the living body over the monument? Or does it explore the choice more fluidly? After all, a substitution is not what Pygmalion requests from Venus:

> If that you Goddes can all things give, then let my wife (I pray)
> (He durst not say bee yoon same wench of Ivory, but) bee leeke
> My wench of Ivory. (X: 298–300)

Ovid implies that Pygmalion dares not ask for an ivory-to-flesh conversion. And although Venus easily determines 'What such a wish as that did meene' (X: 301), Ovid never quite asserts that the quickening of the statue fulfils his request. The epistemological fluidity of the *Metamorphoses,* in which metaphor can become metamorphosis and vice versa, makes it impossible to take the maiden's final form as the final answer.[11] After all, it is the hard-heartedness of the Propoetides that prepares their transformation to stone – 'In which betweene their former shape was diffrence small or none' (X: 260) – which in turn produces Pygmalion's own settling for a woman of stone, who then softens. Ovid's trajectory from metaphor to metamorphosis could always be inverted: could the lesson not be that Pygmalion might long to remonumentalize his wife, preferring a less yielding virtue? Or, criticism of the monumentalizing impulse might be read in certain elements of the Pygmalion story, such as the narrative shift from Pygmalion to his new wife. Once the object of metaphoric thinking, the maiden becomes a subject, seeing 'hir lover and the light at once' in her own first epiphany (X: 320). The former monument becomes first spectacle, then spectator.

Renaissance appropriations of the Pygmalion myth vary in accepting the reversibility of its metamorphosis. Arthur Golding's 1567 translation implies that even a living wife would be monumentalized by ideologies of containment, commenting on the ivory maiden:

The looke of it was ryght a Maydens Looke,
And such a one as that yee would beleeve had lyfe, and that
Would moved bee, if womanhod and reverence letted not. (X: 268–70)

Golding adds a paradox not in Ovid: the statue looks like a maiden, but a desiring one; but if she is desiring, she can be no maiden. On the other hand, John Marston's infinitely cynical version of the Pygmalion story, *The Metamorphosis of Pigmalions Image* (1598), explicitly rejects an ideologically monumentalized woman – or, for that matter, statue. Marston regards stony virtue as a (Petrarchan) game played by a living woman, the narrator's 'relentlesse stone' mistress.[12] Against Golding's protestations, Marston's intrusive narrator tells the reading 'Ladies' that he, (meaning Pygmalion too) wants to 'moue' a woman who wants to be moved (20.5–6). Marston's version of Pygmalion's prayer to Venus is direct where Golding's was ambivalent: 'In changing stone to flesh, make her relent, / And kindly yeeld to thy sweet blandishment (23.5–6).' When she does 'melt (29.3),' the narrator/Pygmalion rewrites the 'mouing blandishment' (29.6) as 'his owne worke' (29.4). Or perhaps the narrator's gamesmanship goes further, and she was never a statue at all; for where most translations began the story by noting that the maiden was made of ivory, Marston's notes that her breast is '*like* polisht Ivory' (8.4, 1, emphasis added). In insisting on flesh, Marston rejects the very possibility of stone-to-flesh transformation. Ironically, by refusing to take the monumental impulse seriously, Marston forestalls the Ovidian spectacle as well.

Marston's libertine insistence on woman-flesh may point to another possibility: perhaps, for early readers, Pygmalion's unvivified statue counted as a man. Why is Pygmalion, who learns to love women, included in the Orpheus books, so preoccupied with the transgression of heterosexual norms? Ovid's sources for the Pygmalion story involve actual intercourse with a statue, a harsher challenge to heterosexuality.[13] If classical culture defines transgression as an adult man's wish to be the penetratee rather than the penetrator, it can hardly admire a man who performs sexual acts on a body of stone, the ultimate impenetrable. Even in Ovid's version, Pygmalion's image of a woman, insofar as it is a statue, may still be masculine in its sexual state. After all, the statue is the hard body that is the classical and Renaissance masculine ideal.[14] Only Pygmalion's unusual choice of ivory grants feminine potential to the statue.[15] The monumentalizing impulse that the Renaissance inherited via Ovid tends to turn a problematic woman not to a dead woman (as is often suggested) but to a dead man.

That the metamorphosis in the Pygmalion tale has the potential to criticize the monumental impulse is confirmed when the last scene of *The Winter's Tale* switches out a life-size sculpture for a living wife. As Rosalie Colie puts it, 'The famous statue is a simulacrum of Hermione ... Hermione transfixed into a memorial record of what she had been.'[16] If the metamorphosis is illusory – if the statue turns out to have been the living Hermione all along, as she herself claims – what must be sacrificed is not just a sculpture perfected, but the impulse to make statues in the first place. The erasure of the statue is a loss to both the making of art, and Leontes' desire to transfix his wife. No wonder Leontes complains bitterly that 'I faw her / (As I thought) dead: and haue (in vaine) faid many / A:prayer vpon her graue' (5.3.3352–4). As Leonard Barkan has astutely argued, theatrical audiences are as reluctant as Leontes to give up belief in seeing a statue revived; the scene begins by evoking 'our faith in Hermione as a statue' so that, 'like Leontes, and Pygmalion,' we can accept 'the triumph of art' before the 'triumph of life.' Ultimately, that triumph of life is also one of theatre, 'four-dimensional' art superior to three-dimensional sculpture.[17] Theatre trumps sculpture in a spectacular demonstration that sculpture is unnecessary, even nonexistent – even, as Pauline Kiernan argues, an idolatrous 'counterfeit.'[18] Eliminate the idolatrous counterfeit, the patriarchal monument, and the original is restored – presentationally rather than representationally. One cog in the wheel of this antimonumental reading is that the 'original' Hermione, re-produced by illusory metamorphosis, is of course also a representation. Her embodiment is human – but if the spectacle of the female human can be represented only by a boy actor, the monumentalization of women is still at work.

Persuasively as Colie, Barkan, and Kiernan handle the play's canonical scenes, I cannot conclude that its celebration of the theatrical body entirely dismisses the monumental impulse. The spectacle on stage still presupposes containment as the condition of the female body.[19] More distinctively, the Folio text underlines gendered monumentalization with textual monumentalization. In this context, *The Winter's Tale* stands out for two features of its plot, redoubled by its format and its editorial state. The play is driven to generate, lose, and find monuments and monumental embedded texts, including the oracle, the indictment, and epitaphs. And it is more concerned with printed texts than is any other play by Shakespeare, thanks to its extended and digressive ballad-selling scene. These features are then apparently fixed in the edifice of the Folio, which takes deliberate steps towards monumentalizing its absent author and his text, participating in the early modern articulation of English authorship.[20] The Folio text is further weighted down by Ralph Crane's famously heavy transcription, with its bold capitals, excessive punctuation, 'Jonsonian' classicisms, and massed stage entrances.[21]

Yet the play cannot achieve the monumental status to which it aspires. That the textual misplacements of 1623 befell a play about losing and finding is peculiar indeed. Here is another, related instance that the textual criticism does not mention: a reader looking for this play in the 1623 Folio will scan the 'Catalogue,' note that *The Winter's Tale* appears on page 304, and turn there to encounter – a blank. (It can be found on pages 277 to 303.) Had this page been numbered, it might have been a monument to its own emptiness – an unoccupied plinth labelled '304.' For a monument, the First Folio *Winter's Tale* certainly makes a spectacle of itself.

'Emprint an Epitaph': The Monumental Text and Its Issue

The wayward monumentality of the First Folio can be compared to the aims of another folio, published in 1631, that deliberately gathered together, from originals in danger of being 'broken downe ... erazed, torne away, and pilfered,' a compendium of English monuments for 'the true vnderstanding of diuers Families in these Realmes.'[22] Its compiler, John Weever, apologized for the sometimes erratic spelling and grammar of his source texts, insisting on their authority: 'if by the copying out of the fame it be any manner of wayes mollified, it is much againft my will, for I hold originalls the beft' (sig. A2v). Weever was collecting *Ancient Funerall Monuments* and their epitaphs, not drama – regrettably, since his documentary standards were so high. We might wish that the Folio publishers had been as thorough as Weever, who asks his readers: 'If thou shalt find any ancient' epitaphs, please 'copie' them out; if a grave-maker, please cc: all future epitaphs for him to 'publish' (unsigned). The ambitions and problematics of Weever's volume resonate intriguingly with those of the Shakespeare folio published just eight years before. Both texts justify a neglected genre by assimilating it to classical and native examples; both encounter complex problems of transcription yet claim to be 'true.' Weever's epistle to the reader, referring to the 'inhumane, *deformidable* act' of monument-breaking (unsigned, emphasis added), seems to echo the First Folio's letter 'To the great Variety of Readers,' which rejects 'diuerfe stolne, and surreptitious copies, maimed, and *deformed*' (Weever, epistle dedicatory, First Folio, sig. A3, emphasis added).

A book that promises to make deformed originals whole and 'true' problematizes its own textual authority. Like the First Folio, *Ancient Funerall Monuments* is caught in paradox: Weever must claim in one breath that his book is secondary to these monuments, which form an irreplaceable record of originals, and in the next that his book will in fact memorialize the lost memorials: 'Bookes then and the Mufes workes are of all monuments the moft permanent; for of all things elfe there is a viciffitude, a change both of critics and nations; as we may thus reade in *Ouids* Metamorphosis' (p. 3). That irony is familiar to readers of the Shakespeare Folio as well, and shapes the wonderful paradox of its title page: 'Published according to the True Originall Copies.' The problem of reconciling originality to true copies is near the heart of Weever's work, for his own statement of purpose turns out to be less than original. The epistle says that ancient monuments are

> broken downe, and vtterly almoft all ruinated ... by which inhumane, deformidable act, the honourable memory of many vertuous and noble perfons deceafed, is extinguifhed, and the true vnderftanding of diuers Families in these Realmes (who haue defcended of thefe worthy perfons aforefaid) is fo darkened, as the true courfe of their inheritance is thereby partly interrupted.

Pages later, Weever quotes a 1560 proclamation made by Queen Elizabeth I, which reports that monuments are being

> fpoiled, broken, and ruinated, to the offence of all noble and gentle hearts, and the extinguifhing of the honourable and good memory of fundry vertuous and noble perfons deceafed; but also the true vnderstanding of diuers Families in this Realme (who haue defcended of the bloud of the same perfons deceafed) is thereby so darkened, as the true courfe of their inheritance may be hereafter interrupted. (sig. F2v)

Weever's epistle follows Elizabeth's proclamation almost word for word, underlining the central thrust of any monumentalist project: monuments trace the 'true understanding' of family descent that might otherwise be 'interrupted.' Tombs tell what other records might obliterate (and no one had more reason to preserve the monumental record than Elizabeth I, heir to the throne through a queen rejected on paper). Ironically, Weever's recycling reduces the proclamation to the ephemeral mode of front matter.

Weever's own lineage is recorded when he names his mentor in memorial history, Robert Cotton. Weever includes an elegy (his own?) on Cotton, but admits that neither verse nor his book will extend Cotton's memory as well as *issue* can:

> He tooke to wife *Elizabeth*, one of the daughters and heires of *William Brocas* Efquire, by whom he had iffue, onely one Sonne, Sir *Thomas Cotton* Baronet, now liuing; who married *Margaret*, Daughter of the Lord *William Howard* ... by whom hee hath iffue. (epistle dedicatory)

These are the words of an epitaph, of course. 'Issue' was a word that Weever had applied, knowingly, to Shakespeare's poems in his 1599 *Epigrammes*: 'Honie-tongued Shakespeare when I saw thine issue / I swore *Apollo* got them and none other.'[23] So, too, in *The Winter's Tale*, also full of monumental bodies and texts, the word '*issue*' appears fourteen times, often in dispute. Hermione's claim that she has returned to see 'the yffue' gives Perdita a lineage denied earlier in the play. Leontes had said to Paulina, 'It is the Iffue of *Polixenes*,' and to Antigonus: 'Ile not reare / Anothers Iffue' (2.3. 1015, 1125–6). Only two sites in the play offer 'true' records of issue: the oracle (to which Leontes says, 'There is no truth at all i'th'Oracle:' [3.2.1321]); and the monument of Hermione, an epitaph embodied.

Anticipating Weever's fleeting claim that texts are 'of all monuments the moft permanent,' issue in this play is frequently traced as a form of print, a 'true Originall Copie.' Leontes says of Mamillius's nose: 'They fay it is a Coppy out of mine'; Paulina describes the newborn Perdita as, 'Although the Print be little, the whole Matter / And Coppy of the Father'; and Leontes tells Florizell that his mother 'did print your Royall Father off, / Conceiuing you' (1.2.197; 2.3.1021–2; 5.1.2880–1). What Leontes and Polixenes want, and seek, is a true copy, an heir. The copy is of the father; the mother, as we know, is merely the vessel of reproduction – as such no-body: '*This receptacle/nurse ... cannot take a form, a morphe, and in that sense, cannot be a body.*'[24] The machine that produces textual copies is the printing press; the machine that guarantees human copies is the monumentalized woman, a container for matter formed on a male model, a female name bound into a man's lineage. The monument acknowledges the female body only in this supposedly bodiless passage from father to heir – issue.

If there is no heir, on the other hand, the monument as memorial to issue is meaningless, and the cost of monument-making – the sacrifice of the living female body – seems too high. After sixteen years mourning a dead wife and 'interrupted' issue at a tomb the play never visits, Leontes gets his monument only *after* his line of issue is recovered. He immediately loses the monument to the living originals of wife and issue at once. Is it the monument or the monumentalized that must be found if the king is to recover his heir? What is resolved about the female body when the play ends with the spectacle of the vanishing monument?

'The babe is counted lost'

The oracle promises that 'The King ſhall liue without an Heire,if that which is loſt,be not found' (3.2.1315–16). But who exactly is lost and who is found in this play? The oracle is less help than we expect, for this play has so many losses of loved ones and of bodies, and a surprising excess of findings as well. Indeed, many scholars have found the play perverse in its failure to fill crucial losses, and its gratuitous replacement of others. *The Winter's Tale* 'cheats our expectations' (Colie, *Shakespeare's Living Art*, p. 278). Even when Gent. 2 asks, 'Ha's the King found his Heire?' Gent. 3 equivocates: 'Moſt true, if euer Truth were pregnant by Circumſtance' (5.2.3039–40). What is found is not a singular male heir, a replacement for Mamillius, or a copy of the king; it is an iteration with a difference, two to make up for one, a collective heir made up of a mere daughter and a dynastically appropriate prince, a collaboration promising further issue. The king has accepted his responsibility for the death of his wife; in a kind of cosmic lagniappe, he gets her back – but her only words are to her daughter. All these re-found bodies are misdelivered: the finding of the heir promised by the oracle takes place offstage, the finding that no one expects is delivered in a misleading spectacle.

As is well known, the peculiar wording of the oracle can be traced to Shakespeare's narrative source, Robert Greene's *Pandosto. Or the Triumph of Time* (1588). Shakespeare's First Folio reads:

Hermione *is chaſt,* Polixenes *blameleſſe,* Camillo *a true Subiect,* Leontes *a*

> *iealous Tyrant, his innocent Babe truly begotten, and the King ſhall liue without an* Heire, *if that which is loſt, be not found.* (3.2.1313–16)

But it is perfectly acceptable for a king to live without an heir, provided that he does not die without one. The stipulation of a living rather than a dying king goes back to Greene's version, in which little differs except the name:

> The Oracle.
>
> Svspition is no proofe: Iealousie is an vnequall Iudge: Bellaria is chaſt: Egiſtus blameleſſe: Franion a true ſubiect: Pandosto treacherous: his Babe an innocent, and the King ſhal liue without an heire: if that which is loſt be not founde. (sigs. C2–2v; *STC* 12285)

Some compositor corrected the problem, consciously or not, in the 1607 edition of the romance (the first published after the death of the heir-less queen Elizabeth):

> the King shall die without an heire: if that which is loſt be not ſound. (sigs. C2–2v)

Oracles are ambiguous by definition, but the textual variant makes this one especially hard to interpret: what will be the life-and-death effects of finding the heir? Should Leontes be seeking an heir, or something *like* it, as Pygmalion would say?

Most critics name Perdita as the 'lost' character whose rediscovery fulfils the oracle. Stephen Orgel, who insists on the cataclysmic loss of Mamillius, accepts her as 'what is found, the essential thing' – though only inasmuch as she and Florizel constitute and promise issue.[25] After all, she is named as a 'lost' child, and her finding is hailed by the public as fulfilling the oracle. Still, some ambiguity—'pregnant by Circumſtance' – remains because the oracle merely lists 'what is lost' while referring to every other character by name. Shakespeare gives Perdita her name in explicit reference to the oracle, although the oracle comes from Greene and the name does not: Hermione's apparition tells Antigonus, as though in conspiracy with the oracle, 'and for the babe / Is counted loſt for euer, *Perdita* / I prethee call't:' (3.3.1474–6). Even that explanation is ambiguous: the babe is 'counted' lost, apparently debited from the family tally, but actually only re-counted to be gone. The 'charracter' that Antigonus leaves with the exposed child does not detail the circumstances of its loss, but prepares for its finding: Antigonus guesses that Apollo wants the child found, and in the land of 'it's right Father,' 'this being indeede the *iffue* / of King *Polixenes*' (3.3.1489, 1486–7, emphasis added).

Often forgotten is the on-stage loss of Antigonus, which Hermione's apparition, again like an oracle, predicts. Even before the bear, Paulina has anticipated Antigonus's loss in her body count for Leontes: 'Ile fpeak of her no more, nor of your Children: / Ile not remember you of my owne Lord, / (Who is loft too:)' (3.2.1420–4). She emphasizes it again sixteen years later:

> Is't not the tenor of his Oracle,
> That King *Leontes* fhall not haue an Heire,
> Till his loft child be found? Which, that it fhall,
> Is all as monftrous to our humane reafon,
> As my *Antigonus* to breake his Graue,
> And come againe to me: who, on my life,
> Did perifh with the Infant
> ...
> Care not for Iffue,
> The Crowne will find an Heire. (5.1.2771–7, 2780–1)

Paulina's methods here converge with those of Hermione's apparition: as Hermione taught Antigonus to misinterpret Apollo's will, Paulina now teaches *her* friend's husband to misinterpret the oracle. For surely Leontes' issuelessness is *not* the tenor of the oracle. Paulina's interpretation uses Antigonus's death as circumstantial evidence for the loss of Perdita, as though, startlingly enough, Paulina and Hermione conspired to kill Antigonus to aid Leontes' misapprehension. In the final moments of the play, Antigonus recurs as a symbol of the confusion of loss and finding, when Paulina's promise to 'lament' her 'Mate (that's neuer to be found againe) / ... till I am loft' is answered by Leontes's ability to 'finde thee' a husband in Camillo (5.3.3347–8, 3356).

The question of who is to be found can hardly be answered by Leontes, who has trouble enough keeping track of how many friends and family members he has lost. When Mamillius dies, he plans his reconciliations with Polixenes, Camillo, and Hermione, without thinking to recall Antigonus and the baby (3.2.1340–1). After Paulina reports Hermione's death, he plans a monument:

> Prethee bring me
> To the dead bodies of my Queene, and Sonne,

One graue ſhall be for both: Vpon them shall
The cauſes of their death appeare (vnto
Our ſhame perpetuall) once a day, Ile viſit
The Chappell where they lye, and teares ſhed there
Shall be my recreation. (3.2.1426–32)

He describes 'one grave ... for both,' yet 'upon *them*' will the 'causes of their [singular] *death* appeare' (emphasis added). Leontes promises to shed 'teares' 'once a day' (3.2.1431, 1430), like Greene's *Pandosto*, who 'would once a day repaire to the Tombe' (sig. C4). But later, Leontes can only recall that he '(in vaine) ſaid many / A:prayer vpon her graue' (5.3.54–5), forgetting the presence of Mamillius in the shared grave. In any case, the tomb over the grave seems, for Leontes as for the audience, to be replaced retroactively by Paulina's statue.

Leontes's body-count problem is inherited from *Pandosto*, whose narrator is equally vague about the number of the king's losses. Pandosto plans a monolithic epitaph for two:

hee caused his wife to bee embalmed, and wrapt in lead with her young sonne Garinter: erecting a rich and famous Sepulchre, wherein hee intombed *them both* ... cauſing this Epitaph to be ingrauen on *her* Tombe in letters of Golde:

¶ The Epitaph.

Here lyes entombde Bellaria faire, Falsly accuſed to be vnchaste:
Cleared by Apollos ſacred doome, Yet ſlaine by Iealousie at last.
What ere thou be, that passest by,
Curſſe him that cauſde this Queene to die. (sig. C4; emphasis added)

The epitaph begins by echoing the oracle in syntax, but ends with a dead queen rather than a living king, forgetting altogether the son who shares the tomb. These two embedded texts, epitaph and oracle, are typographically linked in early editions of *Pandosto*, set off by large-font, centred headings and Roman type within the black-letter narrative. Both oracle and epitaph, in other words, are typographic memorials to lost bodies; both insist that they identify the loss specifically; but both lose count of their bodies. Weever would be horrified to see family members so 'extinguished.' This unreliable monumentalization recurs in the romance's infamous last sentence, which (accidentally?) entombs the newlywed Fawnia with her self-slain father: Prince 'Dorastus ... went with his wife and the dead corpse into Bohemia, where, after *they* were fumptuously entombed, Doraftus ended his daies in contented quiet' (sig. G4; emphasis added). Dorastus's unconscious admission may explain the lapses of Pandosto and Leontes, suggesting that to all these royal husbands, a tomb is a surrogate *preferable* to a living wife. Worse than Pandosto and Dorastus, Leontes, at the start of Act 5, has monumentalized his lost queen and almost forgotten the monument.

The confusion comes to a head when Leontes meets the disguised Florizell and Perdita:

> Moft dearely welcome,
> And your faire Princeffe (Goddeffe) oh: alas,
> I loft a couple, that 'twixt Heauen and Earth
> Might thus haue ftood, begetting wonder,as
> You (gracious Couple) doe: and then I loft
> (All mine owne Folly) the Societie
> Amitie too of your braue Father (5.1.2885–91)

Lost in his rhetoric of replication, Leontes equates the loving couple before him to, first, a puzzling 'lost ... couple,' and then the inapposite pairing of his homosocial bond with Polixenes. Who is this 'lost couple'? Since Mamillius and Florizell were of an age, and since Leontes goes on to wish 'Might I a Sonne and Daughter now haue look'd on, / Such goodly things as you' (5.1. 2938–9), the obvious answer is Mamillius and Perdita. Uncomfortably, Leontes's couple skirts the loss of Hermione, although his bond with her would seem the closest parallel to the heterosexual coupling of Florizel and Perdita. Hermione is reduced to a principle of issue, guarantor of a lost sibling pair that preempts future couplings.

The identification of Perdita reminds Leontes to feel the loss of Hermione, although the recovery of the heir should make her a more secure monument of issue. Gent. 3 reports that Leontes, 'for ioy of his found Daughter; as if that Ioy were now become a Loffe, cryes, Oh, thy Mother, thy Mother:' (5.2.3059–61). Gent. 3, Paulina's steward, underlines the vocabulary of finding and loss as heavily as she would: 'fo that all the Inftruments which ayded to expofe the Child,were euen then loft, when it was found' (5.2.3079–81). When instruments of loss can disappear, the moment of finding has arrived. I would suggest that if the restoration of Hermione is, as much as Perdita's return, the 'finding' that fulfils the oracle, it is not because Leontes has gained a 'true understanding'of loss, but because he is forced to understand *finding*.

'Petrified allegorical drama':[26] Finding the Performative

Jean Wilson reports that Jacobean funeral monuments strive for illusionistic effect. Always representational, some even portray 'the deceased as in life ... taking part in a conversation with his or her spouse' (p. 88). They are deliberately spectacular: 'The sense of our being spectators at a dramatic scene is highlighted in a group of monuments in which the scene is "discovered" for us by attendants ... pulling back a curtain' (p. 88). The reverse illusion is implied in the common stage practice of using actors to portray on-stage statues, which must have left Jacobean viewers uncertain whether the 'actor revealed in the final scene was performing the role of a statue or of Hermione pretending to be a statue' (Barkan, p. 663). These mannerist complexities stymie any separation between monument and spectacle, as they are meant to do. Even the First Folio cannot make the distinction between monument and spectacle. At the start of 5.3, we get the massed entry characteristic of a Crane-transcribed play:

Enter Leontes, Polixenes, Florizell, Perdita, Camillo,
Paulina: Hermione (like a Statue:) Lords, &c.

Hermione is set apart from her living household by Crane's deliberate colons.[27] The ample stage direction informs us that she must enter *as* a statue according to the convention, but the other reading is possible: that she *looks like* a statue. Hermione is like a statue, as Pygmalion requests a wife 'leeke my Wench of Ivory.' It is anachronistic to read Crane's punctuation – :) – as an early modern emoticon, but the stage direction does seem to wink instead of petrify.

Structurally and emotionally, it is the stirring of the statue that completes the play, although critics have resisted the conclusion that this scene confirms the oracle. If that which is lost is found, 'found' is the magic word that allows Hermione to speak. Paulina says, 'turne good Lady; / Our *Perdita* is found' (5.3.3332). Then and only then does the statue speak – to Perdita:

Tell me (mine owne)
Where haſ thou bin preferu'd? Where liu'd? How found
Thy Fathers Court? For thou ſhalt heare that I
Knowing by *Paulina*, that the Oracle

> Gaue hope thou waft in being, haue preferu'd
> My selfe, to fee the yffue. (5.3.3335–40)

As in contemporary theatre jargon, 'finding' is discovering something that was there all along, but required presentation to others. Hermione's lines explain that she and Perdita alike are 'preferu'd' – a word that replaces 'found,' more precisely capturing the experience of being found by others without ever having been lost to yourself. Particularly with an early modern long 's,' 'preferu'd' also graphically links to 'perform'd,' another much-repeated word in this play. Supposedly Julio Romano has performed the statue and Paulina has preserved it; now the statue performs Hermione's preservation. Preserving is not truly metamorphic: it is a spectacle of the body's survival under the pressure of the monumental.

This last scene thus demonstrates the epistemological complexity of the Butlerian performative. 'Finding,' once redefined as preservation, does not require giving up loss, as the oracle's sentence structure misleadingly implied. That which is found *is* still the lost daughter, the almost-statuesque wife. All that must be given up, as Leontes learns, is the impossible demand at the heart of 'issue': that the monument should replace a maternal body for the sake of the heir, becoming a mere record of lineage. 'Finding' means accepting that issue will be disrupted by (excessive) living bodies, that time will yield not a monument-sanctioned copy of the father, but a reiteration that differs, a wrinkled woman or a grown child with her own desires. The man who swore 'Ile not reare / Anothers Iffue' (2.325–6) accepts issuings he could not expect. The former monument to issue looks up and sees her daughter and the light at once, and her claim is ambiguous: has she preserved herself to see the issue of the oracle, preserved herself to see her daughter as issue, been preserved to see herself as issue, been preserved to show what issue must mean?

It is crucial to the logic of the play that it is the women characters – Paulina, Hermione, and Perdita – who find out what it means to 'be found,' and that they must convince Leontes to find only by guiding him through an apparent monumentalization. Monumental hopes are not dispelled in this play. Rather, their satisfaction is performed. Leontes gets his heir, and a fresh copy of his wife. But the actors in this monumental script know that its ivory wenches have been preserved through the agency of women. Hermione deftly minimizes that agency as she revises Paulina's 'Our *Perdita*' to 'my daughter' and then refers Perdita to 'thy Father' (5.3. 3332, 3335). Picking up on Hermione's tacit deference to patriarchal illusions, Leontes' stiff reply struggles to restore norms of issue and gender division. He introduces Hermione to 'This your Son-in-law, / And Sonne vnto the King, whom heauens directing / Is troth-plight to your daughter' (5.3.3363–5), his syntax doing everything it can to suggest that *his* son is marrying *her* daughter. The hollow monumentality of his rhetoric fails to dispel awareness that a disturbing spectacle has just been mounted.

And so Leontes ends the play with a sharp twist against the women who have unsettled the monument, a comment pointing out that their agency, too, is nothing but spectacle. He urges that 'Each one ... anfwere to his part / Perform'd in this wide gap of Time, fince firft / We were diffeuer'd' (5.3.3367–9). Leontes's grammar points out that every one who played 'his part' in this scene has been male; just as the statue is always male, the female character on-stage is always a male. Leontes has gone along with the spectacle, but his last words credit its performance to boy actors rather than to women. Perhaps Paulina and Hermione, celebrants of the performative, would embrace even this arbitrary metamorphosis. Certainly audiences uniformly ignore Leontes's revelation amid the losings and findings this play performs.

The Folio, too, has a complex final move. The bottom half of the last page of the play preserves 'The Names of the Actors' (p. 303). The bold heading, and then the italicized list of characters, are set upon that much-battered tail ornament, a satyr-decorated bracket. In this 'petrified allegorical drama,' Perdita is finally and surely identified as '*Daughter to Leontes and Hermione*,' an identification more explicit and more even-handed than those given by the oracle and by Hermione. The royal household is thus re-monumentalized – except that the Folio heading, like Leontes' last lines, reminds us that these are 'actors.' The modern meaning of that word invites us to think of the all-male players; the early modern meaning, of the characters they played for a few hours. Each player, like each character, has 'perform'd' 'his part' in the collective performance that paradoxically fulfils the monumental script through spectacle. The list joining the oracle and the epitaph as another italicized would-be monument, reveals again how thin is the illusion of the textual monument, how deep the spectacle has gone. That fragile balance between script and spectacle is, precisely, the performative, in which gender and sex are 'tenuously constituted in time ... through a *stylized repetition of acts*' (Butler, *Gender*, p. 140). For Butler, 'the *appearance of substance* is precisely that, a constructed identity, a performative accomplishment which the mundane social audience, including the actors themselves, come to believe and to perform in the mode of belief' (*Gender*, p. 141). What is crucial here is that not only gender identity, but also its social acceptance, is performed; that not only the actors, but also their audiences, are working against and through scripts. The Folio *Winter's Tale* shows actors, characters, and future 'mundane social audiences' that gender and its acceptance are effortful, collaborative, conditional, and volatile, whenever any script is preserved or performed.

NOTES

Thanks to Kim Woosley for her sharp-eyed checking of quotations.

1 Quoted in J.H.P. Pafford, 'Introduction,' *The Winter's Tale*. The Arden Shakespeare (New York: Routledge, 1963), p. xvi.
2 W.W. Greg, *The Shakespeare First Folio: Its Bibliographical and Textual History* (Oxford: Clarendon Press, 1955), pp. 436–9.
3 Alfred W. Pollard, *Shakespeare Folios and Quartos* (1909; repr. New York: Cooper Square Publishers, 1970), pp. 135–6.
4 I follow two powerful readings of monumentality and gender: Abbe Blum, 'Strike all that look upon with mar[b]le': Monumentalizing Women in Shakespeare's Plays,' in *The Renaissance Englishwoman in Print*, ed. Anne M. Haselkorn and Betty S. Travitsky (Amherst: University of Massachusetts Press, 1990), pp. 99–118; and Valerie Traub's chapter, 'Jewels, Statues, and Corpses: Containment of Female Erotic Power,' in *Desire and Anxiety: Circulations of Sexuality in Shakespearean Drama* (New York: Routledge, 1992) esp. pp. 25–49. In aligning practices of textual reproduction with these gendered notions of bodily and ideological reproduction, I note that not only these binaries, but also the associations between them, are always subject to disturbance.
5 My use of 'spectacular' is meant not to invoke Guy Debord's contemporary *Society of the Spectacle*, but to poise the evanescence and superficiality of theatre against the apparent weight and depth of texts.
6 Judith Butler, *Bodies That Matter* (New York: Routledge, 1993), p. x.
7 The influential statement is by Peter Stallybrass, 'Patriarchal Territories: The Body Enclosed,' in *Re-writing the Renaissance*, ed. Margaret W. Ferguson, Maureen Quilligan, and Nancy J. Vickers (Chicago: University of Chicago Press, 1986), pp. 123–42.

8 Judith Butler, *Gender Trouble: Feminism and the Subversion of Identity* (New York: Routledge, 1990), p. 277.

9 William Shakespeare, *The Winter's Tale*, 5.3.3334–5 in *The First Folio of Shakespeare 1623* (New York: Applause Books, 1995). Quotations from the play are from this edition unless otherwise indicated. Note that I have followed the through-line numbers used in this facsimile edition. For the sake of defamiliarization, I have eschewed modernization of the text, even recording irregular spacing of the type. More idiosyncratically, I have adopted 'f' for long 's' to call attention to a certain visual effect discussed below. I am not recommending this substitution as a general practice.

10 *Ovid's Metamorphoses: The Arthur Golding Translation, 1567*, ed. John Frederick Nims (New York: Macmillan, 1965), X: 320. All citations are from this translation.

11 In *Shakespeare and Ovid*, Jonathan Bate argues that Shakespeare tends to adapt Ovid in one direction, reducing physical metamorphosis to emotional metaphor. *The Winter's Tale* is rare in literalizing the softening of Leontes' 'hardened image of his wife' ([Oxford: Oxford University Press, 1993], p. 236).

12 John Marston, 'The Metamorphosis of Pigmalions Image,' in *The Poems of John Marston*, ed. Arnold Davenport (Liverpool: Liverpool University Press, 1961), 21.6. On the Renaissance blending of Petrarchanism with the Pygmalion myth, see Leonard Barkan, *The Gods Made Flesh* (New Haven: Yale University Press, 1986), p. 284.

13 Brooks Otis terms this 'agalmatophily' in *Ovid as an Epic Poet* (Cambridge: Cambridge University Press, 1966), p. 389.

14 On the other hand, Golding's Pygmalion, obsessed with cushioning the statue, full of soft-hearted knowledge of the things girls like, is a familiar Renaissance figure, the man made womanly by lovesickness for a woman.

15 Marina Warner reports that ivory was used 'to depict the flesh of goddesses in ancient sculpture.' See *Monuments and Maidens* (New York: Athenaeum, 1995), p. 228.

16 Rosalie Colie, *Shakespeare's Living Art* (Princeton: Princeton University Press, 1974), pp. 278–9. Recent critics have substantiated Colie's interpretation by arguing that Jacobean audiences read the statue of Hermione in the tradition of English funeral monuments. See Bruce Smith, 'Sermons in Stones: Shakespeare and Renaissance Sculpture,' *Shakespeare Studies* 17 (1985), pp. 1–23; and Catherine Belsey, 'Parenthood: Hermione's Statue,' in *Shakespeare and the Loss of Eden* (New Brunswick, NJ: Rutgers University Press, 1999), pp. 85–127.

17 Leonard Barkan, '"Living Sculptures": Ovid, Michelangelo, and "The Winter's Tale,"' *ELH* 48 (1981), pp. 663–4.

18 Pauline Kiernan, *Shakespeare's Theory of Drama* (Cambridge: Cambridge University Press, 1996), p. 80.

19 See Blum and Traub. Belsey argues that if Hermione's statue is a funeral monument, its coming to life is a 'miracle' that denies the lives lost in the name of what she calls 'family values' and I am calling 'issue' (p. 112).

20 Jeffrey Masten, *Textual Intercourse: Collaboration, Authorship, and Sexualities in Renaissance Drama* (Cambridge: Cambridge University Press, 1997); Kevin Pask, *The Emergence of the English Author* (Cambridge: Cambridge University Press, 1996); and Wendy Wall, *The Imprint of Gender: Authorship and Publication in the English Renaissance* (Ithaca: Cornell University Press, 1993).

21 See Pollard, Greg, and T.H. Howard-Hill, *Ralph Crane and Some Shakespeare First Folio Comedies* (Charlottesville: University Press of Virginia, 1972).

22 John Weever, 'The Author to the Reader,' in *Ancient Funerall Monuments* (London, 1631; *STC* 25223). This passage is from the first page of 'The Author to the Reader,' which is unsigned. The third leaf of the epistle is signed 'A,' although there is no apparent break from the previous page.

23 John Weever, *Ad Gulielmum Shakespeare*, in *The Norton Shakespeare*, ed. Stephen Greenblatt et al. (New York: Norton, 1997), p. 3328).

24 Butler, *Bodies*, p. 41. See also Margreta De Grazia, 'Imprints: Shakespeare, Gutenberg, and Descartes,' in *Alternative Shakespeares 2*, ed. Terence Hawkes (New York: Routledge, 1996), pp. 63–94.

25 Stephen Orgel, 'Introduction,' to [William Shakespeare,] *The Winter's Tale* (New York: Oxford University Press, 1996), p. 79.

26 Jean Wilson, *The Shakespeare Legacy: The Material Legacy of Shakespeare's Theatre* (Godalming: Bramley Books, 1995), p. 88.

27 See T.H. Howard-Hill, '"The Winter's Tale": Typographical Peculiarities in the Folio Text,' *Notes and Queries* (May 1961), p. 176.

Afterword

VALERIE TRAUB

In the Renaissance literature classroom, 'Ovid' is never very far away. But when his name is invoked, it often is in the form of a brief literary allusion that raises more questions than it answers ('after being raped by her brother-in-law, Philomela's tongue was cut out; she was later transformed into a nightingale') or worse, an inert and inexplicable reference to an even more temporally distant text ('see *Fasti*'). In a time when Shakespeare, Spenser, Donne, and Milton have been joined on the syllabus by Isabella Whitney, Mary Wroth, Elizabeth Cary, and Margaret Cavendish, it might seem to be asking too much for students to read English translations of Ovid as well. Why should students and scholars return to the Renaissance Ovid? What are the uses of Ovidianism at this moment?

The essays included in *Ovid and the Renaissance Body* demonstrate compellingly that the reasons for such a 'return' differ from just a decade ago, when the 'attempt to salvage a tradition that is rapidly disappearing' was, among other things, part of Jonathan Bate's motivation for analysing 'Ovid's inspiriting of Shakespeare' in *Shakespeare and Ovid*.[1] The contributors to this new collection are less interested than was Bate in the sources of creative inspiration and the ingenuity of literary allusion, or even in how Renaissance writers renovated, incorporated, and revised Ovidian styles and themes. Rather, these essays treat Ovidianism as a contested cultural resource for the creation of distinctively early modern representations of the body, gender, and eroticism. Insofar as feminist, psychoanalytic, new historicist, and queer scholarship has, over the past twenty years, changed the terms by which these phenomena are understood, a return to the author that early moderns considered the 'preceptor of wanton love' was all but inevitable.[2] Along with another important monograph – Lynn Enterline's *The Rhetoric of the Body from Ovid to Shakespeare*[3] – this volume thus heralds a subtle but significant shift. If one cannot argue that *Ovid and the Renaissance Body* single-handedly enacts an entirely new approach to Ovidian influence, one does sense with its publication that something we might call a 'new Ovidianism' has emerged.

Whatever their arguments with prior scholarship on Renaissance Ovidianism, the contributors to this volume clearly are indebted to the previous generation of work. They have absorbed Bate's views on sexual polymorphousness, boundary-blurring, and inclusivity; William Keach's description of the ambivalent eroticism of Renaissance epyllia, its signature blend of irony, pathos, and comedy; Leonard Barkan's elucidation of the erotics and paradoxes of metamorphosis; and Elizabeth Harvey's insights about male writers' use of the ventriloquized female voice. [4] Focused on 'the cultural production of new subjects, that is, Ovidian identities or Ovidian sexualities' (p. 15), this volume adds to our understanding of the specific 'cultural labour' (p. 77) that Renaissance Ovidianism performed. It has been clear since Keach that Ovid provided Renaissance writers with a diverse repertoire of subjects and objects of desire, including solipsistic rapists, lamenting victims, indifferent adolescents, and aggressive female wooers; and it has been obvious since Barkan that Ovid offered Renaissance writers an enabling, if ambivalent, model for articulating the attractions of homoeroticism.[5] *Ovid and the Renaissance Body* revisits these issues of erotic power and diversity, while also adding to the critical landscape such self-conflicted figures as the hermaphrodite, the narcissist, and the cuckold.

The best of the work included here tackles a theoretical or historical problem in addition to reading Renaissance Ovidianism. Carla Freccero's essay on the love lyric, for instance, not only analyses Ovid's influence on Petrarch and Louise Labé, but advances our understanding of a crucial issue within the history of sexuality (especially as articulated within psychoanalytic and queer theory) – the relations between identification and desire. Arguing that despite the 'pretext of a normative organization of identification and desire according to the binary of sexual difference, Petrarch's is a "perverse" model of desire' (p. 25), she demonstrates that the myth of Narcissus mediates Petrarchan subjectivity, in part by 'invoking the body of the Lady as that which must be seen, silenced, fetishistically fragmented, and collapsed back into the poet's words' (p. 29). That Narcissus is a figure around whom relations of desire and identification revolve is an insight developed in a quite different direction by Mario DiGangi, who anatomizes the link (or lack of a link) between homosexuality and narcissism in *Cynthia's Revels.* Originally entitled *Narcissus, or the fountain of self-love,* Jonson's play satirizes male courtiers by associating self-love not with homoerotic desire but with effeminate manners. Self-love, DiGangi argues, indicates 'a disturbance of proper masculine social protocols' (p. 101) which are particularly important to the aristocracy. In demonstrating how effeminacy in behaviour and dress polices 'boundaries of the aristocratic male body' (p. 99), DiGangi historicizes both homoeroticism and narcissism. So, too, Gina Bloom's analysis of Echo's disembodied agency in George Sandys's translation and commentary of the *Metamorphoses* and Judith Deitch's treatment of Echo in Spenser's *Epithalamion* propose radically different understandings of this figure of the female voice. Deitch argues that 'in Ovid's myth Echo only passively re-sounds other voices' (p. 224), and she sees this 'ineffectual image' of 'doomed repetition' (pp. 224–5) transferred onto the silent bride in Spenser's poem. Arguing that the bride embodies an 'erased corporeality, both ... passive hollow structure waiting to resound and ... container for the masculine poet's procreativity' (p. 229), Deitch maintains that Spenser manages his relation to Ovidian *imitatio* much in the way that Freccero argues Petrarch did: in securing his own authorial identity, he 'leaves the girl behind.' Bloom argues, in contrast, that the coincidence of voice and agency is neither self-evident nor necessarily enabling for women. Reading Echo through early modern philosophies of vocal sound, Bloom probes the contradictions within Sandys's text, revealing that the translation and commentary, caught within contradictory ideologies of gender and vocal production, are at odds with one another. Deconstructing textual instabilities, she argues for a new model of female agency, one that locates vocal effectiveness in the gap between speech and speaker.

What, then, might be said to define Ovidian gender and eroticism in Renaissance texts? If there is an 'Ovidian sexuality' produced in the early modern period, as Stanivukovic contends, what are its defining characteristics? The answers proposed in this volume are multiple and somewhat contradictory. Ovidian sexuality, these essays assert, is ambivalent and ironic; dissident and normalizing; liberatory and entrapping. The lack of critical consensus should not surprise us: the uses of Ovid were contested in the early modern period, just as they are now. Such critical contradictions partly result from the indeterminacy of Ovid's texts, the cacophony of attitudes, passions, and voices they bequeathed to Renaissance writers; partly from each writer's redeployment of Ovidian materials; and partly from each critic's conceptual focus and method. It is not coincidental that several of the figures who come to the fore (Pygmalion's statue, Echo, Narcissus, Hermaphroditus, Ganymede) are those associated with either a silencing of female voices, a merger or dispersal of bodily boundaries, or male homoeroticism – concerns correlated with the well-established interests of, respectively, feminism, queer theory, and gay male studies. Two essays on female homoeroticism – Mark Dooley's on Lyly's revision of the tale of Iphis and Ianthe and Morgan Holmes's on Marvell's *The Nymph Complaining for the Death of her Faun* – augment and complicate this line-up.[6] But critical differences here also stem from political investments. Dooley, for instance, argues that *Gallathea* provides a 'radical alternative to heterosexual marriage' (p. 73), whereas in his reading of the Hermaphroditus myth in Peend and Spenser, Michael Pincombe directly challenges the 'romantic' critical posture of 'enthusiasm' that sees in Ovidianism 'polymorphous liberation' (p. 156). Dooley's appreciation of Lyly's treatment of lesbianism likewise contrasts with Jim Ellis's treatment of heterosexuality in Renaissance epyllia, which, in highlighting the way the narrative voice obtains a position of 'unassailable mastery and masculinity' (p. 54), interprets all female personas as 'props for the construction' of male subjects (p. 55). This emphasis on female containment is reiterated by Elizabeth Sauer, who argues that the 'Ovidian language and scenes of metamorphoses that pervade Milton's poems and prose works are projected onto the unruly, demonic, and the feminine' (p. 219). Such masculinist projections, we know, were common in the early modern period; thus, it is one of the strengths of this collection that it analyses as well the ways men were subject to social and psychic regulation. Like the attempt to police gender protocols through images of effete courtiers, the effort to regulate masculine subjectivity through the figure of the conflicted and dependent husband, Bruce Boehrer argues, exposes the cuckold of Ovidian verse as an exemplary site of masculine 'sexual self contradiction' (p. 172). Tracing the revival of 'Ovid's contemptuous portrait of the willing cuckold' (p. 178) in early modern drama, Boehrer anatomizes the psychic labour involved in managing the contradictions at the heart of patriarchal masculinity.

To the extent that a coherent image of Renaissance Ovidianism emerges from this anthology, it is one founded on a faultline: certain essays celebrate Ovid as an 'erotic boundary-breaker' while others expose him as a masculinist 'master of containment.' It is noteworthy that this subversion/containment divide is most evident when either gender *or* sexuality is critically privileged as the interpretative lens. Ovidian *gender* politics, this volume implies, are largely patriarchal, normalizing, regulatory, containing (for men as well as for women), while Ovidian *erotic* politics are primarily polymorphous, liberatory, sexy, subversive (for women as well as for men). Yet, given the complex and shifting textual, psychological, and erotic dynamics delineated in some of the essays here, any line between Ovidianism as erotic boundary-breaking and Ovidianism as masculinist mastery risks being overdrawn. Indeed, if we think of *Ovid and the Renaissance Body* as staging a critical conversation among contributors, the sense that emerges is that it may no longer suffice to argue that female figures are contained by Ovidian structures of male homosociality, nor to counter this feminist dictum with queer affirmations of erotic multiplicity. Rather, the methods pursued by several of the contributors imply that we need to analyse the ways in which efforts to 'contain' and to 'free' are themselves unstable and contested – in other words, subject to ongoing cultural negotiation. In this respect, we might capitalize on Lori Humphrey Newcomb's distinction between two Ovidian impulses – to monumentalize ('to shape and fix texts, to demand singular control of the art object, to memorialize the body in an exact duplicate, to contain women in immobility') and to spectacularize ('to leave texts behind, to embrace collaboration and proliferation, to celebrate the changefulness of the human body, even the female body,' pp. 240). Looking at the relations between text and performance, Newcomb demonstrates that both impulses are at work in the cultural production of *The Winter's Tale*: 'The fable of the revised statue draws on Ovid's Pygmalion narrative to condemn monumentalization in favour of dramatic, dynamic metamorphosis. But at the same time, the monumentalizing environment of the Folio tends to curb the gender instabilities introduced by this spectacular, Ovidian resolution' (p. 241). That cultural context (e.g., the tension between performance and text) may be crucial in arbitrating the meaning of Renaissance Ovidianism is affirmed as well in Ian Moulton's reading of the cultural reception of Ovid and Ariosto. Arguing that 'Ovidian eroticism celebrates *raptus* – a violent and unpredictable encounter between human and divine,' and that *Orlando Furioso* derives from this its view of sexual passion as 'chaotic and socially disruptive' (p. 113), Moulton traces concern about social disorder in English translations of the *Metamorphoses* and Harington's translation of *Orlando*. The moralizing response to a vernacular Ovid in England arose not so much from the text itself as from a reconfiguration of reading publics: 'Ovidian eroticism becomes dangerous when it circulates in the book market, not in school, and in English, not in Latin' (p. 122).

Just as the dialogue implicit among these essays suggests the need to develop more dynamic models of cultural negotiation and to attend to the specificities of cultural production and reception, it also intimates that now might be the time to rearticulate the conceptual relations between gender and sexuality. If the analytical separation of sexuality from gender promoted by queer theory initially provided a beneficial reorientation and specification, it now seems clear that we need to concentrate efforts on reading gender in terms of eroticism and eroticism in terms of gender – in other words, to find productive ways for queer theory and feminist theory to speak to one another.[7] With its blend of explicit erotic pleasures and profound psychic pains, with its articulation of desiring, resistant, and lamenting female voices and its imagery of masculine prowess, indifference, and dissolution, Renaissance Ovidianism offers a particularly promising site for this engagement. If we consider the transgression of bodily, moral, and epistemological boundaries to be one hallmark of Ovidian eroticism, then we need to ask: what is such polymorphous desire depicted *in the service of*? When and why is erotic multiplicity abandoned in the interests of a normative hetero-erotic and/or patriarchal economy? Does early modern patriarchy support or police homoeroticism, and does the answer to this question differ along gender lines? Freccero's scrutiny of the simultaneously homoerotic and misogynist trajectories of Ovidian desire provides one means of answering such questions; Boehrer's anatomy of the abject cuckold as a site of gender and erotic definition offers another. If we ask how and why Ovidianism can be both polymorphously perverse and misogynous, we might be in a better position to account for the Renaissance vogue of Ovidianism, as well as for our current interests in its spectacular blend of sex and violence.

Given the corporeal violence inherent to the concept of Ovidian metamorphosis, it is striking that, with the exception of Sauer's brief comments on dismemberment in Milton, material violence is hardly mentioned in this volume. Particularly since Jonathan Sawday contends that Ovid's Marsyas, flayed by a punitive Apollo, functions as an apt if grotesque figure for what he calls the Renaissance 'culture of dissection'[8] (not to mention Enterline's new book, which begins 'At the center of Ovid's *Metamorphoses* lie violated bodies'),[9] it seems important for work focused on Ovidian gender and eroticism to trace the way that extreme metamorphic violence (toward both women and men) abets and upsets early modern structures of desire, subjectivity, and agency. The Ovidian transgression of bodily boundaries, after all, is not solely one of ecstasy or hermaphroditic fusion, but also one of mutilation and dismemberment, punishment and revenge. The cost of Lycaon's cannibalistic feast is transmutation into a howling wolf; Actaeon pays for his voyeurism by being mauled by hounds; and Orpheus's scorn of women causes a horde of Bacchae to tear him apart. Any comprehensive account of the impulses and effects of Ovidianism needs to account for its fascination with the erotics of cruelty, including the amplification of such violence in such quintessentially Ovidian texts as *Titus Andronicus* and *The Duchess of Malfi.* Addressing the terror and allure of eroticized violence also might give us some analytical purchase on the question of Ovid's influence (or lack of influence) on women writers. With the exception of Freccero's short treatment of Labé, this volume is silent about women's engagement with Ovid – as either writers or readers. We know from the work of Richard Halpern that women readers delighted in the erotics of Shakespeare's *Venus and Adonis.*[10] Nonetheless, I wonder whether Ovidian eroticism was perceived as too extreme, too tormented, too sensationalistic, and hence, too disturbing or dangerous for women writers – concerned as they necessarily were about the propriety of authorship – to find in Ovid a model to emulate.

Although an anthology is not the place to expect diachronic argumentation, the claims made by these essays suggest that mapping the temporal coordinates of Ovidian gender and sexuality in the early modern period would be a worthy project. Is the female homoeroticism represented in Marvell's ventriloquization of a nymph's lyric lament for her faun the same as that Lyly represents in his play for an all-boy cast almost a century earlier? Does the courtly effeminacy satirized in Jacobean representations of Narcissus take the same form during the Civil War and after the Restoration? As several of the essays here demonstrate, the answers to such questions would be enriched by a sustained examination of an early modern 'culture of Ovid': the pedagogy of the schoolroom, the literary one-upmanship at the Inns of Court, the commercial milieu of the theatre, and scenes of private and public reading. As the gendered and erotic dynamics internal to those sites shift historically, so too would 'Ovidian eroticism.'

Obviously, one volume cannot address every wish. The fact that *Ovid and the Renaissance Body* raises such hopes for future investigation indicates the import of the work included here. As a herald, of sorts, of a new line of inquiry, this book demonstrates the interest in and critical capacity for revitalizing the Ovidian literary allusion. This volume reanimates Ovid and his uses in the early modern period as something more than a distant footnote: more troubling, provocative, dangerous, sexy, and, in all senses of the word, queer.

NOTES

1 Jonathan Bate, *Shakespeare and Ovid* (Oxford: Clarendon Press, 1993), pp. ix and 2.
2 Ibid., p. 32.
3 Lynn Enterline, *The Rhetoric of the Body from Ovid to Shakespeare* (Cambridge: Cambridge University Press, 2000). Asking 'what kind of subjects emerge as a result of this collective "internalizing" of Ovidian narrative' (p. 23), Enterline's feminist analysis of the relations among sexuality, rhetoric, and violence is aligned with the goals of the present volume.
4 See William Keach, *Elizabethan Erotic Narratives: Irony and Pathos in the Ovidian Poetry of Shakespeare, Marlowe, and Their Contemporaries* (New Brunswick, NJ: Rutgers University Press, 1977); Leonard Barkan, *The Gods Made Flesh: Metamorphoses and the Pursuit of Paganism* (New Haven and London: Yale University Press, 1986) and *Transuming Passion: Ganymede and the Erotics of Humanism* (Stanford: Stanford University Press, 1991); and Elizabeth Harvey, *Ventriloquized Voices: Feminist Theory and English Renaissance Texts* (London and New York: Routledge, 1992). Other important work on the Renaissance Ovid published during this period includes Clark Hulse, *Metamorphic Verse: The Elizabethan Minor Epic* (Princeton: Princeton University Press, 1981); Joseph Loewenstein, *Responsive Readings: Versions of Echo in Pastoral, Epic, and the Jonsonian Masque* (New Haven: Yale University Press, 1984); and Lee Pearcy, *The Mediated Muse: English Translations of Ovid, 1560–1700* (Hamden, CT: Archon Books, 1984).
5 The differences in Barkan's treatment of homoeroticism in his books of 1986 and 1991 enact some of the analytical advances that fostered critical work on Ovid and early modern homoeroticism. See Bruce Smith, *Homosexual Desire in Shakespeare's England: A Cultural Poetics* (Chicago: University of Chicago Press, 1991); Gregory Bredbeck, *Sodomy and Interpretation: Marlowe to Milton* (Ithaca: Cornell University Press, 1991); Mario DiGangi, *The Homoerotics of Early Modern Drama* (Cambridge: Cambridge University Press, 1997); Theodora Jankowski, '"Where there can be no cause of affection": Redefining Virgins, Their Desires, and Their Pleasures in John Lyly's *Gallathea*,' in *Feminist Readings of Early Modern Culture: Emerging Subjects*, ed. Valerie Traub,

M. Lindsay Kaplan, and Dympna Callaghan (Cambridge: Cambridge University Press, 1996), pp. 253–74; and Valerie Traub, 'The Insignificance of "Lesbian" Desire in Early Modern England,' in *Erotic Politics: Desire on the Renaissance Stage*, ed. Susan Zimmerman (New York: Routledge, 1992), and 'The Perversion of "Lesbian" Desire,' *History Workshop Journal* 41 (1996): 19–50.

6 For my own analysis of 'Iphis and Ianthe' and *Gallathea*, as well as further analysis of the Calisto story, see *The Renaissance of Lesbianism in Early Modern England* (Cambridge: Cambridge University Press, forthcoming).

7 For a critique of queer theory from the standpoint of gender, see Biddy Martin, *Femininity Played Straight: The Significance of Being Lesbian* (New York and London: Routledge, 1996); and Judith Butler, 'Introduction: Against Proper Objects,' *differences: More Gender Trouble: Feminism Meets Queer Theory* 6.2–3 (1994): 1–26.

8 Jonathan Sawday, *The Body Emblazoned: Dissection and the Human Body in Renaissance Culture* (London and New York: Routledge, 1996).

9 Enterline, *The Rhetoric of the Body*, p. 1.

10 Richard Halpern, '"Pining Their Maws": Female Readers and the Erotic Ontology of the Text in Shakespeare's *Venus and Adonis*,' in *Venus and Adonis: Critical Essays* (New York and London: Garland, 1997), pp. 377–88.

Contributors

Gina Bloom recently completed her dissertation 'Choreographing Voice: Staging Gender in Early Modern England' at the University of Michigan at Ann Arbor. She has published in *Renaissance Drama* and will be Assistant Professor of English at Lawrence University beginning September 2001.

Bruce Boehrer is Professor of English Renaissance literature at Florida State University. He is the author of *Monarchy and Incest in Renaissance England* (1992), *The Fury of Men's Gullets: Ben Jonson and the Digestive Canal* (1997), and articles in, among others, *PMLA, ELH, Journal of English and Germanic Philology*, and *Modern Language Quarterly*.

Judith Deitch is a sessional instructor at the University of Toronto specializing in the intersection of literature and intellectual culture. She has published recently in *Other Voices, Other Views: Expanding the Canon in English Renaissance Studies*, ed. Helen Ostovich et al (1999), and her 1998 doctoral dissertation is entitled 'The Genre of Logic and Artifice: Rhetoric, Dialectic and English Dialogues 1400–1600, Hoccleve to Spenser.'

Mario DiGangi is Assistant Professor of English at Lehman College and the Graduate School, CUNY. He is the author of *The Homoerotics of Early Modern Drama* (1997). His articles appear in *Approaches to Teaching Shorter Elizabethan Poetry* (2000) and *Marlowe, History, and Sexuality*, ed. Paul Whitfield White (1998), as well as in *Shakespeare Quarterly, ELH, Textual Practice*, and *English Literary Renaissance.*

Mark Dooley is Senior Lecturer in English and Cultural Studies at the University of Teesside, UK, where he teaches courses on early modern literature, contemporary popular culture, and gender and sexuality.

Jim Ellis is Assistant Professor of English at the University of Calgary. His essays appear in the collections *The Wit of Seventeenth-Century Poetry*, ed. Ted-Larry Pebworth and Claude Summers (1995); *The Work of Opera*, ed. Richard Dellamora and Daniel Fischlin (1997); *Out Takes*, ed. Ellis Hanson (1999); and in *Renaissance Quarterly* and *English Studies in Canada.* He is currently working on a study of the construction of masculinity in the early modern Ovidian epyllia.

Carla Freccero is Professor of Literature and Women's Studies at the University of California at Santa Cruz. She is the author of numerous articles on early modern continental literature and history, feminist and queer theory, and current U.S. popular culture. Her essays appear in such collections as *Queering the Renaissance*, ed. Jonathan Goldberg (1994), and *Rewriting the Renaissance: The Discourses of Sexual Difference in Early Modern Europe*, ed. Margaret W. Ferguson, Maureen Quilligan, and Nancy J. Vickers (1986). Her publications include *Father Figures: Genealogy and Narrative Structure in Rabelais* (1991), *Premodern Sexualities* (1996, coedited with Louise Fradenburg), and *Popular Culture: An Introduction* (1999). She is currently at work on two books, *Marguarite de Navarre and the Politics of Maternal Sovereignty* and *Early Modern Masculinities.*

Morgan Holmes is the author of several articles on gender and sexuality in early modern British literature and culture, as well as of *Early Modern Metaphysical Literature: Nature, Custom and Strange Desires* (2001). He is a communications consultant in Toronto, Ontario.

Lori Humphrey Newcomb is Assistant Professor of English at the University of Illinois at Urbana-Champaign. She has just completed a book, *Reading Popular Romance in Early Modern England*, on the textual transmission of *Pandosto* and *The Winter's Tale*, and is turning to a new project on early modern material culture, gender, and print.

Raphael Lyne is a Lecturer in English at New Hall, Cambridge, and a Newton Trust Lecturer in the English Faculty, specializing in Renaissance literature, Shakespeare, and the classical inheritance. His book *Ovid's Changing Words: English Metamorphoses 1567–1632*, which includes chapters on Golding, Spenser, Drayton, and Sandys, will be published by Oxford University Press in 2001.

Ian Frederick Moulton is Assistant Professor of English at Arizona State University West. He has published essays on early modern erotic writing and gender identity in *Shakespeare Quarterly*, *English Literary Renaissance*, and in the collection *Marlowe, History, and Sexuality*, ed. Paul Whitfield White (1998). He is the author of *Before Pornography: Erotic Writing, Effeminacy, and National Identity in Early Modern England* (2001).

Michael Pincombe teaches English at the University of Newcastle upon Tyne. He has written extensively on mid-Tudor and Elizabethan topics. He is the author of *Eros and Eliza: The Plays of John Lyly* (1996), and has just completed a book entitled *Elizabethan Humanism* for the Longman Medieval and Renaissance Library (2001).

Elizabeth Sauer is Professor of English, Brock University, Ontario, and has authored *Barbarous Dissonance and Images of Voice in Milton's Epics* (1996), and coedited *Agonistics: Arenas of Creative Contest* (1997); *Milton and the Imperial Vision* (1999 Milton Society of America Irene Samuel Memorial Award winner); and *Books and Readers in Early Modern England: Material Studies* (2001). *Print, Performance, and the Public Sphere in Early Modern England* is in progress, as is *Reading Early Women.*

Goran V. Stanivukovic is Assistant Professor of English at Saint Mary's University, Halifax, Nova Scotia. He has published journal and book articles on sexualities in early modern drama and prose fiction, and on rhetoric; has just completed a critical edition of Emanuel Ford's *Ornatus and Artesia* for the Barnabe Riche Society series; and is currently working on two books: one on early modern sexualities and popular prose romances in England, and a coedited volume on early modern prose fiction and embodiment.

Valerie Traub is Professor of English and Women's Studies at the University of Michigan. She is the author of *Desire & Anxiety: Circulations of Sexuality in Shakespearean Drama* (1992) and coeditor of *Feminist Readings of Early Modern Culture: Emerging Subjects* (1997). Her book *The Renaissance of Lesbianism in Early Modern England* is forthcoming.

Index

www.ingramcontent.com/pod-product-compliance
Lightning Source LLC
LaVergne TN
LVHW090806070826
844660LV00022B/1094
* 9 7 8 1 4 8 7 5 2 4 1 9 7 *